Envy in Politics

PRINCETON STUDIES IN
Political Behavior
Edited by Tali Mendelberg

RECENTLY PUBLISHED IN THE SERIES

Communism's Shadow: Historical Legacies and Contemporary Political Attitudes by Grigore Pop-Eleches and Joshua A. Tucker

Resolve in International Politics by Joshua Kertzer

Democracy for Realists: Why Elections Do Not Produce Responsive Government by Christopher H. Achen and Larry M. Bartels

Envy in Politics

GWYNETH H. MCCLENDON

PRINCETON UNIVERSITY PRESS
Princeton & Oxford

Copyright © 2018 by Princeton University Press

Published by Princeton University Press,
41 William Street, Princeton, New Jersey 08540
In the United Kingdom: Princeton University Press,
6 Oxford Street, Woodstock, Oxfordshire OX20 1TR

press.princeton.edu

All Rights Reserved

Library of Congress Control Number: 2018932150

ISBN 978-0-691-17865-3

British Library Cataloging-in-Publication Data is available

This book has been composed in Sabon Next LT Pro and Hevetica Neu LT Std

Printed on acid-free paper. ∞

Typeset by Nova Techset Pvt Ltd, Bangalore, India
Printed in the United States of America

10 9 8 7 6 5 4 3 2 1

CONTENTS

FIGURES

TABLES

ACKNOWLEDGMENTS

I owe a debt of gratitude to many people for helping me bring this book to fruition. It started as a dissertation project, and I owe special thanks to my advisors in graduate school: Evan Lieberman, Robert Keohane, and Carles Boix. None of them shied from asking me tough questions, and each knew how to help me find my own wings, as it were. Evan's scholarship on South Africa and ethnic politics has inspired me in countless ways. Without Bob's willingness to indulge my half-baked ideas, this project would never have gotten off the ground. Carles's good-humored skepticism about the undertaking at various points was one of my biggest motivators. Leonard Wantchekon became an important fourth reader when he came to Princeton University toward the end of my time there. The final product benefited immensely from his suggestions.

Many other members of the Princeton community helped me formulate early ideas for the project. I would particularly like to thank Mark Beissinger, Mina Cikara, Rafaela Dancygier, John Darley, Amaney Jamal, Atul Kohli, Phillip Petit, Grigore Pop-Eleches, Keith Whittington, and Deborah Yashar for providing feedback, cautions, and advice. The graduate students in the Politics Department were often my most lively interlocutors. Thank you to Graeme Blair, Brookes Brown, Will Bullock, Peter Buisseret, Sarah Bush, Jeff Colgan, Kevin Collins, Michael Donnelly, Sarah El-Kazaz, Sarah Goff, Yanilda Gonzalez, Kristin Harkness, Vinay Jawahar, Kristina Johnson, Noam Lupu, Michael McKoy, Michael Miller, Meredith Sadin, and Teppei Yamamoto. The interdisciplinary group of graduate students in the Fellowship of the Woodrow Wilson Scholars also provided useful suggestions. Three friends deserve special mention: Lauren Davenport, Lisa

McKay, and Kanta Murali have provided me with incredible support, encouragement, and good humor at key moments as this book evolved.

The Mamdouha S. Bobst Center for Peace and Justice, the Fellowship of the Woodrow Wilson Scholars at Princeton, and the MacMillan Center's Program on Democracy at Yale University provided financial support for data collection and writing. While I was a postdoctoral associate at Yale, Susan Stokes, Thad Dunning, Tariq Thachil, Ana De La O, and Elizabeth Carlson provided a space for reflection and gave me useful feedback on different aspects of the project. I presented parts of the work at American Political Science Association annual meetings, Midwest Political Science Association annual meetings, Princeton University, New York University, and Yale University. Peter Loewen, Patrick Emmenegger, Jan-Emmanuel De Neve, John Stephens, Victoria Shineman, and Tumi Makgetla provided valuable discussant comments on early drafts during those workshops and conferences.

The field experiment on participation in collective action was made possible only with the cooperation of an LGBTI advocacy organization. I owe special thanks to its director for his interest in my research questions and his enthusiasm for executing the experiment. The set-up and results from that field experiment were published as "Social Esteem and Participation in Contentious Politics: A Field Experiment at an LGBT Pride Rally" in the *American Journal of Political Science* in 2014. I thank John Wiley and Sons, Inc. for permission to reprint a version of this article in this current volume. Rick Wilson, three anonymous reviewers at *AJPS*, and Don Green provided crucial feedback that greatly improved that article before I expanded it into a section of this book.

For their friendship, help, and guidance in South Africa over the years, I thank Estelle Prinsloo, Gcobani Qambela, Ntobeko Qolo, and Siyabonga Yonzi, as well as Kenneth Chatindiara and Diego Inturralde at Stats SA and the staff at the Cory Library at Rhodes University. Various academics, including Justine Burns and Jonny Steinberg at the University of Cape Town and Patrick Bond at the University of KwaZulu-Natal, offered probing questions and helpful advice at the early stages when I was a graduate student doing fieldwork. Back in 2008, Pumi planted the seed of what would become the main ideas for this book, and some of Jonny Steinberg's writings nurtured that seed as I endeavored to turn it into a research agenda. I also owe a debt of gratitude to the numerous politicians and bureaucrats who took the time to help me.

I finished the book at Harvard University and benefited from being surrounded by many talented colleagues there. Robert Bates's close reading of a draft proved invaluable. He is the master of writing concise, insightful books and encouraged me to keep it short. I have endeavored to follow his lead and advice, albeit quite imperfectly. I would also like to thank Stephen Ansolabhere, Melani Cammett, Dan Carpenter, Amy Catalinac, Ryan Enos, Jeff Frieden, Claudine Gay, Josh Kertzer, Horacio Larreguy, Nancy Rosenblum, Prerna Singh, Dan Smith, Arthur Spirling, Dustin Tingley, and Daniel Ziblatt, among many other colleagues, for their advice and support at various points.

Eric Crahan at Princeton University Press and Tali Mendelberg, the series editor, generously took an interest in and a chance on the book. I owe them as well as two anonymous reviewers tremendous thanks for their comments and encouragement. The book is immensely better as a result. Kelley Friel made excellent copy edits to the draft manuscript.

I could not have accomplished any of this without the support of my family. In particular, my parents, Judith and Charles, and my sister, Emma, inspire me every day with their creativity and passion for learning, research and teaching. My husband, Scott, has been steadfast over the last fifteen years, seeing me through college and graduate school as well as the transition to faculty life. He has accompanied me around the world for travel and fieldwork, challenged me on every idea, and forgiven me my periods of self-doubt. Most important, he has been a full partner in raising our daughter, Eleanor. I hope she will read this book one day and find it worthy of esteem.

Envy in Politics

ONE Introduction

Status Concerns and Political Behavior

This book touches on three long-standing political questions: How do citizens evaluate public policies? Under what conditions do governments act in service of their constituents' material interests or fail to do so? Why (and under what conditions) do citizens participate in politics? Each of these questions is important in its own right. Together they cover much of what politics is about: public opinion, policy implementation, and political participation.

However, the focus of this book is not so much on any one of these puzzles as it is on an insight about human psychology that can help us address these three important political questions and more. The insight is that people care about maintaining and improving their social status within groups. This concern for status comes in many forms: Envy is the inclination to bring down those who are better off. Spite is the inclination to *keep* down those who are worse off. The pursuit of admiration is the inclination to rise in the ranks of others' opinions. Each of these impulses involves a concern for a better *relative* position within the group, even if that means costs to the self and to others. Some of these motivations are considered ugly and undesirable, and others less so, but they are all central components of human psychology. Every person experiences them at some point in her life.

Many explanations of political behavior assume that citizens are motivated by material group- or self-interests, or by broader principles and ideological commitments. Such motivations are undeniably important. Citizens vote at least in part based on a desire to maximize their own material resources and physical safety,[1] and they support policies that protect their social identity groups relative to other groups.[2] Likewise, they participate in politics when the material and physical costs of doing so decrease and when doing so would make them materially better off.[3] They evaluate policies based on partisan commitments,[4] or according to general principles of compassion, fairness, and reciprocity.[5]

Yet scholars of politics should not overlook the ways that people are also motivated by the desire to distinguish themselves from others, particularly within groups. Social psychologists have observed that "one of the most important goals and outcomes of social life is to attain status in the groups to which we belong."[6] John Adams wrote that attaining such status "is as real a want of nature as hunger."[7] These authors join numerous social scientists who have observed the high value people place on achieving distinction within social groups. Within-group status brings

---

[1] E.g., Daniel N. Posner. *Institutions and ethnic politics in Africa*. Cambridge University Press, 2005; Beatriz Magaloni. *Voting for autocracy: Hegemonic party survival and its demise in Mexico*. New York, NY: Cambridge University Press, 2006.

[2] E.g., Evan S. Lieberman. *Boundaries of contagion: how ethnic politics have shaped government responses to AIDS*. Princeton, NJ: Princeton University Press, 2009.

[3] E.g., Emmanuel Teitelbaum. *Mobilizing restraint: Democracy and industrial conflict in postreform south Asia*. Ithaca, NY: Cornell University Press, 2011; Xi Chen. *Social protest and contentious authoritarianism in China*. New York, NY: Cambridge University Press, 2012.

[4] E.g., James N. Druckman, Erik Peterson, and Rune Slothuus. "How elite partisan polarization affects public opinion formation." In *American Political Science Review* 107.01 (2013), pp. 57–79.

[5] E.g., Christina Fong. "Social preferences, self-interest, and the demand for redistribution." In *Journal of Public Economics* 82.2 (2001), pp. 225–246; Kenneth Scheve and David Stasavage. *Taxing the rich: A history of fiscal fairness in the United States and Europe*. Princeton, NJ: Princeton University Press, 2016; Charlotte Cavaillé. "Demand for Redistribution in the Age of Inequality." PhD thesis. Harvard University, 2014.

[6] Cameron Anderson et al. "Who attains social status? Effects of personality and physical attractiveness in social groups." In *Journal of Personality and Social Psychology* 81.1 (2001), p. 116.

[7] Charles Francis Adams. *The works of John Adams*. Boston, MA: Little Brown, 1850, p. 234.

pleasure and a sense of personal power,[8] and is more closely linked to self-reports of well being than many measures of absolute welfare.[9] It informs self-judgment when absolute benchmarks are not otherwise available, as is often the case.[10] Occupying a high within-group status makes people feel good, whatever their absolute circumstances, and, as a result, people sometimes make real sacrifices to preserve or elevate their status.[11]

This book explores how concerns about within-group status shed light on political attitudes and behavior. Although political theorists and researchers in other social sciences have written about envy, spite, and the desire for admiration, within-group status motivations have received little empirical attention in political science.[12] Political scientists have certainly paid attention to emotions (especially fear, anger, and enthusiasm),[13] but emotions related to within-group status have largely been overlooked.

[8] Cameron Anderson et al. "The local-ladder effect: Social status and subjective well-being." In *Psychological Science* 23.7 (2012), pp. 764–771.

[9] Christopher J. Boyce, Gordon D. A. Brown, and Simon C. Moore. "Money and happiness: Rank of income, not income, affects life satisfaction." In *Psychological Science* 21.4 (2010), pp. 471–475.

[10] Leon Festinger. "A theory of social comparison processes." In *Human Relations* 7.2 (1954), pp. 117–140; Susan T. Fiske. *Envy up, scorn down: How status divides us.* New York, NY: Russell Sage Foundation, 2011; Robert H. Frank. *Choosing the right pond: Human behavior and the quest for status.* New York, NY: Oxford University Press, 1985.

[11] Yoram Weiss and Chaim Fershtman. "Social status and economic performance: A survey." In *European Economic Review* 42.3 (1998), pp. 801–820.

[12] A recent exception is Jonathan Renshon. *Fighting for status: Hierarchy and conflict in world politics.* Princeton, NJ: Princeton University Press, 2017, which looks at foreign policy elites' concern for status in international relations, and the implications of these concerns for inter-state conflict.

[13] For examples, see Bethany Albertson and Shana Kushner Gadarian. *Anxious politics: Democratic citizenship in a threatening world.* New York, NY: Cambridge University Press, 2015; Antoine J. Banks. *Anger and racial politics: The emotional foundation of racial attitudes in America.* Cambridge University Press, 2014; Nicholas A. Valentino et al. "Is a worried citizen a good citizen? Emotions, political information seeking, and learning via the internet." In *Political Psychology* 29.2 (2008), pp. 247–273; Ted Brader. *Campaigning for hearts and minds: How emotional appeals in political ads work.* Chicago, IL: University of Chicago Press, 2006; and George E. Marcus. "Emotions in politics." In *Annual Review of Political Science* 3.1 (2000), pp. 221–250, on these emotions.

A rich literature on ethnic and racial politics has taken seriously people's concern for their group's relative position vis-à-vis other groups[14] and studied the emotions that stem from such concerns,[15] but that literature has focused less on individuals' striving for distinction *within* groups or on the political consequences thereof. More recent studies have found that invoking social comparisons can influence voter turnout,[16] and at least one study of distributive attitudes highlights individuals' dislike of being relatively worse off than others,[17] but, given the level of attention that status motivations have received in other social sciences, the insights of these exceptional studies deserve further exploration and application in political science.

This book therefore takes a closer look at the political implications of within-group status motivations, paying particular attention to the influence of envy, spite, and the desire for admiration on politics. It first combines insights from political theory, behavioral economics, psychology, and anthropology to develop a framework for anticipating when and how status motivations might influence political attitudes and behavior. It then applies

---

[14] E.g., Lars-Erik Cederman, Nils B. Weidmann, and Kristian Skrede Gleditsch. "Horizontal inequalities and ethnonationalist civil war: A global comparison." In *American Political Science Review* 105.03 (2011), pp. 478–495; Evan Lieberman. *Boundaries of contagion: How ethnic politics have shaped government responses to AIDS*; Henri Tajfel. "Social psychology of intergroup relations." In *Annual Review of Psychology* 33.1 (1982), pp. 1–39.

[15] See in particular Roger D. Petersen. *Understanding ethnic violence: Fear, hatred, and resentment in twentieth-century Eastern Europe*. Cambridge University Press, 2002, for a discussion of inter-group resentment.

[16] Alan S. Gerber, Donald P. Green, and Christopher W. Larimer. "Social pressure and voter turnout: Evidence from a large-scale field experiment." In *American Political Science Review* 102.01 (2008), pp. 33–48; Costas Panagopoulos. "Affect, social pressure and prosocial motivation: Field experimental evidence of the mobilizing effects of pride, shame and publicizing voting behavior." In *Political Behavior* 32.3 (2010), pp. 369–386.

[17] Xiaobo Lü and Kenneth Scheve. "Self-centered inequity aversion and the mass politics of taxation." In *Comparative Political Studies* 49.14 (2016), pp. 1965–1997. Rather than highlight status motivations per se, Lü and Scheve explore the possibility of "self-centered inequity aversion" which involves citizens wanting to be neither worse off *nor* better off than others.

that framework to a series of political puzzles to see if status motivations help us explain more than we could relying on existing theories of the drivers of political behavior alone. The goal is not to prove that status motivations account for *all* political behavior, or even that they are the most important determinant of political behavior in each case. Rather, the goal is to explore whether status motivations give us additional explanatory leverage over important political questions and enrich our understanding of disparate domains of political behavior.

To be sure, there are at least three reasons that empirical political scientists might have hesitated to study status motivations. But each of these can be overcome. First, it might seem improbable that the concern for status—a fundamental and universal feature of human nature—could explain variation in political behavior.[18] But while envy and other status motivations may be regular features of human experience, the evidence suggests that there is variation in how often these concerns affect *political* opinions and behaviors. For instance, anthropological studies, some of which I discuss below, convincingly illustrate that status concerns are often addressed informally, with no need for the involvement of political processes or institutions. For example, groups establish norms for concealing advantages most likely to excite envy[19] and develop social practices to encourage people to display goodwill

---

[18] Indeed, an earlier literature on relative deprivation—the motivation to make demands on government because one is worse off than others—ran into difficulty because it seemed that relative deprivation was much too prevalent a phenomena to account for variation in political engagement. See Joan Neff Gurney and Kathleen J. Tierney. "Relative deprivation and social movements: A critical look at twenty years of theory and research." In *Sociological Quarterly* 23.1 (1982), pp. 33–47.

[19] As I discuss below, these practices are found throughout the world in both developing and developed countries. They include social conventions for limiting conspicuous consumption, demonstrating modesty about personal accomplishments, and avoiding outpacing other group members. See Jean-Philippe Platteau. "Redistributive pressures in Sub-Saharan Africa: Causes, consequences, and coping strategies." In *Africa's development in historical perspective*. Ed. by Emmanuel Akyeampong et al. New York, NY: Cambridge University Press, 2014, pp. 153–207.

rather than spite toward the less fortunate.[20] These informal mechanisms for managing status motivations are strongest when people know each other well, and when times are relatively "settled," to use Swidler's term.[21] Under such conditions, social rules are relatively uncontested. People can learn which disparities are most likely to excite envy and spite, utilize established mechanisms for conferring admiration, and follow established social practices for managing status conflict without demanding that policies and political institutions do it for them. By contrast, in "unsettled" times,[22] when social conventions for managing status motivations are weak, there are no longer strong rules for addressing status motivations without help from policies and political institutions. Since status motivations are most likely to shape political preferences and actions under these conditions, we can use this insight to better account for variation in political behavior.

A second reason that political scientists might have hesitated to examine status motivations is that they are sometimes hidden. Many status motivations, particularly envy and spite, are antisocial since they involve wishing that others had less.[23] Other status motivations—like the desire for admiration—are not antisocial per se, but people may feign that they are not a priority.[24]

[20] Practices for mitigating envy and spite could also include "feeling rules" that define when and where it is socially appropriate to experience envy and spite and when and where it is instead best to suppress it: Arlie R. Hochschild. *The managed heart*. Berkeley, CA: University of California Press, 1983.

[21] Ann Swidler. "Culture in action: Symbols and strategies." In *American Sociological Review* (1986), pp. 273–286.

[22] Swidler defined "unsettled times" as periods of "social transformation" when "people are learning new ways of organizing individual and collective action, practicing unfamiliar habits until they become familiar." See ibid., p. 278. In other words, they are periods during which social rules and practices that were previously taken for granted become contested and reworked. In the applications section of this book, I consider the period just after the transition from apartheid as one example of a time when communities within South Africa were experiencing "unsettled times," though to varying degrees.

[23] Benedikt Herrmann, Christian Thöni, and Simon Gächter. "Antisocial punishment across societies." In *Science* 319.5868 (2008), pp. 1362–1367.

[24] Geoffrey Brennan and Philip Pettit. *The economy of esteem: An essay on civil and political society*. Oxford, UK: Oxford University Press, 2004.

Thus, people may report status motivations less often than they report other concerns. They may even use other labels when describing their own feelings, perhaps saying that rather than envying others, they are concerned about "fairness."[25] But the fact that status motivations may not be reliably self-reported does not mean that we cannot identify their observable implications in political attitudes and actions apart from self-reports.[26] As I discuss in greater detail below, concerns about within-group status manifest when people self-centeredly try to avoid disadvantageous inequality for themselves and try to preserve advantageous inequality for themselves. The observable implications are thus distinct from those of prosocial motivations (which would not lead to preserving advantageous inequality) and from those of broader fairness principles (which would not be so self-centered), even if individuals might claim otherwise. We can look for these observable implications in attitudinal, observational, and experimental data.

Third, political scientists may have hesitated to examine status motivations because they seemed too close to self-interest. Since within-group status is sometimes associated with material benefits (economic opportunity, influence), the observable implications of status-motivated behavior may seem to be indistinguishable from the pursuit of absolute material welfare, especially over the long term. Indeed, in early human societies, high status within small groups may have guaranteed mating partners as well as control over resources;[27] in other words our concerns about within-group status may have functional, evolutionary origins. Yet, regardless of the origins of status motivations, concerns about within-group

---

[25] Paul Hoggett, Hen Wilkinson, and Phoebe Beedell. "Fairness and the politics of resentment." In *Journal of Social Policy* 42 (July 3, 2013), pp. 567–585. I further discuss the conceptual distinctions between envy, spite, and fairness below, as well as in the Elaborations chapter of the book.

[26] Rational choice research does not usually require actors to articulate the costs and benefits of a particular action explicitly—only that they act as if they had.

[27] Steven R. H. Beach and Abraham Tesser. "Self-evaluation maintenance and evolution." In *Handbook of social comparison: Theory and research*. Ed. by Jerry Suls and Ladd Wheeler. New York, NY: Springer, 2000, pp. 123–140; Weiss and Fershtman, "Social status and economic performance: A survey."

status have become so hardwired in our psychology that today we pursue them even when doing so might not incur material benefits in either the short or long term.[28] This book focuses specifically on instances in which the empirical implications of within-group status motivations diverge from those of material self-interest.

Each of the applications in this book begins with questions about why some people's political attitudes and behaviors diverge from their material interests. Why do some citizens support taxation and redistribution policies that are personally costly to them? Why do some governments fail to implement funded policies that would make constituents materially better off? Why do citizens contribute their time and energy to collective political action instead of free-riding off of the efforts of others? While taking other variables—state capacity, people's social identities, their concerns for fairness and risk, their party affiliations and larger ideas about what government should do—into account helps a great deal, unexplained variation remains.

A close look at the observable implications of status motivations gives us additional leverage over these questions. A citizen's puzzling opposition to redistribution policies that would put more money in her pocket is explained in part by the fact that the policy at issue would benefit her neighbors even more and thus reduce her local status. Policies that are generally welfare enhancing may be stymied because politicians perceive that citizens do not want policies that advantage others, even though they would benefit, too. In the domain of contentious politics, participation may be individually costly but promise higher within-group status to some, drawing those people into the fray. In all of these examples, if we allow that people sometimes prioritize status over other interests and principles, we can use variation in who faces these trade-offs, along with insights about the conditions under which

[28] David M. Buss. "Evolutionary biology and personality psychology: Toward a conception of human nature and individual differences." In *American Psychologist* 39.10 (1984), pp. 1135–1147.

status motivations become politically salient, to explain more about puzzling political behavior than we otherwise could.

I use the terms "status motivations" or "status concerns" throughout the book rather than "status emotions." The book focuses specifically on the influence of envy, spite, and the desire for admiration on the goals people pursue—on the things they want from political activity and from public policies.[29] I thus use the term "status motivations" rather than "status emotions" to make clear this particular focus. Status emotions also perform other functions that I do not discuss. For instance, status emotions can provide information to the self and to others ("affect-as-information"),[30] and can influence information processing and belief formation.[31] I return to a discussion of these other functions in the conclusion.

The evidence in the book comes primarily from two countries—the United States and South Africa. I chose these countries because at first glance both seemed unlikely places for

---

[29] The arguments in this book need not contradict rational choice theories. Rational choice models are compatible with a variety of goals. Much of political science research has focused on other goals, such as the desire to maximize absolute economic well-being and to retain the material benefits of office, and the desire to enact particular policies for the good of others or for principled reasons. This book suggests that we also consider an additional goal: maintaining and enhancing within-group status.

[30] Conor M. Steckler and Jessica L. Tracy. "The emotional underpinnings of social status." In *The psychology of social status*. Ed. by Joey T. Cheng and Jessica L. Tracy. New York, NY: Springer, 2014, pp. 201–224. The authors outline several ways in which the experience and display of status emotions sends information to the person experiencing the emotions about his/her status and conveys this information to others. For instance, experiencing envy or shame not only motivates a person to pursue a higher status within her group; it also communicates to the person that he/she is in a lower-status position. Furthermore, the person's (often unconscious) display of these emotions (e.g., lowering of the head or hunching of the shoulders to denote shame) communicates to others that she is in a low-status position.

[31] Christopher Oveis, Elizabeth J. Horberg, and Dacher Keltner. "Compassion, pride, and social intuitions of self-other similarity." In *Journal of Personality and Social Psychology* 98.4 (2010), pp. 618–630. The authors found that people experiencing pride processed information in ways that led them to perceive themselves as even higher status than they were.

within-group status concerns to matter. Narratives of individual enrichment are strong enough in the United States that they might undermine any desire for within-group status at the expense of personal fortune. The American Dream is that all individuals, if they work hard enough, can "make it." This narrative accomplishes two things. First, it elevates absolute wealth above all other goals. Second, it implies that if a person simply works hard enough, he can rise to the top of the economic hierarchy. He should not need to cut others down in the process. The book also looks at South African politics in the late 1990s and early 2000s, soon after the transition from apartheid that removed barriers to power and fortune for a majority of South Africans. Other scholars have predicted that such transitions leave a warm glow, at least for a little while.[32] According to this logic, citizens should be so heartened by seeing others like them succeed that they refrain from competing for within-group status. For this reason, early post-apartheid South African politics also seem an unlikely place to find a strong influence of within-group status concerns on political behavior. Both countries have histories of severely racist institutions and racial segregation that have strengthened perceptions of linked fate among members of the same races and ethnicities.[33] Although within-group inequalities are real and pervasive in both countries, political rhetoric has often focused on differences and inequalities between groups, masking inequalities within them. As a result, one might not generally expect US or South African citizens to compete with other group members for status, especially not at the expense of their own material welfare or that of their group.

[32] Albert O. Hirschman and Michael Rothschild. "The changing tolerance for income inequality in the course of economic development." In *The Quarterly Journal of Economics* 87.4 (1973), pp. 544–566.

[33] Michael C. Dawson. *Behind the mule: Race and class in African-American politics.* Princeton University Press, 1994; Martin Gilens. *Why Americans hate welfare: Race, media, and the politics of antipoverty policy.* Chicago, IL: University of Chicago Press, 2009; Donald L. Horowitz. *A democratic South Africa?: Constitutional engineering in a divided society.* Vol. 46. University of California Press, 1991; Anthony W. Marx. *Making race and nation: A comparison of South Africa, the United States, and Brazil.* Cambridge University Press, 1998.

While the two countries share attributes that provide tough tests for theory, they also differ in important respects. Both countries are democracies, where citizens' motivations and actions are most likely to have an observable effect on public policy and governance patterns. Yet one has been a democracy for some time, while the other's democracy is newer; one has an advanced industrialized economy, while the other is newly industrialized and considered a developing country by some. Some scholars have argued that status concerns affect behavior only in very rich industrialized democracies, where people have moved beyond worrying about basic resources on a daily basis.[34] The evidence in this book suggests otherwise. Examining these two countries together helps to focus on how status motivations are features of the human experience rather than markers of particular societies.

This book joins other work that seeks to integrate the complexities of human psychology into our understanding of comparative political behavior. Alongside scholarship on social identities, prosocial motivations, and cognitive biases, among other subjects, this book suggests ways to move beyond "homoeconomicus" assumptions that political actors are primarily concerned with material self-interest. My goals are to enrich our descriptions of political behavior and to explore whether (and how) insights about status motivations give us analytic purchase over important puzzles in politics.

DEFINITIONS

Before combining insights from political theory and other social sciences to further develop the main arguments, a discussion of key concepts is in order. As a category, status motivations all involve doing well relative to other people on some socially valued

---

[34] Andrew E. Clark, Paul Frijters, and Michael A. Shields. "Relative income, happiness, and utility: An explanation for the Easterlin paradox and other puzzles." In *Journal of Economic Literature* 46.1 (2008), pp. 95–144.

dimension of income, assets, attributes, actions, or achievements. Status can be assessed on many dimensions, but I focus here on two: an economic one and an attitudinal one. People might enjoy occupying a higher relative economic position: earning more money, owning more property, or having more material possessions compared to members of their social groups. But they might also desire to be highly regarded, to enjoy a high place in the opinion of others. I bundle both of these desires together as examples of status motivations.[35] I assume that when human beings pursue status goods, they do so rationally[36] and that they generally care about both their rank compared to others and the disparities between themselves and others. That is, I assume that people care about their relative position in both an ordinal and a cardinal sense.[37]

Status motivations can be further disaggregated into specific components. For instance, envy is a status motivation that is felt specifically in response to "upward comparisons"—that is, when a person is worse off than others in her group. Of course, colloquially, the word "envy" is used in many different ways.[38] But I use the term here specifically to indicate a feeling of hostility

---

[35] Since this study provides a first cut at whether status motivations influence political attitudes and behavior, for simplicity, I treat income and admiration here largely as independent dimensions on which within-group status can be measured. However, in some contexts, higher levels of income may denote competence and thus also bestow admiration upon an individual, or the pursuit of relative income and the pursuit of admiration may be linked.

[36] As discussed above, one could also explore how status motivations distort rationality. In *Othello*, for instance, Shakespeare writes, "Trifles light as air seem to the jealous confirmation strong as proofs from holy writ." That is, status motivations like jealousy may also distort how we process information or perceive the intentions of others. This line of exploration should be pursued in future research but is beyond the scope of this book.

[37] Daniel John Zizzo and Andrew J. Oswald. "Are people willing to pay to reduce others' incomes?" In *Annales d'Economie et de Statistique* (2001), pp. 39–65; Colin Camerer. *Behavioral game theory: Experiments in strategic interaction.* Princeton, NJ: Princeton University Press, 2003.

[38] Colloquially, it is used to mean anything from a vague or benign wish to have what someone else has ("I envy your trip to the Bahamas!") to a desire to see someone else harmed. See Fiske, *Envy Up, Scorn Down: How Status Divides Us.*

toward the greater success of others—a wish for those with more to have less,[39] even if that would mean few benefits (or even negative consequences) for the envier. Envy is thus only one type of concern for relative, rather than absolute, welfare. A related emotion, spite, is felt specifically in response to "downward comparisons"—that is, in response to others who are worse off. Spite is a wish for those with less to continue to have less, or to become even worse off, relatively speaking.[40] In other words, it is a wish to preserve or improve one's relative position. Like envy, spite is an antisocial motivation that seeks to improve one's own status by ensuring that others have less.[41] But not all status motivations are explicitly antisocial. For instance, the desire for admiration represents the wish to occupy a high status in the opinion of others.[42] It is a desire for social distinction in an attitudinal sense, to be seen as more estimable than others are. While it does not necessarily involve a wish for others to become less well off materially, it, too, entails a concern for one's relative position. These are the status motivations discussed in this book.[43]

---

[39] The goods in question might be "positional" in the sense that their value stems from their ranking relative to alternatives, but they need not be: Fred Hirsch. *Social limits to growth*. New York, NY: Routledge, 1976. A house provides shelter against bad weather, which is valuable to an individual even if others do not also desire the house. Nevertheless, a person may experience envy when seeing others occupying houses. See Fiske. *Envy up, scorn down: How status divides us*, chapter 3, for evidence that individuals compare status on the basis of non-positional goods such as health, marriage quality, depression, and risks of accidents.

[40] Ernst Fehr, Karla Hoff, and Mayuresh Kshetramade. "Spite and development." In *American Economic Review* 98.2 (2008), pp. 494–499.

[41] Herrmann, Thöni, and Simon Gächter. "Antisocial punishment across societies."

[42] Brennan and Pettit. *The economy of esteem: An essay on civil and political society*.

[43] Other examples of status motivations include shame (the painful feeling when one performs or behaves in a manner that is disesteemed by others), schadenfreude (the pleasure at seeing someone envied brought low), and vanity (the overestimation of one's own achievements relative to others). These motivations deserve further exploration in future research but are beyond the scope of this study. On schadenfreude, see Mina Cikara. "Intergroup schadenfreude: Motivating participation in collective violence." In *Current Opinion in Behavioral Sciences* 3 (2015), pp. 12–17.

As discussed above, status motivations can be difficult to measure through self-reports. People rarely admit that they want to see
others made worse off just to increase their own status. Even in the
case of the desire for admiration, people may sometimes deny that
their actions are influenced by wanting the esteem of others rather
than by other goals.[44] However, status-motivated behavior does
have distinctive markers, and people can still discern envy, spite, or
the desire for esteem as motivations for the behavior of others just
by their body language. There are even studies of the subtle (and
automatic) facial cues that signal when someone experiences envy
or spite.[45] While I describe status motivations in terms of inner
feelings and desires, their analytic usefulness does not depend
on self-reports. The antecedents and behavioral manifestations of
status motivations can be used to explain political patterns.

The behavioral markers of status motivations also help differ-
entiate them from other concepts in political science, such as
fairness, inequality aversion, and social pressure.[46] I further discuss

[44] For instance, Elster (1983) worries that admiration is subject to a teleological
paradox, according to the old adage "nothing is so unimpressive as behavior that is
designed to impress" (quoted in Brennan and Pettit, *The economy of esteem: An essay
on civil and political society*, p. 36). The worry is that people may admire people's
actions and traits unless those actions are openly motivated by the desire to win
admiration. While these concerns may be valid, this research reveals that people
act on explicit promises that their political actions will be admired by in-group
members.

[45] See Fiske, *Envy Up, Scorn Down: How Status Divides Us*, pp. 36–42, for one
discussion.

[46] The concept of relative deprivation, which was an important variable in
earlier political science research, particularly on rebellion, is perhaps closest to
the concept of status motivations discussed here: Ted Robert Gurr. *Why men rebel*.
Princeton, NJ: Princeton University Press, 1970. Relative deprivation refers to the
discontent people feel when they are worse off than others, or when there is a
disjuncture between people's expectations and the reality of their circumstances:
Walter Garrison Runciman. *Relative Deprivation and Social Justice: A Study of
Attitudes to Social Inequality in Twentieth-century England*. Berkeley, CA: University
of California Press, 1966; Gurney and Tierney, "Relative deprivation and social
movements: A critical look at twenty years of theory and research." I discuss the
distinction between relative deprivation and status motivations in the Elaborations
chapter. One difference is that relative deprivation scholarship focused on how
relative deprivation motivated people to try to demand more for themselves in

these conceptual distinctions in the Elaborations chapter of the book, but it is important to remember that when a person is influenced by status motivations, she responds to the differences between what *she* has and what others have, and between how *she* is seen and how others are seen, and she then behaves in ways that are intended to increase those differences in her favor. In other words, she is concerned about her own status—about decreasing inequality that is disadvantageous for her—not about reducing inequality in general and not about ensuring that all people are treated according to standardized principles. She is striving for *distinction*, not simply trying to conform to the average behavior of others. Of course, all of these various concerns—for status, for fairness, for conforming to norms—are likely to influence the political opinions and behaviors of a given person at some point in her life. The focus here on status motivations does not suggest that other concerns never shape political behavior. Rather, I argue that we can use insights about the antecedents and consequences of envy and other status motivations in conjunction with these other motivations in order to gain a richer and deeper understanding of political behavior.

In the next section, I draw on other disciplines and authors to gather insights about the nature of status motivations, the conditions under which they are most salient, and the consequences they tend to have. Doing so helps me formulate expectations about when (and how) status motivations might influence political behavior.

Origins of the Argument

The argument in this book draws inspiration from the writings of political theorists and the empirical research of behavioral economists, psychologists, and anthropologists. This section briefly discusses relevant ideas and findings from these literatures in order to

---

absolute terms. This book focuses on the effects of people's concerns about relative position itself.

construct a framework for thinking about the potential effects of status motivations on political behavior.

I use findings from these other disciplines in the following ways. From both political theory and behavioral economics, I draw the insight that envy and other status motivations are pervasive and distinguishable from considerations of material self-interest, as well as from other common distributive preferences, such as a concern for fairness. Political theorists suggest in general terms that envy, spite, and the quest for admiration might alter politics by introducing motivations that are contrary to the pursuit of basic material interests. Behavioral economists then go further to demonstrate empirically that people are willing to pay personal costs and to diverge from fairness principles to improve their status within groups. I then use insights from behavioral economics, psychology, and anthropology studies to consider the conditions under which status motivations are likely to motivate political behavior, and the groups within which people are likely to gauge their own status. Research in psychology tells us that comparisons among similar people are those that most often give rise to status concerns; that is, status comparisons are most intense among neighbors, coethnics, coworkers, and friends. Behavioral economics research underscores that visible disparities to which we are frequently exposed provoke envy and spite. And research in anthropology suggests that when social ties are weak and during times of transition, status motivations are less well addressed through nonpolitical mechanisms. They are thus likely to result in more political forms of conflict. These insights about the conditions under which status motivations are (1) provoked and (2) likely to spill over into politics are key for explaining variation in political behavior.

POLITICAL THEORY

The political theory literature uses multiple terms to describe status motivations. For instance, Rousseau refers to *amour-propre*, and

Hobbes discusses the competition for honor and dignity. Rawls uses the term "envy" explicitly, as do Aristotle, Mill, Tocqueville, and Smith. Grant describes "status passions," a category in which she includes vanity, pride, envy, jealousy, and the desire for honor and glory.[47] Yet these thinkers agree that people care about their relative position, often for its own sake. From varying perspectives and with varying degrees of detail, they argue that this concern can affect people's political attitudes and actions.

For instance, in his *Discourse on the Origin and Foundations of Inequality*, Rousseau distinguishes between two kinds of self-love or self-concern—*amour-de-soi* and *amour-propre*.[48] The first focuses on self-preservation, basic needs, and material interests. Human beings want to survive: they seek security and material welfare— the kinds of goals we take for granted in contemporary empirical political science. The second, potentially more troublesome, kind of self-love (amour-propre) focuses on distinction from others: it is rooted in social comparison.[49] Amour-propre is the desire to be better than other people—to be recognized as such, and even to sacrifice in order to harm others so that one can surpass them in relative terms. Therefore, amour-propre can be troublingly destructive. It can be punishing to others and, paradoxically, to the self.

Hobbes also writes about the human tendency to be concerned with relative position. In *Leviathan* he explains that humans are

---

[47] Grant defines status passions as "those that aim at distinction or recognition relative to others": Ruth W. Grant. "Passions and interests revisited: the psychological foundations of economics and politics." In *Public Choice* 137.3-4 (2008), p. 453.

[48] Jean-Jacques Rousseau. *The Basic Political Writings*. Trans. by Donald A. Cress. Indianapolis, IN: Hackett, 1987.

[49] As Kolodny writes, even if amour-de-soi can be comparative as well, it is comparative in a different sense: "Perhaps all forms of self-concern, such as concern for one's health, are desires that one's actual condition compare well with certain *possible* conditions, which someone, oneself or another, might enjoy. But amour-propre is a 'comparative' desire, whereas the desire for health is 'absolute,' in the stricter sense that it is a desire that one's actual condition compare well with the *actual* conditions of others." Niko Kolodny. "The Explanation of Amour-Propre." In *Philosophical Review* 119.2 (2010), pp. 165–200, p. 169.

different from animals, in part, because other creatures "have no other direction than their particular judgments and appetites," whereas:

> Men are continually in competition for honour and dignity... and consequently amongst men there ariseth on that ground, envy and hatred, and finally war.... *Man, whose joy consisteth in comparing himself with other men, can relish nothing but what is eminent.*[50]

In other words, the concern for distinction from others is uniquely human. While other animals are driven by appetites for survival and basic needs,[51] man goes further: he also desires to be distinguished, even if that means conflict. In a way, man's politics arise precisely from these relative position concerns. While other social animals can live fairly peacefully without a common power, the competition among humans for honor and dignity often forces them to submit to a governing authority in order to avoid being in a constant state of war.

To be sure, the distinction between self-interest and this concern for eminence is blurrier for Hobbes than it is for Rousseau.[52] For Hobbes, the pursuit of relative position can be entangled with the pursuit of long-term self-interest, an alternative account of status motivations to which I return in the "Elaborations" chapter of the book. Only by exceeding others in all things (property, physical strength, and reputation) can an individual be assured that others

[50] Thomas Hobbes. *Leviathan*. New York, NY: Oxford University Press, 1998, part 2, chapter 17, emphasis added

[51] We know now from studies of both chimpanzees and dogs that other animals actually also exhibit status motivations. See, for example, Friederike Range et al. "The absence of reward induces inequity aversion in dogs." In *Proceedings of the National Academy of Sciences* 106.1 (2009), pp. 340–345; and Sarah F. Brosnan, Hillary C. Schiff, and Frans B. M. de Waal. "Tolerance for inequity may increase with social closeness in chimpanzees." In *Proceedings of the Royal Society of London B: Biological Sciences* 272.1560 (2005), pp. 253–258.

[52] Grant. "Passions and interests revisited: the psychological foundations of economics and politics."

will not destroy him or her in the future. But Hobbes acknowledges that status motivations sometimes diverge from long-term interests. For instance, human beings desire social distinction even after their deaths, despite the fact that "after death, there be no sense of the praise given us on earth."[53] Although social status after one's death clearly serves no instrumental purpose, Hobbes recognizes that it is still valued: "Men have present delight therein, from the foresight of it ... which though they now see not, yet they imagine; and any thing that is pleasure to the sense, the same also is pleasure in the imagination."[54] Hobbes concedes that humans sometimes pursue a higher relative position for its own sake, even when doing so incurs no material benefits.

Drawing on the works of Rousseau and Hobbes, Grant urges political scientists and policy makers not to ignore what she calls "status passions":

> A political order that succeeds in impartially adjudicating interests and providing for economic security and growth, difficult as this may be, will have done only part of the job. ... The notion that such a political order has completed the job is the source of dangerous blindness. Politics must allow somehow for the satisfaction of desires for distinction.... It must contend with anger and ambition, hatred, envy and contempt.... A successful political order cannot afford to ignore any of the full array of human passions and purposes.[55]

Grant reminds us that these sorts of concerns give rise to social interactions that can be more deeply conflictual than the simple pursuit of interest. "People will choose to hurt a rival, rather than

<hr/>

[53] See also Brennan and Pettit. *The economy of esteem: An essay on civil and political society*.

[54] Hobbes. *Leviathan*, part 1, chapter 11.

[55] Grant. "Passions and interests revisited: The psychological foundations of economics and politics," p. 476.

to attain the original object of their desire," she writes.[56] "Amour-propre leads people to seek satisfaction, not in their own benefit, but rather in harming others."[57] Thus understanding politics means grappling with status motivations, too.

Other thinkers have also discussed status motivations. For instance, Rawls writes of envy as "the propensity to view with hostility the greater good of others.... We envy persons whose situation is superior to ours .... and we are willing to deprive them of their greater benefits *even if* it is necessary to give up something ourselves."[58] Both Alexis de Tocqueville and John Stuart Mill discuss envy explicitly in *Democracy in America* and *On Liberty*, respectively.[59] Tocqueville describes those who are envious: "There is no superiority...not irksome in their sight."[60] Mill calls envy "that most anti-social and odious of all passions"[61] and places it among the moral vices that must be regulated because they "involve a breach of duty to others."[62] Here, again, concerns about one's relative position are treated as distinct motivations that are different from both self-interest and prosocial other-regarding preferences. These thinkers acknowledge that status concerns are sometimes important and powerful enough to require government intervention.

Even Adam Smith, while dismissing some status motivations, underscores others. In *The Wealth of Nations* he acknowledges antisocial status emotions like envy and spite but speculates that they may not be terribly consequential. "Envy, malice or resentment, are the only passions which can prompt one man

[56] Ibid., p. 454.

[57] Ibid., p. 459.

[58] John Rawls. *A theory of justice*. New York, NY: Oxford University Press, 1971, 532, emphasis added. He goes on, "So understood envy is collectively disadvantageous: the individual who envies another is prepared to do things that make them both worse off, if only the discrepancy between them is sufficiently reduced."

[59] Alexis de Tocqueville. *Democracy in America*. Trans by Henry Reeve. New York, NY: Adlard and Saunders, 1838; John Stuart Mill. *On Liberty and Other Essays*. New York, NY: Oxford University Press, 1998.

[60] Tocqueville. *Democracy in America*, book 1, chapter 13.

[61] Mill. *On Liberty and Other Essays*. p. 87.

[62] Ibid.

to injure another.... But the greater part of men are not very frequently under the influence of those passions, and the very worst men are so only occasionally. As their gratification too, how agreeable soever it may be to certain characters, is not attended with any real or permanent advantage it is in the greater part of men commonly restrained by prudential considerations."[63] On the one hand, Smith here recognizes the distinction between envy and self-interest, noting that envy's satisfaction is "not attended with any real or permanent advantage." On the other hand, he speculates that for this reason, envy (and presumably spite) will be overridden in many people by more "prudential considerations."[64] But while Smith downplays antisocial status motivations in *The Wealth of Nations*,[65] he highlights human beings' desire for admiration in *The Theory of Moral Sentiments*, in which he emphasizes the desire for "favorable regard" as an end in itself:

> Nature, when she formed man for society, ... taught him to feel pleasure in their favourable, and pain in their unfavourable regard. She rendered their approbation most flattering and most agreeable to him *for its own sake*.[66]

Human beings have a basic desire to achieve distinction in the eyes of others, and to actually live up to that distinction (not just appear to), according to Smith. They have a desire for this kind of status, even when it does not bring other benefits. Thus, even Smith, who is often considered the paramount writer about self-interest in politics and the economy, gives space and attention to status motivations.

[63] Adam Smith. *An inquiry into the nature and causes of the wealth of nations.* Ed. by Edwin Cannan. London, 1904, p. V.1.45

[64] As I discuss below, behavioral economics studies suggest that Smith is wrong here.

[65] *The wealth of nations* focuses on the relationship between self-interest and the public interest. That Smith downplays the importance of motivations that are contrary to self-interest in this work may be no coincidence.

[66] Adam Smith. *The theory of moral sentiments.* Cambridge: Cambridge University Press, 2002, 116, emphasis added.

Several political theory texts thus make clear that status motivations are (1) different from material self-interest and (2) help explain political behavior.[67] However, to my knowledge, few political theorists note that the quest for status is often parochial—that is, that it most often happens locally and within groups.[68] An exception is Aristotle, who argues that envy is more likely among social peers and intimates. In *On Rhetoric* he writes:

> We envy those who are near us in time, place, age or reputation.... We do not compare with men who lived a hundred centuries ago ... or those who dwell near the Pillars of Hercules, or those whom, in our opinion or that of others, we take to be far below or far above us.[69]

In other words, in Aristotle's view, comparisons among social and economic peers, rather than cross-class comparisons, are the most salient. As I discuss below, much modern social science research supports this understanding of status motivations, and it is an important insight for teasing out the observable implications of status motivations in political behavior.

Political theorists also seldom offer clear guidance on the conditions under which status motivations are more likely to be inflamed, or, more important, the conditions under which

---

[67] While political theorists contend that envy helps us understand politics as it *is*, some warn against using it to inform our notion of how politics *ought to be*. A good example is Rawls, who spends the better part of a chapter in *A theory of justice* trying to prove that his notion of justice as fairness is *not* derived from human beings' propensity for envy: Rawls. *A theory of justice*, chapter 8, sect. 80. I will briefly discuss these normative concerns later in the book.

[68] For instance, for Rousseau, amour-propre entails global comparisons: it is the desire to be recognized as superior by *all* others. See Kolodny. "The explanation of amour-propre." p. 171. Similarly, Rawls describes envy as cross-class hostility—a feeling of the disadvantaged toward the most advantaged, the mega-rich: Jeffrey Edward Green. "Rawls and the forgotten figure of the most advantaged: In defense of reasonable envy toward the superrich." In *American Political Science Review* 107.01 (2013), pp. 123–138.

[69] Aristotle. *Complete works of Aristotle: The revised Oxford translation.* Trans. by Jonathan Barnes. Vol. 1. Princeton, NJ: Princeton University Press, 2014, book 10.

status motivations are likely to be a force in politics specifically. One exception is Tocqueville, who argues that in times of great change, men care most about the disparities between themselves and others. In these times, a concern for status "swells to the height of fury":

> This occurs at the moment when the old social system, long menaced, completes its own destruction ...and when the barriers of rank are at length thrown down....Tell them not that by this blind surrender of themselves to an exclusive passion they *risk their dearest interests*: they are deaf.[70]

Like the other thinkers mentioned, Tocqueville recognizes that people can be so concerned about not being outdone by others that they pursue status at the expense of their own interests— especially when the social, economic, and political system is in flux. Thus, in his view, envy and other status motivations are likely to be most consequential in unsettled times. This argument resonates with more recent findings in anthropology and psychology, which I discuss below.

BEHAVIORAL ECONOMICS

While political theorists conceptualize status concerns as distinct from other interests, studies in behavioral economics go furthest in precisely identifying such divergences. For instance, these studies show that individuals sacrifice real income in order to achieve first place,[71] to stay out of last

---

[70] Tocqueville. *Democracy in America*, book 2, chapter 1, emphasis added.

[71] Bernardo A. Huberman, Christoph H. Loch, and Ayse Önçüler. "Status as a valued resource." In *Social Psychology Quarterly* 67.1 (2004), pp. 103–114. The authors conducted an experiment with an investment round followed by a lottery round. Investing more in the first round increased a subject's chances of moving on but decreased her chances of actually winning the lottery round. In a "status condition," the researchers promised a tag that read "winner" as well as applause

place,[72] or to lower the income of those better off than they regardless of their rank in the income hierarchy.[73] Zizzo and Oswald allowed subjects in their lab in Britain to "burn" the money of other subjects after it was allocated through a betting round. Eliminating ("burning") the money of other players was costly in this one-shot game; doing so meant that a subject walked out of the lab with a higher relative position but less money in his pocket (and no hope of turning that higher relative position into future material benefits). Contrary to Adam Smith's speculation that few people would allow envy to win out over self-interest, Zizzo found that over 60 percent of the subjects engaged in burning behavior.[74]

Research from all over the world finds similar evidence of real sacrifices to enhance one's relative position. In India, Fehr et al. found that in single-shot trust games with third-party

---

to the player who invested the most money in the first round. They found that people invested much more money in the first round when they were promised status rewards (compared to a control condition) even though, by doing so, they lowered their expected earnings by about 18% on average. The study participants did not know each other's identity, so they could not expect these status rewards to translate into other material rewards outside the lab.

[72] Ilyana Kuziemko et al. " 'Last-place aversion': Evidence and redistributive implications." In *Quarterly Journal of Economics* 129.1 (2014), pp. 105–149, conducted an experiment in which participants were ranked according to monetary endowments. In each round, the person in last place had to choose between a guaranteed payment that almost never improved her relative position and a gamble that *might* allow her to leapfrog the person above her in the ranking. Earnings were the equivalent in expectation. A majority of the time, the person in last place chose the gamble. The researchers also used survey evidence to show that Americans who are wage laborers employed just above the minimum wage are the *most* likely to oppose increasing the minimum wage.

[73] Zizzo and Oswald. "Are people willing to pay to reduce others' incomes?"

[74] Daniel John Zizzo. "Inequality and procedural fairness in a money burning and stealing experiment." In *Research on Economic Inequality* 11 (2004), pp. 215–247, also finds that money burning is higher when wealth is arbitrarily acquired (randomly assigned) than when it is earned (through an experimental task), but that money burning occurs no matter the procedural allocation. Burning is thus not solely due to fairness concerns. Below I further discuss the empirical distinctions between envy and concerns for fairness, and their possible interaction.

punishment,[75] third parties frequently punished the other players at a cost to themselves, regardless of how the first and second parties had behaved toward each other.[76] The cost paid by the punisher was always slightly less than the cost he imposed, thus improving his relative position. Third-party players explained their willingness to punish in post-experiment surveys by saying, "I wanted to destroy [player] B," or "I was jealous of B; that is why it is important to impose a loss on him."[77] The authors described the phenomenon they observed as spite, which they defined as "the desire to reduce another's material payoff for the mere purpose of increasing one's relative payoff."[78] In rural Ethiopian villages, Kebede and Zizzo conducted money "burning" experiments and found a similar willingness to eliminate the earnings of advantaged players, even at a personal cost.[79]

Behavioral economists have also demonstrated empirically that status motivations can be distinguished from concerns for fairness. Kirchsteiger showed how envious motivations can be distinguished from fairness concerns in ultimatum games used in laboratory experiments.[80] In ultimatum games, one player decides how much of his endowment to share with another person. The second person then decides whether to accept or reject the first

[75] In a trust game, one player is given an amount of money and asked to choose some fraction of it (or all of it) to send to a second person. The amount of money the first person sends is doubled or tripled and then the second person has to decide how much of the new amount to send back to the first player. In Fehr et al.'s version, a third person watches the transaction and is allowed to punish the other players for how they choose to play the game.

[76] Fehr, Hoff, and Kshetramade. "Spite and development."

[77] Ibid., p. 496.

[78] Ibid., p. 494.

[79] Bereket Kebede and Daniel John Zizzo. "Social preferences and agricultural innovation: An experimental case study from Ethiopia." In *World Development* 67 (2015), pp. 267–280.

[80] Georg Kirchsteiger. "The role of envy in ultimatum games." In *Journal of Economic Behavior & Organization* 25.3 (1994), pp. 373–389. See also David K. Levine. "Modeling altruism and spitefulness in experiments." In *Review of Economic Dynamics* 1.3 (1998), pp. 593–622; and Keith Jensen. "Punishment and spite, the dark side of cooperation." In *Philosophical Transactions of the Royal Society of London B: Biological Sciences* 365.1553 (2010), pp. 2635–2650.

person's offer. If she rejects the offer, neither player gets anything. The "homoeconomicus" expectation is that the second person should accept any offer. And yet many studies have found that people all over the world reject substantial offers that are less than equitable.[81] Kirchsteiger argues that while people might be tempted to conclude that these rejections are driven by fairness concerns, that conclusion "is misleading, because ...people are not concerned about *every* deviation from a fair share. They are only concerned if this deviation is disadvantageous for *themselves*."[82] He shows that the same people who reject unequal offers in an ultimatum game give far less than equal shares to someone worse off than they in a dictator game.[83] In other words, many people protest inequality that is disadvantageous to them but do not seek to rectify inequality that is disadvantageous to others. This is not to say that people are never concerned with fairness. Brañas et al. recently demonstrated that fairness concerns, envy, and spite can all be identified in patterns of play in the ultimatum game.[84] However, the distinguishing features of status motivations versus concerns for fairness relate to whether people apply distributive principles self-centeredly while maximizing their own relative position (status motivations), or whether they apply distributive principles widely and consistently (fairness). Status motivations and fairness concerns are both important explanatory factors that can be distinguished empirically.[85]

Thus, behavioral economists have gone furthest in showing empirically that status motivations have observable implications

[81] Joseph Patrick Henrich. *Foundations of human sociality: Economic experiments and ethnographic evidence from fifteen small-scale societies*. Oxford, UK: Oxford University Press, 2004.

[82] Kirchsteiger. "The role of envy in ultimatum games." p. 377, emphasis added.

[83] A dictator game involves the same set-up as an ultimatum game except that the second person has no choice but to accept the offer.

[84] Pablo Brañas-Garza et al. "Fair and unfair punishers coexist in the Ultimatum Game." In *Scientific Reports* 4 (2014).

[85] Anna Dreber and David G. Rand. "Retaliation and antisocial punishment are overlooked in many theoretical models as well as behavioral experiments." In *Behavioral and Brain Sciences* 35.01 (2012), p. 24.

that are distinct from the pursuit of self-interest and from other other-regarding preferences, such as a preference for equity or fairness. Behavioral economists have also shown that communities can develop mechanisms to manage the envy and spite of others. For instance, Boltz et al. show through a series of laboratory experiments in Senegal that villagers who are wary of the envy and spite of neighbors and extended kin take deliberate steps to hide their income and assets.[86] They do so at a cost to themselves, forgoing potential income in order to decrease potential hostility from neighbors and friends. In these tightly knit communities, people develop conventions and strategies to anticipate and mitigate the status motivations of others, a point to which I return when discussing anthropological studies below.

One other insight from behavioral economics is that many status motivations are felt more strongly when interpersonal disparities are highly visible. Gershman argues that envy is likely to be strongest where people's assets are not easily hidden.[87] It is difficult to be envious of disparities one cannot observe. But where differences in assets are highly visible, the disadvantaged are constantly reminded of their low status. Gershman finds that, at least among preindustrial societies, the more visible the assets, the more likely there is to be frequent punishment of the most advantaged members of the community. Working in rural villages in Ethiopia, Kebede and Zizzo make a similar argument.[88] They find that the rate of money burning in a village correlates with investment in conspicuous forms of economic activities, such as rain harvesting and fertilizer adoption. Envy and spite are both

---

[86] Marie Boltz, Karine Marazyan, and Paola Villar. "Preference for hidden income and redistribution to kin and neighbors: A lab-in-the-field experiment in Senegal." In Unpublished Paper, Paris School of Economics (2015). The authors use the term "social pressure to redistribute" but refer to parts of the anthropological literature on envy as motivation.

[87] Boris Gershman. "The economic origins of the evil eye belief." In *Journal of Economic Behavior & Organization* 110 (2015), pp. 119–144.

[88] Kebede and Zizzo. "Social preferences and agricultural innovation: An experimental case study from Ethiopia."

problematic when disparities are visible and frequently observed by those living in close proximity to one another.

PSYCHOLOGY

There is a rich body of psychological research on status motivations. Festinger, an early pioneer of "social comparison theory," wrote that it is difficult for us to assess our own abilities in isolation, so we tend to compare ourselves with others and use them as our benchmarks, even when doing so makes us feel worse about ourselves.[89] Indeed, most social comparisons are "spontaneous, effortless, and unintentional" and therefore "relatively automatic" rather than calculated.[90] To a large extent, we cannot avoid internally engaging in, and reacting to, social comparisons even when they do not make us feel good or improve our material situation.

For psychologists, envy is a pained response to an "upward" comparison (i.e., with those who are doing better than we are), whereas spite is a response to a "downward comparison" (i.e., with those who are worse off).[91] Following James's notion that emotions have response tendencies, psychologists have documented that both emotions are accompanied by a tendency to harm others.[92] Psychologists have documented evidence of envy and

[89] Festinger. "A theory of social comparison processes."

[90] Daniel T. Gilbert, R. Brian Giesler, and Kathryn A. Morris. "When comparisons arise." In *Journal of Personality and Social Psychology* 69.2 (1995), pp. 227–236.

[91] David K. Marcus et al. "The psychology of spite and the measurement of spitefulness." In *Psychological Assessment* 26.2 (2014), pp. 563–574; Thomas A. Wills. "Downward comparison principles in social psychology." In *Psychological Bulletin* 90.2 (1981), pp. 245–271.

[92] William James. *Principles of psychology*. New York, NY: Dover, 1890. As Amy Cuddy et al. "Stereotype content model across cultures: Towards universal similarities and some differences." In *British Journal of Social Psychology* 48.1 (2009), pp. 1–33, and Fiske. *Envy up, scorn down: How status divides us*, make clear, the more benign feeling that may colloquially be referred to as envy can lead people to associate with the envied others. But the more malicious feeling of envy (the focus of this book) is likely to lead to harm when acted upon. Spite (or contempt, in Fiske's terminology) can lead either to active harm or to neglect of someone worse off.

spite in numerous societies, in both the developed and developing world,[93] although different terminology is sometimes used. For instance, Feather wrote several papers on a phenomenon in Australia he called "Tall Poppy Syndrome," wherein when one or more individuals rise above their friends and peers, those peers seek to "cut" them down, even if such behavior is costly.[94]

The psychological literature helps clarify the types of comparisons that are likely to give rise to status concerns. Reinforcing Aristotle's intuition, psychologists have often concluded that salient social comparisons, including envious ones, are made among "similar" others[95]—among neighbors, classmates, coworkers, family members and coethnics.[96] Individuals less often gauge their status against other individuals who are geographically remote,[97] or against people who are vastly and visibly different from them in background, experience, or abilities.[98]

Research in psychology tells us that we tend to envy, spite, and desire the admiration of "similar" others for two reasons: evaluation and visibility. We seek comparisons that help us determine the level of self-esteem we ought to carry. In-group members provide us with information that is relevant to our self-esteem. We believe these people to be somewhat similar to us either in capability or disposition. "People who are similar to us provide

[93] Cuddy et al. "Stereotype content model across cultures: Towards universal similarities and some differences."

[94] Norman T. Feather. "Attitudes towards the high achiever: The fall of the tall poppy." In *Australian Journal of Psychology* 41.3 (1989), pp. 239–267.

[95] Festinger. "A theory of social comparison processes."

[96] See also Fiske. *Envy up, scorn down: How status divides us*; John Knight, Song Lina, and Ramani Gunatilaka. "Subjective well-being and its determinants in rural China." In *China Economic Review* 20.4 (2009), pp. 635–649; Wills, "Downward comparison principles in social psychology."

[97] Claudia Senik. "Direct evidence on income comparisons and their welfare effects." In *Journal of Economic Behavior & Organization* 72.1 (2009), pp. 408–424; Knight, Lina, and Gunatilaka. "Subjective well-being and its determinants in rural China."; Geeta Gandhi Kingdon and John Knight. "Community, comparisons and subjective well-being in a divided society." In *Journal of Economic Behavior & Organization* 64.1 (2007), pp. 69–90.

[98] Fiske. *Envy up, scorn down: How status divides us*.

us with a proxy self."[99] When they achieve more, have more, or are more, highly regarded, it indicates something bad about us.[100] The logic is that if *they* obtained that wealth or won that esteem, *we* could (and should) have won it, too.[101] Anderson et al. call this "the local ladder effect."[102]

There are certain types of groups with whose members we tend to assume we share similar capabilities, such as coworkers with similar responsibilities to ours,[103] and members of our same age cohort.[104] In addition, coethnicity can be used as a relatively low-cost and sometimes automatic heuristic for gauging similarity on a variety of dimensions.[105] In the presence of salient ethnic group boundaries, shared ethnicity may be used as a signal that two individuals share similar backgrounds. A person may also believe that his coethnics have similar capabilities, even though these judgments are often based on stereotypes.[106] Falling behind a coethnic is particularly likely to highlight failure in oneself, because, according to the same logic discussed above, given these

---

[99] Ibid., p. 82.

[100] We "envy those whose possession of or success in a thing is a reproach to us: these are our neighbours and equals; for it is clear that it is our own fault we have missed the good thing in question; this annoys us, and excites envy in us" (Aristotle, *On Rhetoric*, book 10).

[101] Robert F. Bales et al. "Channels of communication in small groups." In *American Sociological Review* 16.4 (1951), pp. 461–468. The authors note that the attention to status within proximate groups of similar others may stem from early stages of evolution, when humans had to focus on surviving within face-to-face groups. They note that striving for this kind of within-group status occurs in non-human, small-group species as well.

[102] Anderson et al. "The local-ladder effect: Social status and subjective well-being."

[103] Frank. *Choosing the right pond: Human behavior and the quest for status.*

[104] Senik. "Direct evidence on income comparisons and their welfare effects."

[105] Mary J. Rotheram-Borus. "Adolescents' reference-group choices, self-esteem, and adjustment." In *Journal of Personality and Social Psychology* 59.5 (1990), pp. 1075–1081.

[106] Brenda Major. "From social inequality to personal entitlement: The role of social comparisons, legitimacy appraisals, and group membership." In *Advances in Experimental Social Psychology* 26 (1994), pp. 293–293; Jennifer Crocker and Brenda Major. "Social stigma and self-esteem: The self-protective properties of stigma." In *Psychological Review* 96.4 (1989), pp. 608–630.

similarities, one might (and should) have achieved a similar level of success.[107]

The people most frequently visible to us also provide easily available, and often automatic, comparisons, even if they are not always informative. "We [often] compare so spontaneously that we do it automatically, and we use whoever is at hand."[108] While we may not have deep relationships with our neighbors, and while they may differ from us in some ways, they and their possessions are highly and frequently visible to us and foster automatic comparisons. We constantly gather information about the clothes they wear, the cars or bicycles they own, the houses they live in, and their public conduct—whether we intend to or not.[109] Social comparisons vis-à-vis neighboring coethnics are likely to be even more salient because they stem from both availability and an assumption of similarity.[110]

Yet, just because comparisons arise relatively automatically does not mean there are no mechanisms for regulating emotions and the behavior that result from them.[111] Emotions have response tendencies,[112] but actual behavioral responses vary; they are not predetermined.[113] Efforts to suppress negative emotions often

---

[107] Wendi L. Gardner, Shira Gabriel, and Laura Hochschild. "When you and I are 'we,' you are not threatening: the role of self-expansion in social comparison." In *Journal of Personality and Social Psychology* 82.2 (2002), pp. 239–251. Moreover, this reference group—unlike some of the others—is also arguably exogenously assigned to the individual.

[108] Fiske. *Envy up, scorn down: How status divides us*, p. 84.

[109] Knight, Lina, and Gunatilaka. "Subjective well-being and its determinants in rural China"; Kingdon and Knight. "Community, comparisons and subjective well-being in a divided society."

[110] Erzo F. P. Luttmer. "Neighbors as negatives: Relative earnings and well-being." In *Quarterly Journal of Economics* 120.3 (2005), pp. 963–1002; Peter Salovey and Judith Rodin. "Some antecedents and consequences of social-comparison jealousy." In *Journal of Personality and Social Psychology* 47.4 (1984), pp. 780–792.

[111] Emily A. Butler, Tiane L. Lee, and James J. Gross. "Emotion regulation and culture: Are the social consequences of emotion suppression culture-specific?" In *Emotion* 7.1 (2007), pp. 30–48.

[112] James. *Principles of psychology*.

[113] Ross Buck. "Social and emotional functions in facial expression and communication: The readout hypothesis." In *Biological Psychology* 38.2 (1994), pp. 95–115.

backfire, only heightening the negative emotional experience.[114] People use other strategies to try to decrease their feelings of envy and spite, or to stop themselves from harming others if they experience these emotions. Psychologists have found that one such strategy involves turning attention to a different dimension of assets or traits so as to lessen the dependence of our self-esteem on comparisons based on the first dimension.[115] For instance, students who are envious of a more academically accomplished peer might remind themselves that they are better at sports. Alternatively, students hoping that a less accomplished student will mess up on a test so that they can stay ahead might remind themselves that they are already more popular than that other student. Another strategy involves switching reference points. An individual might seek to contain his envy either by switching reference groups to find more favorable comparisons, or by turning inward to rely more on himself.

These internal strategies have limitations. Status motivations arise from comparisons along dimensions relevant to the "self-concept."[116] This means that switching the dimension of comparison and downplaying the importance of the original dimension requires a shift in fundamental beliefs about what constitutes the self, which can be quite difficult to achieve. Switching reference groups can also fail if one is constantly exposed to the group that induced the original status comparisons. For instance, unless one has enough resources and opportunities to move, it can be difficult to avoid invidious comparisons with neighbors. Avoiding interactions with others is also difficult because it can be rather

---

[114] Daniel M. Wegner, Ralph Erber, and Sophia Zanakos. "Ironic processes in the mental control of mood and mood-related thought." In *Journal of Personality and Social Psychology* 65.6 (1993), pp. 1093–1104.

[115] Salovey and Rodin. "Some antecedents and consequences of social-comparison jealousy"; Richard H. Smith. *Envy: Theory and research.* Oxford, UK: Oxford University Press, 2008; Julie J. Exline and Anne L. Zell. "Antidotes to envy: A conceptual framework." In *Envy: Theory and research. Series in affective science.* Ed. by Richard H. Smith. Oxford, UK: Oxford University Press, 2008, pp. 315–331.

[116] Salovey and Rodin. "Some antecedents and consequences of social-comparison jealousy."

lonely.[117] The reality is that there are few reliable strategies for internally regulating status motivations.

Thus, more important than internal regulation alone is the influence of social context on our management of status motivations.[118] From observing and interacting with others people learn whether and how to control their emotions, and in front of whom.[119] Social conventions convey whether and which emotions are appropriately felt and publicly expressed.[120] As Gross writes, "Emotion regulation is almost always a social affair."[121] Social conventions regularly govern the management of the internal experience of status motivations as well as their action tendencies.

Research in psychology provides some limited insights into the conditions under which social conventions might *not* be able to mitigate status motivations. For instance, in times of upheaval and transition, people are very attuned to and unavoidably bothered by new disparities within groups.[122] This pattern might be related to the psychology of attention. When people filter the vast amounts of information about their environment, they are selective, and they pay particular attention to change. On average individuals are more attuned to elements of their social environment when those elements have recently shifted.[123] For instance, we pay more attention to ethnic diversity when our

---

[117] Salovy and Rodin do however find that the "self-reliance" strategy tends to be the most successful way to reduce envy.

[118] Buck. "Social and emotional functions in facial expression and communication: The readout hypothesis."

[119] Joseph J. Campos et al. "Reconceptualizing emotion regulation." In *Emotion Review* 3.1 (2011), pp. 26–35.

[120] Hochschild. *The managed heart.*

[121] James J. Gross. "The emerging field of emotion regulation: An integrative review." In *Review of General Psychology* 2.3 (1998), pp. 271–299, p. 279.

[122] Salovey and Rodin. "Some antecedents and consequences of social-comparison jealousy"; Fiske, *Envy Up, Scorn Down: How Status Divides Us.*

[123] Daniel Kahneman and Amos Tversky. "Prospect theory: An analysis of decision under risk." In *Econometrica: Journal of the Econometric Society* (1979), pp. 263–291.

communities have recently become more or less diverse.[124] Similarly, we are likely to pay more attention to our relative position within groups when that position has recently or dramatically changed.

Despite these clues, research in psychology does not generally offer in-depth exploration of the social conventions governing status motivations. Nor does it explore in depth the contexts in which those social conventions are likely to be robust or to break down. For more thorough responses to these questions, I turn to research in anthropology.

ANTHROPOLOGY

A rich set of anthropological studies explores the ways people navigate, give meaning to, and regulate differences in wealth and status. These studies are particularly useful for learning about both social conventions that communities use to manage status motivations and the conditions under which those conventions break down.

One noteworthy finding that emerges from the anthropological literature is that societies all over the world share the view that there is danger in having advantages over others, due to the interpersonal hostility those advantages might provoke. In tight-knit and settled communities, this view is regularly translated into social conventions that anticipate and mitigate envy, spite, and the pursuit of admiration. For instance, practices meant to ward off the "evil eye" are pervasive.[125] Other documented strategies for avoiding hostility from others who may be less advantaged include avoiding contact with individuals who are thought to be particularly envious, shunning compliments, hiding evidence

---

[124] Daniel J. Hopkins. "The diversity discount: When increasing ethnic and racial diversity prevents tax increases." In *Journal of Politics* 71.01 (2009), pp. 160–177.

[125] Alan Dundes. *The evil eye: A casebook* Vol. 2. Madison, WI: University of Wisconsin Press, 1981.

of prosperity (livestock, pregnancy, fancy clothes, salaries), and avoiding leadership positions.[126]

These kinds of social conventions developed to manage status motivations appear in anthropological accounts across a range of societies, from Northern Pakistan[127] to the Philippines,[128] to New York.[129] Ghosh notes that in an Egyptian town where avoiding the evil eye was an explicit practice, individuals would walk far out of their way to avoid passing the windows of families thought to be particularly envious.[130] They would keep their livestock in the back rooms of their house, rather than outside, so that neighbors would not see them. Some chose to plant corn, even when they could afford to buy more-profitable livestock, in order to avoid becoming wealthier than their neighbors. Status motivations were observed to be a salient social concern that structured everyday activities. They shaped how people displayed their attributes and assets, as well as individual choices about what to prioritize and in what to invest. In these small communities, where people knew each other well, they developed ways to hide advantages or to forgo opportunities to gain them if such advantages might provoke hostility from others. In other tight-knit communities, people with advantages are constrained by social convention to demonstrate generosity rather than spite vis-à-vis others—giving money away to neighbors and relatives, throwing parties, and otherwise demonstrating goodwill.[131]

Anthropological accounts thus give insight into the conditions under which social practices for managing status motivations

---

[126] George M. Foster, et al. "The anatomy of envy: A study in symbolic behavior [and comments and reply]." In *Current Anthropology* (1972), pp. 165–202.

[127] Exline and Zell. "Antidotes to envy: A conceptual framework."

[128] George M. Guthrie. "A social-psychological analysis of modernization in the philippines." In *Journal of Cross-Cultural Psychology* 8.2 (1977), pp. 177–206.

[129] Dundes. *The evil eye: A casebook.*

[130] Amitav Ghosh. "The relations of envy in an Egyptian village." In *Ethnology* 22.3 (1983), pp. 211–223.

[131] Harri Englund. "Witchcraft, modernity and the person: The morality of accumulation in central Malawi." In *Critique of Anthropology* 16.3 (1996), pp. 257–279.

break down. As both Tocqueville and contemporary psychologists suggest, status motivations seem to be more likely to affect political life under conditions of social and economic transition, or flux.[132] During these periods, new interpersonal disparities appear at the same time that the rules for regulating responses to these disparities break down or are contested. These periods are the "unsettled" ones described by Swidler, in which "people are learning new ways of organizing ... action, practicing unfamiliar habits until they become familiar."[133] In such times, the meaning of new types of inequalities can become unclear and troubling: "Does the fact that he is suddenly better off than I mean that I am being left permanently behind?" "Does it mean he and I can no longer have the same relationship?" The social "feeling rules" governing the regulation of action tendencies from social comparisons falter.[134] While most religions and social systems prohibit acting on (or even feeling) status concerns, those rules can become considerably weaker in unsettled, transitionary periods. In South Africa, Ramphele describes life in a Cape Town township in the early 2000s, only a few years after the transition from apartheid.[135] The formal legal and economic barriers to advancement had only just recently been removed for black South Africans. New (though still limited) opportunities were available to young black South Africans in some parts of the country (including Cape Town), but new social conventions had not yet been developed to deal with them. Ramphele notes that it was clear that under these conditions "climbing the ladder of success" was a suddenly contested act that could have open social repercussions. She writes:

> As soon as the individual reaches the upper levels [of the ladder], they [those at the bottom] start doubting the wisdom of their action [in letting him climb]: what if the

[132] Tocqueville, *Democracy in America*.

[133] Swidler. "Culture in action: Symbols and strategies," p. 278.

[134] Hochschild. *The managed heart*.

[135] Mamphela Ramphele. *Steering by the stars: Being young in South Africa*. Cape Town, SA: Tafelberg, 2002.

individual reaches the top and forgets about them? They are then apt to pull the ladder away and let the individual come crashing down.[136]

During periods of transition and transformation, new inequalities emerge, leaving many feeling uncertain, potentially betrayed, and without social rules to make sense of them and guide behavior. In these situations, the "local ladder effect"[137] is likely to influence what people want from policy and political institutions. Because social conventions that might otherwise have anticipated and addressed status motivations are weak, third-party intervention may be needed.

ζ

The insights from these disciplines offer an analytic framework for thinking about the politics of status motivations. The research in these fields makes clear that status motivations are common in most, if not all, societies. Political theorists distinguish status motivations from self-interest and argue that status motivations are likely to be politically relevant. Behavioral economists go the furthest in empirically demonstrating that people can be willing to sacrifice both long- and short-term interests, as well as principles of fairness, in order to enhance their within-group status. Psychologists show that status comparisons are relatively automatic responses and that many are accompanied by an action tendency toward harm that is difficult to suppress internally. Anthropologists have documented social practices in tightly knit communities designed to respond to those action tendencies.

These disciplines thus point to the conditions under which status motivations are both (1) salient and (2) successfully regulated without the involvement of political institutions and policy. They show that status motivations can be particularly potent

---

[136] Ibid., p. 105.
[137] Anderson et al. "The local-ladder effect: Social status and subjective well-being."

among people who expect to be similar to one another and where interpersonal differences are highly visible and frequently observable. Termed the "local ladder effect," this means that social comparisons can be particularly potent within social groups and neighborhoods. However, the anthropological literature makes clear that there are social conventions in many contexts for managing, and even suppressing, status motivations within groups. Particularly in settled times and where social ties are strong, people follow clear social rules about whether, when, and how disparities should be regulated and negotiated.

When these social conventions break down (e.g, during "unsettled" times of economic and social transition) or when they have not yet developed (e.g., where people do not know each other well), policy and political institutions are likely to have to contend with status motivations in a meaningful way. Because social institutions are failing to manage "status passions" in such situations, people may turn to policy, political institutions, and political engagement for redress, or political elites may take advantage of the situation to promise status rewards for specific types of political behavior. Under these conditions, people's political preferences are more likely to reflect their willingness to pay a personal cost to improve their within-group relative position; people should be more likely to support policies and actions that make them relatively better off within local social groups, even if they are made worse off in absolute terms. In the rest of the book, I explore whether there is empirical support for these claims.

Overview of the Book

This book is a series of "essays" in Montaigne's sense of the word— that is, of attempts to explore how attention to status motivations might give us additional leverage over puzzles in political science. I do this from an empirical, not just a theoretical, point of view, but I do not attempt to examine any single puzzle, example, or case in as great a depth or with as much analytic precision as I would if the book were focused on that puzzle alone. The goal is instead to look for observable implications of status motivations across a range of puzzles that might not otherwise be considered in tandem. Therefore, the brushstrokes in the rest of the book are necessarily broad.

I consider three different puzzles from comparative politics: Why do citizens sometimes support redistribution and taxation policies that go against their material self-interests? Why do politicians sometimes fail to implement funded policies? Why do citizens sometimes participate in contentious political events even though it is individually costly to do so? The applications in the book involve, broadly, what citizens want from government, what they get from government, and whether (and when) they participate in politics. Thus, while these applications do not cover *all* of political behavior, they touch on core aspects of both the demand and supply sides of government. In each case, I argue that understanding more about the psychology of status motivations in its various manifestation—envy, spite, and the desire for admiration—can help shed additional light on citizens' and politicians' puzzling behavior. In each case, I argue that people often formulate preferences and take political actions that hurt their material interests when doing so promises a higher within-group status. Even if it is personally costly, they oppose higher taxes, oppose the implementation of funded policies, and engage in collective action when doing so will make them *relatively* better off within local reference groups. Status motivations are certainly not the only non-interest-based explanation, but they can be a useful one.

I focus on evidence specifically from South Africa and the United States because they provide hard tests of the argument. Since both countries are well known for salient racial divisions, one might expect citizens of these countries to privilege the welfare of their groups rather than to bicker over interpersonal disparities *within* groups. The United States is also known to celebrate rags-to-riches success stories. Thus we might expect that the relative success of others would generally be positively received rather than incite envy. If status motivations help us illuminate aspects of political behavior in these countries, I suspect they would do so elsewhere as well.

The applications bring together different sources of evidence (surveys, case studies, an experiment) to investigate the usefulness of the framework from a variety of different angles. Experiments often get us closest to identifying and isolating the fine-grained micro-foundations of political behavior. But such tools are not always available, and they do not always help us directly aggregate implications of individual-level motivations to the meso- or macro-level outcomes we seek to understand. My hope is that by leveraging different types of evidence, all of which are imperfect in their own ways, I might encourage political scientists using various methodological perspectives and working in various political contexts to consider whether envy and other status motivations might shed light on the phenomena they investigate. My contention is that the framework is not methodologically specific. Likewise, my exploration of within-group status dynamics in both "developed" and "developing" country settings is meant to suggest the applicability of this approach to disparate contexts. Status motivations are provoked by particular situations, but they are not specific to particular types of societies.

One could certainly read each of the applications in isolation, but my hope is that the whole is greater than the sum of its parts. After discussing the three specific empirical applications, I take a step back again and elaborate on conceptual, explanatory, and normative aspects of the main argument that carry across specific puzzles. I revisit how we can distinguish status motivations from other variables in the existing literature: from fairness concerns, relative deprivation, and inequality aversion. I also discuss alternative interpretations of the observable implications of status motivations. For instance, could all of the empirical puzzles in the applications sections have been accounted for by a theory of long-term self-interest or by people's sorting into groups and across space? I show that these alternative accounts are not fully satisfying. I also discuss alternative approaches to studying status motivations that I have largely set aside: (1) taking a dispositional rather than situational approach, and (2) focusing on *between-*group, rather than within-group, status concerns; finally, I briefly discuss potential normative concerns; for instance, since status motivations are often ugly inclinations, is it morally appropriate to consider appeasing status motivations when designing policy? The Elaborations chapter of the book is broad and wide-ranging but should be useful to anyone considering status motivations as a potential explanation for puzzling political behavior.

I conclude by offering thoughts on scope conditions, more general implications, and extensions for future research. The book is meant to be probing rather than definitive. My goal is to offer a different way of thinking about politics by considering status motivations as independent influences on political attitudes and behavior. Future research can then apply the arguments advanced here to other places and domains of political behavior and can further develop, or correct, the book's main ideas.

TWO Applications

In 2011 the *New York Times* published an article on the regulation of tombstones and burial sites in Chengdu, China.[1] The local government in Chengdu had imposed limits on the size of burial plots and the height of tombstones, restricting them to 1.5 square meters and 100 centimeters, respectively. Other local governments had placed limits on funeral expenditures and razed elaborate tombs. Public officials were trying to limit the extravagance with which some Chinese elites were burying their dead.

The new local regulations were not motivated by a scarcity of space or the need to generate revenue, the article reported. Instead, public officials were trying to manage the reactions of those being made to feel both poorer and less respected by the burial displays. A local resident interviewed for the article explained, "Ordinary people who walk by and see these lavish tombs might not be able to keep their emotions in balance." Public officials feared that those left behind by their neighbors might become envious and respond with hostility. Politicians were stepping in because social conventions no longer seemed to be keeping social conflict in check. The article detailed the dramatic ways that economic inequality had increased in these localities in recent decades.[2] The nouveau riche were behaving in ways that were insensitive

[1] Sharon LaFraniere. "China curbs fancy tombs that irk the poor." In *New York Times* (Apr. 2011), A1.

[2] It points out that inequality has dramatically increased in some parts of China over the last three decades and that, countrywide, the 90:10 income ratio effectively doubled between 1988 and 2007.

to the less well off. Social conventions for managing reactions to inequality were breaking down.

In many ways, this account resonates with insights about status motivations described in the introduction of this volume. People are sensitive to their local relative position, both in terms of their economic standing and in terms of the respect they are shown (or not shown). Government officials seek to regulate visible forms of economic disparities in order to minimize the hostility of neighbors, broadly defined, against neighbors. These efforts arise in the wake of economic and social shifts that have created new patterns of wealth and destabilized social conventions.

But, of course, this example does not on its own establish that the argument advanced in this book is correct. First, it is difficult to verify the role of status motivations in this kind of anecdotal account. The account provides little insight into whether citizens are willing to pay personal costs in order to reduce the position of others and improve their own—that is, whether they are concerned with relative position per se. Second, it might not be all that surprising that status motivations could shape policy in China. China has a communist economic system, where efforts to manage economic disparities might be par for the course.[3] The Chinese government has been known to engage in forms of social engineering to manage and shape the behavior and social interactions of citizens,[4] particularly for the purposes of avoiding eruptions of social conflict.[5]

However, there are ways to look systematically for the political implications of status motivations, and we can look for these observable implications in more surprising places. In the following applications, I look for evidence of the main arguments in two

[3] Helmut Schoeck. *Envy*. Boston, MA: Liberty Press, 1969.

[4] Luigi Tomba. "Creating an urban middle class: Social engineering in Beijing." In *China Journal* 51 (2004), pp. 1–26.

[5] Gary King, Jennifer Pan, and Margaret E. Roberts. "How censorship in China allows government criticism but silences collective expression." In *American Political Science Review* 107.02 (2013), pp. 326–343.; c.f., Chen. *Social protest and contentious authoritarianism in China*.

capitalist democracies: South Africa and the United States. I focus on three different political puzzles: Why do some citizens support redistribution and taxation policies that are contrary to their material interests? Why do politicians sometimes fail to implement funded policies that would make most of their constituents better off in absolute terms? Why do citizens participate in contentious politics when it is individually costly to do so? If Lasswell was right that "politics is who gets what, when, and how," these applications touch on many core areas of political science research.[6] The findings resonate with the anecdotal account from China even though the applications do not target conspicuous consumption specifically. As in the anecdotal account, people's concerns for their within-group status have consequences for political preferences and behavior, especially when social conventions for managing status motivations are weak or when elites explicitly prime status rewards.

As discussed in the introduction, the following are essays in the French sense of "attempts." Rather than examining a single political puzzle and seeking one primary explanation for it, I work the other way around: I start with one insight about human psychology and tease out its implications for several political puzzles. The applications explore why people take political positions and actions that are, on balance, materially costly for them. They share the insight that when status concerns are unmanaged by informal social mechanisms or are explicitly primed by elites, they can lead people to make material sacrifices in order to secure a higher status. Otherwise, the applications proceed quite differently. The puzzles are varied, as are the manifestations of status motivations (envy, spite, the desire for esteem) that I use to explain them. I have pursued diversity, at times at the expense of cohesion. My hope is that the results highlight the disparate domains (and ways) in which status motivations can influence politics.

---

[6] Harold Lasswell. *Politics: Who gets what, when, how*. New York, NY: Peter Smith, 1936.

Preferences over Redistribution

Democratic citizens across the economic spectrum often support redistribution policies that are contrary to their self- and class interests. Many poor people in highly unequal democracies do not support high levels of redistribution, even though they would benefit from such a policy. Likewise, many rich citizens of democracies are content to pay disproportionate levels of income tax, even though such policies leave less money in their pockets.[7]

Indeed, despite high and growing levels of economic inequality in the United States and South Africa, both exhibit considerable variation in the attitudes of the poor toward redistribution, and the rich often support high taxes.[8] In South Africa, despite a history of extreme economic and racial inequality, Wegner and Pellicer estimated that only a third of poor black South Africans support efforts to increase redistribution while more than half of the rich (black or white) support or are neutral toward such efforts.[9]

An extensive literature examines why some citizens support redistribution policies that would make them materially worse off. Some explanations reconceptualize material self-interest to focus on long-term and group interests, while others reach beyond material interests to focus on alternative motivations such as altruism and a desire for fairness. I do not discount these alternative explanations and discuss them in more detail below. Instead, my

---

[7] Seminal works have expected individuals' support for taxes and redistribution to decrease as their incomes rose. See Allan H. Meltzer and Scott F. Richard. "A rational theory of the size of government." In *Journal of Political Economy* 89.5 (1981), pp. 914–927.

[8] See, e.g., Larry M. Bartels. *Unequal democracy.* New York, NY: Russell Sage Foundation, 2008; Gilens. *Why Americans hate welfare: Race, media, and the politics of antipoverty policy*; Jeremy Seekings and Nicoli Nattrass. "Class, distribution and redistribution in post-apartheid South Africa." In *Transformation: Critical perspectives on southern Africa* 50.1 (2002), pp. 1–30; Jennifer L. Hochschild. *What's fair? American beliefs about distributive justice.* Cambridge, MA: Harvard University Press, 1986.

[9] Eva Wegner and Miquel Pellicer. "Demand for redistribution in South Africa." In *Special IARIW-SSA Conference on Measuring National Income, Wealth, Poverty, and Inequality in African Countries, Cape Town, South Africa.* 2011.

goal is to explore the possibility that status motivations are also part of the story.

Progressive taxation and redistribution affect a person's pocketbook as well as her relative position within local social groups: a person who is rich by national standards is often surrounded in her day-to-day life by even richer people. Even though she is doing well in absolute terms, constant reminders of her local relative disadvantage can affect her happiness and incite her envy. Where she has strong, established ties with her neighbors, there might be social conventions for managing these feelings. In the absence of such mechanisms, more progressive taxation can be a vehicle for reducing some of the disparity between her richer neighbors and herself, thus lessening her envy, even though it is costly to her. Similarly, a person who is poor by national standards is often surrounded by even poorer people. While more progressive taxation would make her better off in an absolute sense, she might oppose such policies because it would reduce her local relative advantage. In short, some variation in preferences over redistribution might be explained by the dynamics of envy and spite within local reference groups.

The main observable implication of this argument is that a citizen's preferences regarding national distribution policies should be influenced by how well off she is *within her local reference group*, controlling for alternative factors. The worse off a citizen is compared to neighbors similar to herself, for instance, the more supportive she should be of increasing taxation and redistribution, because it will improve her local within-group status, even if those policies would be costly to her personally and to her social identity groups as a whole. Likewise, the better off a citizen is compared to neighbors similar to herself, the less supportive she should be of greater redistribution, because it would hurt her local within-group status, even if greater redistribution might benefit her in absolute terms. These patterns should be strongest where citizens lack robust social mechanisms for addressing status motivations without the involvement of official policies—that is, where social ties are weak.

Will this relationship between local relative position and support for greater redistribution hold net of other important alternative explanations of variation in preferences over redistribution? Such explanations include different conceptualizations of self- and group material interest over both the short and long term. Poor people who are optimistic that they will one day become rich might oppose higher taxes on the rich in order to maximize their future income.[10] Those who are at greater risk of unemployment or other negative income shocks might support redistribution as a social safety net.[11] People who have coping mechanisms for dealing with economic adversity, such as those who are more religious, might be less supportive of redistribution.[12] Those concerned about larger social ills, such as crime, may believe that supporting social spending will reduce their vulnerability to such ills.[13] People might also focus on maximizing the average income of their social identity groups. Poor individuals who are members of a rich group might oppose greater redistribution because they care about group welfare in absolute terms or relative to that of out groups.[14] Those who identify strongly with the nation as a whole

---

[10] Roland Benabou and Efe A. Ok. "Social mobility and the demand for redistribution: The Poum hypothesis." In *Quarterly Journal of Economics* 116.2 (2001), pp. 447–487.

[11] Karl Ove Moene and Michael Wallerstein. "Earnings inequality and welfare spending: A disaggregated analysis." In *World Politics* 55.04 (2003), pp. 485–516; Thomas Cusack, Torben Iversen, and Philipp Rehm. "Risks at work: The demand and supply sides of government redistribution." In *Oxford Review of Economic Policy* 22.3 (2006), pp. 365–389.

[12] Kenneth Scheve and David Stasavage. "Religion and preferences for social insurance." In *Quarterly Journal of Political Science* 1.3 (2006), pp. 255–286.

[13] David Rueda and Daniel Stegmueller. "The externalities of inequality: Fear of crime and preferences for redistribution in Western Europe." In *American Journal of Political Science* 60.2 (2015), pp. 472–489. General perceptions of how the national economy is performing, rather than one's personal economic situation, might also influence support for redistribution: Mitchell Killian, Ryan Schoen, and Aaron Dusso. "Keeping up with the Joneses: The interplay of personal and collective evaluations in voter turnout." In *Political Behavior* 30.3 (2008), pp. 323–340.

[14] Gilens. *Why Americans hate welfare: Race, media, and the politics of antipoverty policy*; Alberto Alesina and Edward L. Glaeser. *Fighting poverty in the US and Europe: A world of difference* Vol. 26. Oxford, UK: Oxford University Press, 2004;

might be more likely to perceive redistribution as in their group's (that is, the nation's) interest.[15]

Such explanations also include non-interest-based motivations. Perhaps people diverge from their self- and group interests because they feel empathy for the poor,[16] or because they want taxation policy to be guided by certain universal principles of fairness and reciprocity, even if that means personal costs to themselves.[17] These concerns do not relate to one's *own* position within local groups but rather to helping others and making sure no one is unduly advantaged or disadvantaged. In addition, partisanship, or principled views about the size and role of government, might play a role.[18]

Although the set of existing explanations is dense, puzzling variation remains. For example, figure 2.1 divides survey respondents[19] into groups for which interest-based explanations have straightforward expectations; for example, the poor who belong

Erzo Luttmer. "Group loyalty and the taste for redistribution." In *Journal of Political Economy* 109.3 (2001), pp. 500–528; Dawson, *Behind the mule: Race and class in African-American politics*.

[15] Moses Shayo. "A model of social identity with an application to political economy: Nation, class, and redistribution." In *American Political Science Review* 103.02 (2009), pp. 147–174.

[16] Alberto Alesina and Paola Giuliano. "Culture and institutions." In *Journal of Economic Literature* 53.4 (2015), pp. 898–944.

[17] Lü and Scheve. "Self-centered inequity aversion and the mass politics of taxation"; Scheve and Stasavage. *Taxing the rich: A history of fiscal fairness in the United States and Europe*; Cavaillé. "Demand for Redistribution in the Age of Inequality"; Leslie McCall. *The undeserving rich: American beliefs about inequality, opportunity, and redistribution*. New York, NY: Cambridge University Press, 2013; Fong. "Social preferences, self-interest, and the demand for redistribution." I consider variation in individual-level preferences in a cross-section. Some notions of fairness better explain changes in public opinion over time. Scheve and Stasavage focus on historical periods when compensatory notions of fairness become more salient. Cavaillé argues that concerns about reciprocity can explain changes in attitudes over time.

[18] Lawrence Bobo. "Social responsibility, individualism, and redistributive policies." In *Sociological Forum* 6.1 (1991), pp. 71–92; Stanley Feldman. "Structure and consistency in public opinion: The role of core beliefs and values." In *American Journal of Political Science* (1988), pp. 416–440.

[19] Unless otherwise noted, all survey analyses come from the *Afrobarometer Data [South Africa][Round 2]*, Cape Town, 2002, or from Tom W. Smith et al. *General*

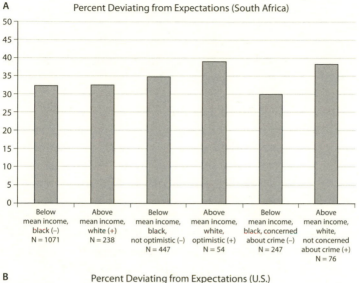

A   Percent Deviating from Expectations (South Africa)

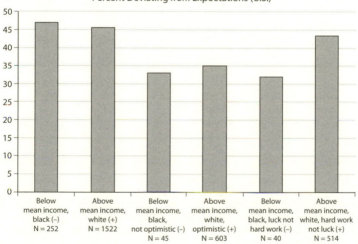

B   Percent Deviating from Expectations (U.S.)

FIGURE 2.1: Puzzling Preferences Over Redistribution: Illustrations
Note: Afrobarometer Data [South Africa][Round 2]. Cape Town, 2002; GSS 2006 (using weights WTSSNR). Bars denoted with a (−) show the proportion of that category that opposes greater redistribution, while (+) indicates support for greater redistribution. See also the Technical Notes at the end of the book.

to poor groups (who are expected to support greater redistribution) or the rich who belong to rich groups (who are expected to oppose greater redistribution).[20] It then divides respondents into subgroups: the poor in poor groups who are *not* optimistic about their future incomes, and the rich in rich groups who *are* optimistic about their future incomes.[21] The figure also separates out poor respondents who are members of poor groups and concerned about crime, rich respondents who are members of rich groups and not concerned about crime, poor respondents from poor groups who believe that success is *not* simply due to hard work, and rich respondents from rich groups who believe that economic success *is* due to hard work.[22] It then graphs the share of respondents in each category that does *not* answer questions about redistributing income in the way expected by existing theories.[23] For example, it graphs the share of poor respondents from poor groups that *opposes* greater redistribution and the share of rich respondents from rich groups that *supports* redistribution. These figures are illustrative only, as some of these categories contain small numbers of respondents. Nevertheless, it is interesting

---

social survey (GSS). Chicago, IL, 2006, because these waves include the largest number of questions relevant to status and to alternative explanations.

[20] Individuals were classified as rich (poor) if they reported a household income above (below) the average household income level for all respondents in each country survey.

[21] For details on coding in all surveys, see the Technical Notes, starting with table E.1.

[22] Unfortunately, the Afrobarometer wave did not include a question about these types of fairness concerns.

[23] In the Afrobarometer, support for redistribution is coded as strong agreement that income inequalities should be avoided, which is an imperfect question for gauging preferences over government policies. However, I use other measures of preferences over redistribution in the analyses below. These measures show even higher rates of puzzling answers than the rates shown in figure 2.1. In the GSS, support for redistribution is coded as agreement that the government should equalize (scores 1, 2, or 3 on a 7-point scale in the original measure). For a group of respondents not asked the question about government-led redistribution, I code support as a response that taxes on "those with high incomes" are "much too low" or "too low."

that at least 30 percent of respondents in each category exhibit unexpected preferences.

To examine whether status motivations contribute to our understanding of preferences over redistribution, I thus looked for the observable implications of status motivations within nationally representative surveys and censuses while trying to account for existing explanations as much as possible. While an experiment might have provided the cleanest identification of the effects of status motivations on support for redistribution, it is difficult to manipulate people's real economic positions within groups in a meaningful way without reducing the treatment to hypotheticals. Nationally representative surveys of political attitudes, paired with census data, allow an examination of the observable implications of the theory outside of the lab while providing large enough samples to account for a variety of other explanations.

I examined the relationship between local relative position and preferences over inequality and redistributive policy using survey data from the Afrobarometer research network in South Africa and the General Social Survey (GSS) in the United States, matched to demographic data drawn from official censuses and community surveys. I define coethnic neighbors—people in the same race group and living in the same immediate area as the individual respondent—as the local reference group.[24] In South Africa, I also examined the relationship between subjective local relationship position vis-à-vis neighbors and support for redistribution using data from a round of the South African Social Attitudes Survey (SASAS), discussed in more detail below.

---

[24] The same immediate area is operationalized as municipality in South Africa and as Public use Micro Area (PUMAs) in the US. As discussed earlier, research in social psychology convincingly demonstrates that status concerns often arise within this reference group for reasons of evaluation and visibility. Where race is salient, it is often used as an indicator of similarity, and neighbors are more likely to be frequently exposed to each other's material assets. An additional methodological advantage of using this reference group is that assignment to a race or ethnic group in these two countries is arguably more ascriptive and thereby less subject to self-selection than assignment to other types of reference groups (such as coworkers or close friends).

I used a relatively similar procedure to construct measures of local relative position for both South African and US respondents. In South Africa, I matched individual responses to the 2002 wave of the Afrobarometer with data on the distribution of pre-tax household income among respondents' coethnics in the same municipality from the 2001 census.[25] Income tax is set largely at the national level in South Africa; municipalities do not levy separate income tax. Municipalities collect revenue from utilities usage and debate rates for property taxes, but these latter rates are reviewed by a national ministry and limited by nationwide caps and ratios.[26] If an individual were concerned about her post-tax-and-transfer income, she should evaluate her relative position within the nation as a whole rather than her economic position among coethnics in the same municipality.[27] For each respondent, I used her reported pre-tax household income[28] and the distribution of incomes reported among her coethnics (those in her same race group)[29] in her municipality in the 2001 census to calculate the income density of coethnics above and below her in the income hierarchy. I then subtracted the income density of those poorer than she from that of those richer than she to produce a measure of her local relative economic position.[30] An increase (decrease) in this measure means that the person is more

[25] Though respondent's municipality is larger than I would like, the results using respondents' subjective assessments of their relative position vis-à-vis their neighbors show the same pattern. I use census data collected prior to the conduct of the Afrobarometer wave to reduce concerns about reverse causality.

[26] Riël Franzsen. *Property taxation in South Africa*. United Kingdom: Ashgate, 1999.

[27] Below, I show that respondents do not simply use local economic position as a heuristic for national relative position.

[28] Reported in brackets in response to Q90 in the Afrobarometer. Respondents were assigned to the mid-point of the bracket or to 110% of the lower bound of the highest bracket (for which there was no upper bound). Since the Afrobarometer solicited reports of monthly income, this midpoint was multiplied by 12 to generate an estimate of annual income and divided by 100 for ease of exposition.

[29] There are four race categories, originally defined by the apartheid government: Black/African, Coloured, Indian/Asian, and White/European.

[30] Total within-group income disparity above her is equal to $\frac{1}{n-1}\sum_{j\neq i} x_j - x_i$, where n is the total number of coethnic (coracial) households in respondent i's

disadvantaged (advantaged) relative to her coethnic neighbors—that is, there is more income distributed "above" her than "below" her. I call the variable "local relative disadvantage."

I followed a similar procedure for the United States. I matched responses from the 2006 GSS to data on pre-tax household incomes in 2005 from the American Community Survey's Public Use Microdata Areas (PUMAs).[31] PUMAs do not levy taxes or rates. If individuals were interested in maximizing their post-tax-and-transfer income rather than maximizing their status within local reference groups, they would not use their relative position within this geographical unit to evaluate redistribution policy. Yet the evidence suggests they do. I constructed a measure of local relative position by comparing each respondent's income to the income density of coethnics in her PUMA who were better off and worse off than she.[32] I subtracted the income density of her coethnic neighbors who were worse off than she from that of her coethnic neighbors better off than she. This variable measures the extent to

---

municipality, x_i is equal to the annual pre-tax household income respondent i reported for 2001 in the Afrobarometer, and x_j is the pre-tax household income reported in the 2001 national census for each coethnic household in the municipality richer than i. Total within-group income disparity below her is equal to $\frac{1}{n-1} \sum_{k \neq i} x_i - x_k$ where x_k is the pre-tax household income reported in the 2001 national census for each coethnic household in the municipality poorer than i.

[31] This required matching census tract indicators, sensitive data from the GSS (governed by a sensitive data protection plan and with Institutional Review Board approval), to 5% PUMAs, which have 100,000 to 150,000 people in them.

[32] Relevant variables from the GSS are INCOME and RACE/HISPANIC. These are the major census categories for race and ethnicity, though I do not claim that they capture all possible definitions of "coethnic." From the Community Survey, the relevant variable is household income (FTOTINC). Both the GSS and the Community Survey reported household income in brackets. I used the midpoints of each bracket. For the top bracket (which has no upper bound), I used 110% of the lower bound. Combining RACE and HISPANIC, I used four racial categories: Black, White, Non-White Hispanic, and Other. Similar to the procedings for South Africa total within-group, income disparity below a respondent was calculated as $\frac{1}{n-1} \sum_{j \neq i} x_i - x_j$ (divided by 1,000 for ease of exposition) where n is the total number of coethnic households in respondent i's PUMA, x_i is equal to the annual pre-tax household income of respondent i, and x_j is the pre-tax household income reported in the 2005 Community Survey for each household in the municipality that is poorer than i.

which each respondent is relatively disadvantaged (i.e., has more wealth above than below her) in her local area.

I then examined how well local relative disadvantage correlated with preferences over redistribution and reducing inequality, controlling for other possible influences on those preferences. The South African survey did not have a direct question either about tax rates or about levels of redistributive spending. In order to leverage a question that measures satisfaction with economic inequality under the current government, I thus used a question that asked respondents to compare the "present economic system with the economic system a few years ago" in terms of "the gap between the rich and the poor." I created a binary measure indicating dissatisfaction with the level of inequality under the current government that takes a value of 1 if a respondent said "much worse" or "worse" rather than "better" or "much better" in response to that question, and 0 otherwise. (See the Technical Notes at the end of the book for more details on the coding of survey variables).

In the United States, I used two measures of support for redistribution. Both questions were more directly about redistribution policy—that is, explicitly about tax rates and social spending—than any questions in the South African surveys. The first was a dummy variable indicating whether a respondent wanted to see more progressive taxation enacted or not. The variable was coded 1 if the respondent said "For those with high incomes, taxes are much too low or too low" and "For those with low incomes, taxes are too high or much too high."[33] The second measure of support for redistribution came from a question about whether the government should make incomes more equal through either taxation or social spending.[34] I coded support for redistribution as

---

[33] Combining these statements into a single measure ensures that the preferences being measured are truly progressive (that respondents do not prefer higher taxes on everyone, or prefer lower taxes for the poor as well as the rich). If I measure support for higher taxes only on those with high incomes, the results do not change.

[34] The question was worded as follows: "Some people think that the government in Washington ought to reduce the income differences between the rich and the poor, perhaps by raising the taxes of wealthy families or by giving income assistance

choosing the highest level of agreement with the statement "The government ought to reduce the income differences between rich and poor."

Readers might wonder whether an individual's local relative economic position is simply a proxy for her perceptions of inequality within the country as a whole.[35] Perhaps individuals simply cannot gauge national levels of inequality, so they use their position within smaller geographical areas and within ethnic groups as a cognitive shortcut to assess how much they are likely to gain or lose from national redistribution policies. If so, an association between preferences over reducing inequality and local relative disadvantage would not be evidence of envy or spite, but rather of calculations of self-interest.

This is a reasonable concern, but perceived national relative position and local relative disadvantage are not identical in either country and can be separated in the empirical analyses. South African respondents in the Afrobarometer were asked, "In general, how do you rate your living conditions compared to those of other South Africans?" Respondents could answer on a five-point scale. The correlation between answers to this question and respondents' relative local disadvantage was very low ($r = 0.079$). Figure 2.2, which plots the distribution of local relative disadvantage for each type of response about national position, illustrates that, with a few exceptions, the distribution of local relative disadvantage in South Africa is quite similar across rankings of national position.[36] In the United States, respondents were asked, "Compared with

---

to the poor. Others think that the government should not concern itself with reducing income differences between the rich and the poor. Here is a card with a scale from 1 to 7. Think of a score of 1 as meaning that the government ought to reduce the income differences between rich and poor, and a score of 7 meaning that the government should not concern itself with reducing income differences. What score between 1 and 7 comes closest to the way you feel?" For the purposes of analysis, I reversed the scoring.

[35] Stephen Ansolabehere, Marc Meredith, and Erik Snowberg. "Mecro-economic voting: Local information and micro-perceptions of the macro-economy." In *Economics & Politics* 26.3 (2014), pp. 380–410.

[36] Looking at the distributions in figure 2.2 one might be concerned about the influence of outliers, given the long tails. However, the results below are robust to dropping outlying respondents for whom local relative disadvantage is more than

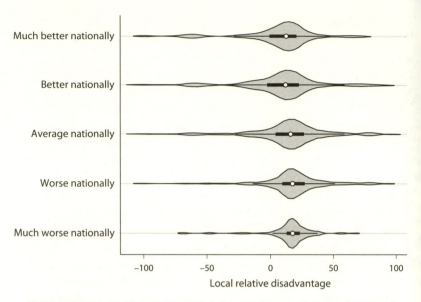

FIGURE 2.2: Violin Plot of Local Relative Position v. Perceived National Position (South Africa)

American families in general, would you say your family income is far below average, below average, average, above average, or far above average?" In figure 2.3 the distribution of local relative disadvantage is shown for each category of response to this question. The figure shows that local relative deprivation is more closely correlated with perceived national relative position in the United States than it is in South Africa. Americans who see themselves as far above average or above average in the nation as a whole are distributed toward the lower end of local relative disadvantage, compared to people who see themselves as average, below average, or far below average. Nevertheless, perceived relative national position and relative local position are not equivalents here either. At almost every level of relative local disadvantage, people report being far below average, below average, average, above average,

---

two standard deviations below and above its mean. The results in column 2 lose statistical significance with the smaller sample size.

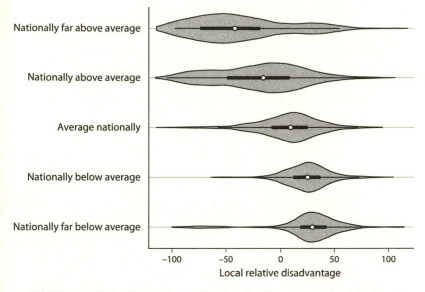

FIGURE 2.3: Violin Plot of Local Relative Position v. Perceived National Position (United States)

and far above average in the nation as a whole. Important, I controlled for perceived national position in the analyses of both surveys, and doing so does not change the main results.

Table 2.1 displays the results of logistic regressions assessing the association between support for redistribution and local relative disadvantage, controlling for other explanatory factors emphasized in the literature. For each measure of support for redistribution in both countries, I first regressed support for redistribution on both relative local disadvantage and a measure of pocketbook self-interest: either absolute income or perceived national relative position, or both. I then introduced other control variables. In the South Africa data, available control variables included race group membership, attachment to the nation as a whole, expectations about future income,[37] and respondents' views on whether the

---

[37] Specifically of respondents' children's future income. See Benabou and Ok. "Social mobility and the demand for redistribution: The Poum hypothesis."

national economy as a whole was doing well. Other controls (unlisted in the table) included whether they thought addressing "crime and safety" was a top priority, sex, age, education, frequency of religious attendance, urban residence, and whether the respondent's profession involved skilled or unskilled work.[38] This Afrobarometer wave did not include many questions that directly addressed principles of fairness, with the exception of a question asking how often the respondent's identity group is treated unfairly by the government, which I also included as a control. In the United States, available control variables other than household income and perceived relative national position included respondents' race group membership (white is the reference category), their expectations about their future income, level of religious attendance, education, age, and marital status. Since US political parties differ in their positions about the size of government, I controlled for respondents' partisan leanings as well.[39]

The US data provided measures of other alternative explanations as well, particularly those concerned with principled positions, fairness, and concern for the relative position of one's group vis-à-vis outgroups.[40] Approximating principled positions about the role of government, a question asked respondents whether the government should "do everything possible" to improve the lives of the poor or whether "each person should take care of himself."

[38] The latter is an approximation of Iversen et al.'s concept of skill specificity. See Torben Iversen and David Soskice. "An asset theory of social policy preferences." In *American Political Science Review* 95.4 (2001), pp. 875–894.

[39] Political parties do not divide as straightforwardly on these issues in South Africa.

[40] Others have argued that, in the US context, people who believe in the principle of limited government, or believe that income is generally earned through hard work, or exhibit resentment toward black Americans are likely to oppose greater redistribution. See Bobo. "Social responsibility, individualism, and redistributive policies"; Feldman. "Structure and consistency in public opinion: The role of core beliefs and values"; Fong. "Social preferences, self-interest, and the demand for redistribution"; Stanley Feldman and Leonie Huddy. "Racial resentment and white opposition to race-conscious programs: Principles or prejudice?" In *American Journal of Political Science* 49.1 (2005), pp. 168–183; Luttmer. "Neighbors as Negatives: Relative Earnings and Well-Being."

Measuring people's beliefs in the fairness of the pre-tax income distribution, another question asked whether the respondent believes that "people get ahead by their own hard work" or that "lucky breaks or help from other people are more important."[41] Last, I incorporated two measures of attitudes toward poorer groups. The first is a question that asked respondents whether they agree that black Americans should "work their way up ... without special favors" as other minority groups have done. The second creates an index of four questions that asked whether respondents believe that economic differences between black Americans and white Americans are due to a lack of will, education, innate ability to learn, or discrimination. There is a fair amount of missing-ness in some of these control variables. I thus first estimated the models employing list-wise deletion. In the last column of the table, I then used multiple imputation.

Table 2.1 demonstrates that the worse off a person is, on balance, compared to coethnics in her local area, the more dissatisfied she is with inequality and the more she wants the government to take steps to reduce it, even if that policy would be personally costly for her. By contrast, the better off a respondent is compared to surrounding coethnics, the more satisfied she is with inequality in the country as a whole and the less she wants her government to take steps to reduce it, holding other material interest- and non-interest-based explanations constant. The table reports estimated changes in the predicted probability of supporting more redistribution associated with a one-standard-deviation change in continuous and ordinal variables and with a one-unit change in binary explanatory variables. The magnitude of the changes in predicted probability associated with a one-standard-deviation change in local relative disadvantage is substantively significant. For instance, in the South Africa survey, it is comparable to

[41] The variable is coded 1 if the respondent said, "Hard work most important" and 0 if the respondent said, "Hard work, luck equally important" or "Luck most important." The results do not change if "Hard work, luck equally important" is coded 1 instead.

TABLE 2.1 Change in Predicted Probability of Supporting Redistribution

	Dissatisfied with inequality (SA)	Dissatisfied with inequality (SA)	Progressive taxation (US)	Progressive taxation (US)	Govt redistribute (US)	Govt redistribute (US)	Govt redistribute (US)	Govt redistribute (US)
Local relative disadvantage	0.028**	0.031*	0.059**	0.058*	0.024***	0.029**	0.027**	0.019*
	(0.014)	(0.017)	(0.027)	(0.034)	(0.008)	(0.012)	(0.013)	(0.010)
Household income	0.025*	0.029**	0.010	0.079*				−0.013
	(0.015)	(0.015)	(0.027)	(0.042)				(0.013)
Perceived national position	−0.036***	−0.024*			−0.051***	−0.044***	−0.014	−0.035***
	(0.013)	(0.014)			(0.010)	(0.014)	(0.014)	(0.010)
Black		0.045		0.123		−0.021	0.060*	0.001
		(0.050)		(0.088)		(0.040)	(0.035)	(0.024)
Hispanic				−0.160*		0.068	0.065	0.029
				(0.095)		(0.050)	(0.042)	(0.028)
Democrat				0.104**		0.078***	0.077***	0.091*
				(0.047)		(0.021)	(0.022)	(0.019)
Pessimism about the future		0.045***				0.058***	0.060***	0.040***
		(0.016)				(0.013)	(0.013)	(0.008)
National pride		−0.020*						
		(0.011)						
Economy good		−0.037**						
		(0.016)						

TABLE 2.1 Continued.

	N = 1,863	N = 1,423	N = 1,215	N = 575	N = 1,654	N = 803	N = 765	N = 1,943
Individual should help self					-0.070*** (0.018)			-0.107*** (0.013)
Hard work			-0.040 (0.055)		0.015 (0.025)			-0.003 (0.013)
Blacks should work way up							-0.051*** (0.011)	-0.029*** (0.007)
Racial resentment index							-0.047 (0.049)	-0.011* (0.007)

Notes: Afrobarometer Data [South Africa][Round 2]. Cape Town, 2002. South African Census, Version 1.1. Pretoria 2011. General Social Survey 2006. American Community Survey. Washington, DC, 2005. * p < 0.10, ** p < 0.05, *** p < 0.01. Standard errors in parentheses, clustered by municipality or PUMA. WTSSNR probability weights included for the US; results for SA are robust to using withinwt. For South Africa, dummy variables set to values for a black, skilled, urban male; for the US, dummy variables set for a white, married, male Democrat. Other controls included in full models but not listed are religious service attendance, female, education, and age (also in SA: urban, unskilled, crime a top priority, my group often treated unfairly). The last column shows estimates after multiple imputations, across three datasets, using Stata 14's MI program.

the magnitude of the changes associated with a one-standard-deviation change in perceived national relative position and to the magnitude of the change associated with being proud of one's national identity. In the US survey, it is more than half the size of the change associated with racial resentment.

Local relative disadvantage thus improves our account of preferences over redistribution even in these unlikely countries. In the United States, as one might expect, Democrats are more likely than non-Democrat-leaning Independents and Republicans to support redistribution. Black Americans are more likely than white Americans to support redistribution, and Hispanics are less or equally likely to do so. Those who believe themselves to be better off in relation to the nation as a whole are less supportive of government-led redistribution. Likewise, those who believe that individuals should take care of themselves (rather than being taken care of by the government) and who believe that black Americans need to "work their way up ... with no special favors" are less likely to support government-led redistribution. But even in a place like the United States—where group and partisan commitments are strong, and where principled debates about the size and role of the government rage—citizens' local within-group status helps understand patterns of support and opposition to redistribution. The better off citizens are relative to their coethnic neighbors, the less supportive they are of redistribution, and vice versa.

But do these patterns help us account for the puzzling preferences presented in figure 2.1? There I highlighted categories of respondents for whom the predictions based on short-term, long-term, and group interests were clear but also clearly incomplete. In tables 2.2 and 2.3, I revisited these categories to estimate the change in predicted probability of supporting redistribution that would be associated with local relative position for these types of respondents. In table 2.2, I controlled for the material interest- and non-interest-based alternative explanations accounted for in table 2.1. In table 2.3, I controlled for all variables in column 6 of table 2.1.

TABLE 2.2 Estimated Change in Predicted Probability of Dissatisfaction with Inequality for Different Categories of Respondents in South Africa

	Black/(much) worse than national average/ not optimistic	Black/(much) worse than national average/ concerned about crime
Local relative advantage	−0.011*	−0.010*
(SE)	(0.006)	(0.005)
Pride in the nation	−0.023**	−0.016**
(SE)	(0.010)	(0.007)

	White/(much) better than national average/ optimistic	White/(much) better than national average/ Not concerned about crime
Local relative disadvantage	0.032*	0.046*
(SE)	(0.019)	(0.027)
Pride in the nation	−0.019**	−0.030**
(SE)	(0.009)	(0.013)

Note: Afrobarometer Data [South Africa][Round 2]. Cape Town, 2002. South African Census, Version 1.1. Pretoria, 2001. * $p < 0.10$, ** $p < 0.05$.

TABLE 2.3 Estimated Change in Predicted Probability of Strongly Supporting Government-Led Redistribution for Different Categories of Respondents in the United States

	Black/(far) below national average/ not optimistic	Black/(far) below national average/ not hard work
Local relative advantage	−0.041**	−0.022**
(SE)	(0.016)	(0.009)
Individual should help self	−0.159**	−0.104***
(SE)	(0.018)	(0.013)

	White/(far) above national average/ optimistic	White/(far) above national average/ hard work
Local relative disadvantage	0.020***	0.026**
(SE)	(0.009)	(0.011)
Individual should help self	−0.076**	−0.060***
(SE)	(0.017)	(0.016)

Note: General Social Survey (2006). American Community Survey. Washington, DC, 2005. * $p < 0.10$, ** $p < 0.05$, *** $p < 0.01$.

I found that in each of these categories, the observable implications of status motivations are estimated to be associated with people's preferences over redistribution.[42] For black South Africans who are much worse or worse off than the average South African and who are not optimistic about their children's future incomes, the model estimates that being *better* off than coethnic neighbors[43] is associated with a *reduction* in dissatisfaction with inequality that is half the change associated with having stronger national pride, a very important correlate of preferences over redistribution.[44] Likewise, for white South Africans who are much better or better off than the average South African and who are optimistic about their future incomes, being *worse* off than coethnic neighbors is estimated to be associated with an *increase* in dissatisfaction with inequality of greater a magnitude than the change associated with having stronger national pride.

In the United States, black Americans who report having incomes far below or below the national average and who do not believe their incomes will improve might generally be expected to favor redistribution based on their short-term, long-term, and group interests. But these respondents are estimated to be less likely to strongly support redistribution if they are better off, relatively speaking, than their coethnic neighbors. The magnitude of the change in the probability of supporting redistribution that is associated with local status is statistically significant but smaller than that associated with believing in economic individualism. The same is true for the association between relative local advantage and support for greater redistribution among black Americans in a low relative position in the nation as a whole who do not believe that economic success is simply due to hard work. For these

[42] As in figure 2.1, the caveat is that some categories are small.

[43] The inverse of relative local disadvantage.

[44] Shayo. "A model of social identity with an application to political economy: Nation, class, and redistribution"; Evan S. Lieberman. "How South African citizens evaluate their economic obligations to the state." In *Journal of Development Studies* 38.3 (2002), pp. 37–62.

respondents, advantage relative to coethnic neighbors is estimated to be associated with a decrease in support for greater redistribution. Relative local position is also estimated to be associated with variation in preferences over redistribution among rich, optimistic respondents from wealthier groups and among rich respondents from wealthier groups who believe that economic success is due to hard work. These categories of respondents might not be expected to support greater redistribution based on their short-term, long-term, and group interests or their concerns for fairness. But for these respondents, being relatively worse off than their coethnic neighbors increases their support for redistribution, controlling for many alternative explanations. Status motivations improve our understanding of variation in preferences over redistribution across these categories of respondents.

Possible criticisms of using municipalities and PUMAs to approximate objective local relative position include that municipalities and PUMAs are too large, that they might not sufficiently overlap with people's perceived reference groups,[45] and that respondents might have misreported their pre-tax incomes in these surveys. To address these concerns, I examined data from the nationally representative South Africa Social Attitudes Survey (SASAS) conducted in South Africa in 2005, in which people were asked about their subjective reference groups ("Whom do you compare your income mostly with?"). A plurality responded, "Neighbors or others in the village/township" (figure 2.4), which is consistent with my contention that local groups are often the most salient reference groups. A much smaller share of respondents reported comparing their incomes to "People in South Africa as a whole" or to people in other geographic areas or other groups, such as work colleagues. In table 2.5. I show that the salience of neighbors as a reference group in fact conditions the relationship between local relative disadvantage and preferences over redistribution.

[45] Cara J. Wong. *Boundaries of obligation in American politics: Geographic, national, and racial communities*. New York, NY: Cambridge University Press, 2010.

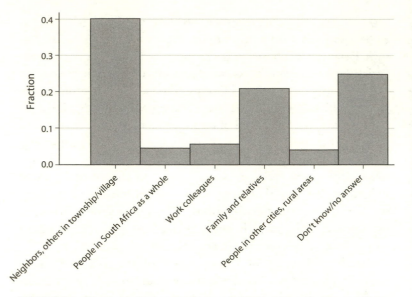

FIGURE 2.4: Economic Reference Groups in South Africa. Survey question: "Whom do you compare your income mostly with?"(Source: South African Social Attitudes Survey 2005.)

Respondents in the SASAS were then asked about their subjective relative position within their local areas, "How does your household income compare with that of other households in your neighborhood or village?" (Respondents could choose "Much above average," "Above average," "Average," "Below average," or "Much below average".) To check whether the main patterns hold when using a different measure of relative disadvantage within local reference groups, I used answers to this question as a subjective measure.

I used two measures of support for redistribution in this survey. Respondents were asked to agree or disagree with the following statements: "In South Africa, incomes are too unequal" and "The government should take more responsibility to ensure that everyone is provided for." Two binary measures of support for redistribution were thus coded as 1 if the respondent strongly agreed with the given statement. Both measures take a value of 0 if the respondent gave a substantive answer but did not agree strongly with the statement.[46]

This survey also provided questions measuring alternative explanations for preferences over redistribution. To account for self- and group interest–based explanations, the regressions below controlled for household income before taxes (five brackets), a dummy variable for being a black South African, answering "It makes me feel proud to be called a South African"(binary), the optimistic belief that one's living conditions will improve in the next twelve months (binary), frequency of religious attendance (eight-point scale), beliefs that the economy has improved (binary), concern about crime (binary),[47] employment status (binary), age, sex (binary), urban (binary), and education, all of which might be expected to influence preferences over redistribution. In South Africa it could also be the case that people who are having a harder time adjusting to legal racial equality under the post-apartheid government would also be more reluctant to contribute taxes and support social spending on what they see as an illegitimate political order.[48] In other words, the degree to which a respondent has racially insular views could influence his or her level of support for redistribution. While the Afrobarometer wave did not measure racial insularity, the SASAS included such a measure by asking respondents whether they agree or disagree that people should marry within their own race group,[49] and so I included this measure as a control in the analysis of subjective relative local position.

---

[46] That is, 0 indicates the respondent answered the question with an indication of simple "agreement" or "disagreement" and did not say "I don't know."

[47] "Please tell me what you think are the 3 most important challenges facing South Africa today?" The variable is coded 1 if the respondent mentioned crime as one of her top three concerns.

[48] Lieberman. "How South African citizens evaluate their economic obligations to the state."

[49] "Please tell me to what extent you agree or disagree with these statements. People should marry someone of the same race group."

TABLE 2.4   Change in Predicted Probability of Strongly Agreeing That Inequality Is Too High and Government Should Do More, Using Subjective Relative Position (South Africa)

	Incomes too unequal	Incomes too unequal	Govt. should address	Govt. should address
Worse off than neighbors	0.072***	0.072**	0.129***	0.122***
	(0.023)	(0.028)	(0.023)	(0.027)
Household income (categorical)	0.040***	0.027*	−0.006	−0.008
	(0.012)	(0.017)	(0.012)	(0.016)
Black		0.031		0.003
		(0.036)		(0.035)
Economy improved		−0.006		0.012
		(0.015)		(0.014)
Prioritize crime		−0.017		0.013
		(0.028)		(0.027)
No interracial marriage		0.011		0.024**
		(0.010)		(0.009)
National pride		0.210***		0.238***
		(0.028)		(0.028)
Unemployed		−0.037		0.005
		(0.027)		(0.027)
Optimistic		0.012		0.001
		(0.029)		(0.028)
Religious attendance frequency		0.020		0.021*
		(0.013)		(0.013)
	N = 2173	N = 1703	N = 2259	N = 1766
p-value associated with log-likelihood ratio test of fit with and without worse off than neighbors	(0.002)	(0.010)	(0.000)	(0.000)

Notes: South Africa Social Attitudes Survey 2005. * p< 0.10, ** p< 0.05, *** p< 0.01. Standard errors in parentheses. Province fixed effects included. Change in predicted probability is shown for a one-standard-deviation change in continuous independent variables and for a one-unit change in dummy variables. All other variables are set at their means (if continuous); dummy variables set to values for a black, employed, urban male. Other controls included in the second column are sex, education, age, and urban.

Table 2.4 shows that controlling for these alternative explanations, the same patterns hold using a subjective measure of relative local position. Based on log-likelihood ratio tests, I can consistently reject the null hypothesis that including subjective relative local deprivation does not improve the goodness of fit of the models. Table 2.4 shows the estimated change in the predicted probability of saying that inequality is too high or that the government should be more involved in addressing distributional issues associated with this subjective measure of relative local disadvantage. There is a robust seven percentage point difference in the predicted probability of saying that incomes are too unequal between an individual who perceives that she is worse off than her neighbors and one who perceives that she is as well (or better) off than her neighbors. There is a robust twelve percentage point difference in the predicted probability of supporting government's doing more in this area between those who feel worse off than their neighbors and those who feel as well or better off.

The magnitude of the changes in predicted probability associated with this subjective measure of relative disadvantage is substantively significant. The changes are greater than those associated with a one-standard-deviation change in household income or religious service attendance. They are a third or more than half the size of the change in predicted probability associated with being proud to be a South African, which, as in the analysis of objective relative position in the Afrobarometer data above, is a highly robust correlate of redistributive preferences. Admittedly, it is more difficult to discount the possibility of reverse causality here than in the analyses using objective relative local position, particularly because the questions about inequality and the government's role in redistribution were asked in SASAS prior to questions about social comparisons and relative local position. Nevertheless, the evidence is consistent whether the reference group is defined objectively or subjectively.

Indeed, if I split respondents into those who feel they are much worse off than their neighbors, those who feel they are not that different from their neighbors, and those who feel they are much better off than their neighbors, the patterns are also consistent with the observable implications of status motivations, particularly among those who claim that local comparisons are salient to them. Table 2.5 shows the results of regressing strong agreement that the government should do more to take care of those who need it on an indicator for feeling much worse off than neighbors as well as on an indicator for feeling much better

TABLE 2.5 Change in Predicted Probability of Strongly Agreeing Government Should Do More Using Two Categorical Values of Relative Position, by Who Engages in Local Comparisons

	All	Compare with neighbors/ within village	Use other reference groups	(All)
Much worse off than neighbors	0.129**	0.129*	0.080	0.046
	(0.072)	(0.071)	(0.140)	(0.141)
Much better off than neighbors	−0.084	−0.220	0.665*	0.654**
	(0.130)	(0.153)	(0.375)	(0.314)
Privileges local comparisons				−0.102
				(0.087)
Local comparisons* much worse				0.091
				(0.154)
Local comparisons* much better				−0.879**
				(0.349)
Household income (categorical)	0.018	0.024	0.031	0.026
	(0.032)	(0.031)	(0.107)	(0.031)
Black	0.038	−0.078	0.431	0.025
	(0.066)	(0.071)	(0.310)	(0.074)
Economy improved	0.033	0.065**	−0.242**	0.042
	(0.030)	(0.032)	(0.100)	(0.032)
Prioritize crime	0.023	0.022	−0.096	0.014
	(0.050)	(0.057)	(0.128)	(0.054)
No interracial marriage	0.038*	0.033	0.052	0.036
	(0.031)	(0.030)	(0.026)	(0.024)
National pride	0.258***	0.286***	0.302*	0.269***
	(0.048)	(0.057)	(0.173)	(0.053)
Unemployed	0.011	0.022	−0.112	0.016
	(0.027)	(0.055)	(0.123)	(0.052)
Optimistic	0.039	−0.013	0.417**	0.019
	(0.054)	(0.062)	(0.174)	(0.059)
Religious attendance frequency	0.019	0.018	0.095	0.024
	(0.025)	(0.030)	(0.067)	(0.029)
	N = 1553	N = 1116	N = 191	N = 1307

Notes: South Africa Social Attitudes Survey 2005. * p< 0.10, ** p< 0.05, *** p< 0.01. Standard errors in parentheses. Benchwgt included as probability weights, and province fixed effects included. Change in predicted probability is shown for a one-standard-deviation change in continuous independent variables and for a one-unit change in dummy variables. All other variables are set at their means (if continuous); dummy variables set to values for a black, employed, urban male. Other controls included in the second column are sex, education, age, and urban.

off than neighbors, with those reporting being not that different from their neighbors as the reference group. The first column of table 2.5 includes all respondents who gave substantive answers to these questions. The second column includes only those respondents who say they compare their incomes mostly with neighbors and others in the township or village. The third column includes only respondents who say they compare their incomes within other types of reference groups other than family (e.g., with people in South Africa as a whole, with work colleagues, with people in other cities). The fourth column pools respondents and adds interaction terms between making local comparisons (including with relatives) and feeling much worse off and much better off.

Table 2.5 shows that among people who engage in local comparisons (with neighbors, others in the village or township, or with relatives), feeling much worse off than neighbors *increases* support for redistribution and feeling much better off than neighbors *decreases* support for redistribution. In the smaller subsamples, I lose some statistical power, so these associations do not always meet conventional levels of statistical significance, but the directions of the relationship are clear: among those who engage in local comparisons, preferences over redistribution are linked to both wanting to decrease one's relative local disadvantage and wanting to preserve or increase one's relative local advantage (columns 2 and 4). These patterns are consistent with status motivations—that is, with the desire to maximize one's relative position (both to decrease personal disadvantage and to increase personal advantage) within salient reference groups.

By contrast, among the few respondents who do not report engaging in local social comparisons—that is, those who instead compare themselves to South Africans in general, or to coworkers or people in other cities or towns—the patterns are not consistent with local status motivations. For these respondents, feeling much better off than their neighbors is actually linked to *higher* support for redistribution (see columns 3 and 4). This pattern is more consistent with what one might expect from motivations grounded in altruism, inequity aversion, or fairness toward neighbors than with local status motivations, that is those who do not judge their own incomes relative to their neighbors' want more redistribution when they feel both worse and better off than their neighbors. People not seeking distinction within local reference groups have preferences that would reduce both their relative local disadvantage and their relative local advantage. Rows 2 and 5 of column 4 show that while people who do not engage in local comparisons and who feel better off than their neighbors are more likely to support redistribution (row 2), people who do engage in local comparisons and who feel better off than their neighbors are less likely to support redistribution (row 2 in conjunction with row 5), which is consistent with the observable implications of status motivations. In other words, the status motivations described in this book do a particularly good job of accounting for preferences over redistribution among people who report engaging in local social comparisons, as a theory of status motivations would expect.

Is there also evidence that the political salience of status motivations varies? Earlier I argued that status motivations are most likely to be politically salient where they are socially unmanaged, and that they are likely to be socially unmanaged where social ties are weaker or weakening.

These surveys also show that within-group status is more strongly associated with preferences over redistribution where social ties are weaker. As a rough first cut, I observe that the relationship between local relative disadvantage and redistributive preferences is much stronger in urban areas than in rural areas. Table 2.6 uses data from the GSS to examine heterogeneity in the association of local relative position and preferences over redistribution in rural and urban areas. The change in the predicted probability of supporting government-led, progressive redistribution associated with local relative disadvantage is much smaller in rural than in urban areas. If we believe that rural communities are more likely to exhibit stronger social ties than urban communities,[50]

[50] Sandra L. Hofferth and John Iceland. "Social capital in rural and urban communities." In *Rural Sociology* 63.4 (1998), pp. 574–598; Claude S. Fischer. *To*

TABLE 2.6 Heterogeneous Effects of Local Relative Position in Rural v. Urban Areas

	Support progressive taxation	Support govt. redistribution
Local relative disadvantage	0.057**	0.017
	(0.027)	(0.011)
Rural	0.060	−0.001
	(0.052)	(0.023)
Rural* local relative disadvantage	−0.026**	−0.015**
	(0.013)	(0.006)
	N = 1208	N = 1620

Notes: General Social Survey 2006. *American community survey.* Washington, DC, 2005. * p<0.10, ** p<0.05. Robust standard errors in parentheses, clustered by PUMA. Probability weights WTSSNR are included. Changes in predicted probability associated with a one-standard-deviation change for continuous variables and with a one-unit change for dummy variables are shown. Continuous variables are set to their means. Dummy variables are set to white, married, male Democrat. Controls included in both columns are household income, Democrat, black, Hispanic, other race, religious service attendance, female, education, age, and marital status. Additional controls included in the second column are perception of relative national position, pessimism about the future, and the view that individuals should help themselves.

then these results are consistent with the argument that individuals in places with stronger social ties find informal (nonpolitical) ways to manage status motivations rather than rely on policies to mitigate relative disparities.

Of course, urban and rural are only proxies for the strength of social ties and thus for the presence of robust mechanisms for managing envy and spite without the involvement of policy. There is evidence that these indicators are useful proxies. Others have found that rural respondents in the United States consistently score higher on neighborhood social ties than respondents from metropolitan and other urban areas.[51] In the 2006 GSS, some respondents were asked how frequently they spend an evening with friends inside the neighborhood versus outside the neighborhood. A significantly larger share of respondents in rural (61%)

---

dwell among friends: Personal networks in town and city. Chicago, IL: University of Chicago Press, 1982.

[51] E.g., Avery M. Guest and Susan K. Wierzbicki. "Social ties at the neighborhood level: Two decades of GSS evidence." In *Urban Affairs Review* 35.1 (1999), p. 103.

than in urban (53%) areas reported spending more time socializing with friends in their neighborhood than outside of it (p = 0.029). In South Africa there is also evidence of more regular neighborhood interactions in rural areas. While the 2002 Afrobarometer wave does not ask directly about strength of attachment to neighbors, a larger percentage of respondents in rural areas (64%) than in urban areas (54%) report they have attended a neighborhood meeting (p = 0.00). Rural respondents are more likely to come together in forums where social conventions might be developed and reinforced.

However, the SASAS in South Africa directly asked respondents about the strength of their local ties ("To what extent do you feel attached to the following types of people? Those who live in your neighborhood?"). Most people responded that they are slightly or very attached to their neighbors, but a significantly lower percentage of respondents in urban areas (64%) than in rural areas (79%) said they are very attached rather than slightly or not attached to people living in their neighborhoods (p = 0.00). Figure 2.5 illustrates the difference in distributions of responses to this question across urban and rural localities.

When I used this latter, direct measure of the strength of local social ties, the expected patterns held. For respondents in the SASAS who are very attached to their neighbors, the association between relative local deprivation and preferences for redistribution is close to nil. Instead, relative local position is robustly associated with support for redistribution among respondents who do not have such strong, stable social ties (see table 2.7).[52] The observable implications of status motivations in politics hold among people who do not have strong social ties to their neighbors. For these people, that is for those who are unlikely to have developed

---

[52] One could argue that weaker attachments to neighbors is a symptom rather than a moderator of envious and spiteful relationships. This is another reason to use both the direct measure of the strength of social ties and proxies that are less subject to this concern. Either way, these patterns are consistent with the argument that status motivations are linked to the ways in which people evaluate redistributive policies.

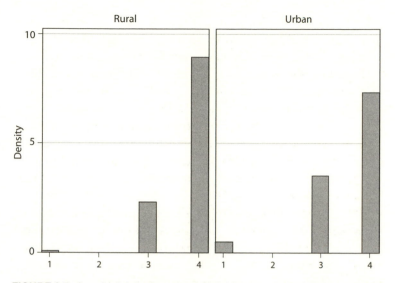

FIGURE 2.5: Level of Attachment to Neighbors in Rural v. Urban Areas (South Africa). Question: "On a scale from 1 (not attached at all) to 4 (very attached), how attached are you to those who live in your neighborhood?"

Source: South African Social Attitudes Survey 2005.

TABLE 2.7 Heterogeneous Effects of Local Relative Position on View That Incomes Are Too Unequal, Depending on Strength of Social Ties

	Incomes too unequal
Worse off than neighbors	0.242***
	(0.082)
Very attached to neighbors	0.112**
	(0.055)
Locally worse off* very attached	−0.253***
	(0.092)
	N = 1782

Notes: South African Social Attitudes Survey 2005. * $p<0.10$, ** $p<0.05$, *** $p<0.01$. Standard errors in parentheses. Probability weights "benchwgt" included to account for any differences in the probabilities of urban and rural respondents selecting into the sample. Province fixed effects included. The change in predicted probability is shown for a one-unit change in the independent variables. Other controls were included because they were significant predictors of support for redistribution in the previous model or are theoretically prominent explanations: pride in the nation, opposition to interracial marriage, household income, race group dummy variables.

robust informal mechanisms to regulate envy and spite within local reference groups, relative local disadvantage (advantage) is associated with higher (lower) support for redistribution.

Together, these pieces of evidence illustrate how status motivations can help account for puzzling variation in preferences over redistribution policy. Even in two countries where other influences (concerns for income, group welfare, fairness, prospects of upward mobility, partisanship) are expected to be the dominant explanations, citizens' attitudes toward redistribution are consistently and meaningfully associated with their local, within-group status. The worse off people are than their coethnic neighbors, the more supportive they are of greater redistribution (regardless of how personally costly this support is); the better off people are than their coethnic neighbors, the less supportive they are of redistribution. When redistribution would improve their within-group status, citizens are more likely to act enviously and support greater redistribution; when redistribution would hurt their within-group status, citizens are more likely to act spitefully and be less supportive of greater redistribution, all else equal. The patterns hold most robustly where social ties are weak.

This essay thus provides an initial demonstration that attention to status motivations can shed light on puzzling political behavior. I return to discuss larger implications of these findings in the conclusion. However, I will briefly note here that these findings invite us to think beyond our frequent focus on inter-group interest competition. Public discourse sometimes makes references to a "politics of envy" that is quite different from the way envy functions in my account. The conventional conception of the politics of envy is one of class warfare, in which the poor want to tear down the rich as a class. Farm seizures in Zimbabwe, expropriation policies in Russia, proposals for higher taxes on the wealthy in the United Kingdom, and anti-structural adjustment movements in Latin America have all been described this way.[53]

---

[53] See Peter Godwin. *When a crocodile eats the sun*. New York, NY: Little Brown, 2007; Nicholas Watt and Shiv Malik. "Nick Clegg wealth tax 'the politics of envy,'

By contrast, in this book's account, envy and spite involve local social comparisons among neighbors, within groups, and within social strata: the rich compare themselves to the even richer; the poor compare themselves to the even poorer. Instead of stoking class warfare, envy and spite here help explain variation in views among the rich and among the poor. Indeed, if anything, the findings in this essay suggest that envy and spite can dilute the common material interests of the poor and of the rich as class groups. Envy and spite can have implications across groups (a point I discuss further later in this book). But both scholarship and public discourse often miss the implications of local, interpersonal envy and spite, and thus overlook an important part of redistributive politics.

Government Underspending

Underspending is a remarkably pervasive political phenomenon. It is surprisingly common for governments to fail to spend money allocated for policy implementation. For example, states in India have regularly underused their allocated budgets, reportedly spending only 64–80 percent of central transfers between 1997 and 2006.[54] Some Latin American states spent, on average, only half of their allocated social sector budgets between 1995 and 2002.[55] South Africa's finance minister reported that at both the national and local levels the South African government spent only 68 percent of allocated funds in 2010–2011.[56] By my calculations, the record in previous years was no better. Just over a third of all

---

says senior Tory." In *Guardian* (Aug. 2012) and "The politics of envy." In *Economist* (May 6, 1999).

[54] Mark Sundberg and Mandakini Kaul. "Bihar: Towards a development strategy." In *World Bank, India* (2005); Bihar. *"White Paper on State Finances and Development."* Tech. rep. Finance Department, Government of Bihar, 2006.

[55] José R. López-Cálix et al., *Creating fiscal space for poverty reduction in Ecuador: A fiscal management and public expenditure review.* Inter-American Development Bank, 2005, p. 80.

[56] See "Gordhan wars on underspending," *Mail and Guardian*, February 22, 2010.

municipalities in South Africa consistently underused their capital budgets every year between 2003 and 2006, leaving on average 48 percent untouched over that period. These patterns are not unique to India, South Africa, and parts of Latin America. By some estimates, underspending is at least as frequent a problem in developing countries as overspending is.[57]

At least in South Africa, underspending is not fully accounted for by existing explanations. Failures to implement policies are often explained by corruption,[58] lack of state capacity,[59] or ethnic diversity.[60] These explanations are important but not satisfying on their own. Arguments based on corruption are not fully satisfying, because the money is transparently left in the bank rather than pocketed. Figure 2.6 then shows the high degree of variation that persists when accounting for other existing explanations, such as the size and quality of government bureaucracy (proxied for by the logged number of bureaucratic staff and the chief bureaucrat's years of experience),[61] racial diversity (proxied for by the percentage of black-headed households in the 2001 census), and level of economic diversity (proxied for by income decile dispersion

[57] Douglas M. Addison. "The quality of budget execution and its correlates." In *World Bank Policy Research Working Paper* 1.6657 (2013).

[58] Susan Rose-Ackerman. *Corruption and government: Causes, consequences, and reform*. Cambridge, UK: Cambridge University Press, 1999.

[59] Daniel Ziblatt. "Why some cities provide more public goods than others: A subnational comparison of the provision of public goods in German cities in 1912." In *Studies in Comparative International Development* 43.3-4 (2008), pp. 273–289.

[60] William Easterly and Ross Levine. "Africa's growth tragedy: Policies and ethnic divisions." In *Quarterly Journal of Economics* (1997), pp. 1203–1250; Robert D. Putnam, Robert Leonardi, and Raffaella Y. Nanetti. *Making democracy work: Civic traditions in modern Italy*. Princeton, NJ: Princeton University Press, 1994; James Habyarimana et al. *Coethnicity: Diversity and the dilemmas of collective action*. New York, NY: Russell Sage Foundation, 2009; Luttmer, "Group loyalty and the taste for redistribution"; Evan S. Lieberman and Gwyneth H. McClendon. "The ethnicity-policy preference link in sub-Saharan Africa." In *Comparative Political Studies* 46.5 (2013), pp. 574–602.

[61] Both measures come from the South African Municipal Demarcation Board's Annual Reports, which are available starting in 2003. State capacity is shown not to be a particularly satisfying explanation for underspending in other countries as well. For instance, in India, both higher-capacity states like West Bengal and lower-capacity states like Bihar have regularly underused their allocated budgets.

in the 2001 census). I regressed the percentage of the allocated capital budget spent, averaged over the years 2003 to 2006,[62] on these explanatory variables. I also included the percentage of the population living in informal housing, to account for variation in the population's objective need for municipal spending, and I included the dominant party's (the African National Congress, ANC's) percentage of the vote secured in the previous local election, since municipalities with more support for the nationally dominant party might be given more support for policy implementation from the center.[63]

Although these are all reasonable explanations of spending patterns, figure 2.6 shows that there is variation still to be explained. The figure plots residuals from the regression model against actual values of average percentages of the capital budget spent. Points above the dashed line are observations that are overpredicted by the model and points below the dashed line are observations underpredicted by it. Notably, the existing explanations both overpredict spending for municipalities that underspent their budgets (upper left corner of the figure, where the bulk of the observations lie) and underpredict spending for a few municipalities that on average spent more than their allocated budgets (lower right corner of the figure). The vast majority of observations are of underspending (i.e., appear to the left of 100

---

[62] Expenditure data were provided by the South African National Treasury's Municipal Liaison Office. I analyzed these years because, as discussed below, they help address the threat of reverse causality to the main theory. The average over these years is used here for simplicity of exposition, but there is a great deal of unexplained variation in each year. The statistical analyses are supplemented by case studies in part due to considerable levels of missing data in the expenditure reports. There were also a few observations of vast overspending (e.g., 1000% of the allocated budget) that may not be reliably reported; I exclude observations reporting spending of more than 200% of the budget. Below, I also discuss these overspending outliers, which may actually be consistent with theory.

[63] Servaas Van der Berg. "Consolidating South African democracy: The political arithmetic of budgetary redistribution." In *African Affairs* 97.387 (1998), pp. 251–264. The regression included province fixed effects, since provinces oversee municipal spending, and controlled for the size of the population (logged number of households).

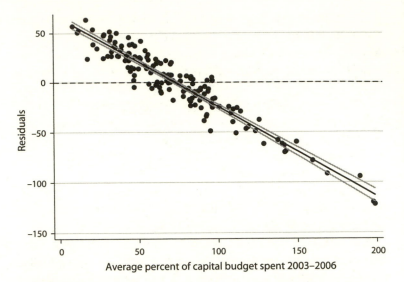

FIGURE 2.6: Variation to Be Explained in South African Municipal Underspending

Note: Residuals denote predicted values minus actual values of the average percentage of the capital budget spent 2003–2006. The x-axis displays actual values of average rates of spending. Gray lines show 95% confidence interval around the line of fit. Explanatory variables in the OLS regression included: % HH black (2001), % population in informal housing (2001), vote share ANC (2000), logged number of staff (2003), municipal manager's years of experience (2003), income decile dispersion (1996) and logged number of households (2001). Unreliable estimates of vast overspending and municipalities with missing values were excluded. Province fixed effects are included.

on the x-axis), and more than half of these are overpredicted by the model that relic on existing explanations.

Paying attention to status motivations can help us understand more of this puzzling variation in government spending.[64] This is because, all else equal, status motivations should increase public opposition to policies that make some people better off than others, which is often what government spending, particularly on individually and household-targeted goods, does. Consider two possible scenarios. In the first, people are only weakly motivated

---

[64] Status motivations most straightforwardly help make sense of puzzling underspending, though I return to the phenomenon of overspending below as well.

by the desire for higher within-group status, though they do value self and group material interests in absolute terms. In this scenario, one would expect opposition to spending policies from people who stand to lose materially because of the policies, and support from people who stand to gain materially. In the second scenario, within-group status motivations are also salient and are unmanaged by nonpolitical mechanisms.[65]

In this second scenario, one would expect people who stand to gain both resources and status from the policies to support spending, just as they would in the first scenario. Likewise, one might continue to expect opposition from people who stand to lose both resources and status. But one might expect more overall opposition in the second scenario overall because of those who are not hurt materially by the policy but nevertheless fear losing status. For these people, while they stand to lose no resources— and perhaps even stand to gain—others will benefit more from the policies and thus leave them in a worse relative position.[66] In

---

[65] Where social mechanisms for managing status motivations are robust, people might find ways to informally redistribute the goods among themselves, thereby reducing local disparities created by the policies between recipients and nonrecipients. For examples in Senegal, see Marie Boltz, Karine Marazyan, and Villar. "Preference for hidden income and redistribution to kin and neighbors: A lab-in-the-field experiment in Senegal." In South Africa, individuals to whom the government has granted single-family low-income homes (known as the Reconstruction and Development Programme, or RDP) might allow worse-off (nonrecipient) families to live in shacks behind or beside the house and use the amenities (electrical wires, outdoor plumbing) that come with the house. See Charlotte Lemanski. "Augmented informality: South Africa's backyard dwellings as a by-product of formal housing policies." In *Habitat International* 33.4 (2009), pp. 472–484. These "backyard shacks" arguably provide informal ways to mitigate disparities among neighbors. Lemanski notes that RDP house recipients will usually charge rent from the backyard shack dwellers, but she also concludes from her fieldwork that the "landlords" are initially motivated by a compulsion to help those who have not yet received a house.

[66] While it is possible that policies could also gain additional support from people who stand to gain status but lose resources, I set aside that possibility because the municipal policies considered here distribute basic household and individually targeted goods that convey economic status. It is not clear that losing such goods could result in status gains.

other words, in a scenario in which within-group status concerns are salient, we might expect similar patterns of support and opposition plus additional opposition from those who might lose status. Because of (real or perceived) pressure from these additional corners, politicians in this scenario may be more likely to strive to implement policies in ways that make everyone somewhat better off in absolute terms and minimize status losses.[67] Indeed,

---

[67] For instance, consider spending on low-income housing. Suppose there are two types of citizens in a municipality: (1) citizen (N) who currently lives in a shack and qualifies for a government-built house and (2) citizen (W) who already lives in a house, either government built or purchased. Suppose these two types of citizens are from the same reference group and therefore might care about their relative position vis-à-vis each other. Suppose there are n citizens of type N and w citizens of type W. Now consider citizen preferences over the implementation of a housing project that would benefit j individuals and for which government funding has already been allocated. The citizens (N) each have a probability ($p > 0$) of receiving a house if the project is implemented. Living in a shack yields a payoff of 0, and living in a formal house of any kind yields a payoff of 1. Assume that an *in-situ* housing upgrade (typical of South Africa) does not harm those who do not receive a house but yields them no major material benefit. If citizens do not care about their status, W_i has an expected utility of 1 if the housing project is implemented and 0 if it is not. N_i has an expected utility of p if the housing project is implemented and an expected utility of 0 if it is not. Very simply, citizens of type W are indifferent between the two actions and, as long as p is greater than 0, citizens of type N prefer implementation to the status quo. If, however, citizens of both types suffer a loss of status when others in their reference group have more than they do and gain in status when others in their reference group have less, opposition to implementation increases. Let's assume that utility takes the following form: $U_i(x) = x_i - \alpha_i \frac{1}{c-1} \sum_{j \neq i} max\{x_j - x_i, 0\} + \beta_i \frac{1}{c-1} \sum_{i \neq j} max\{x_i - x_j, 0\}$, where x_i is the payoff to citizen i of living in a formal or informal house, x_j is the payoff to others in her reference group, c is the total population of the reference group, and $\alpha_i = \beta_i = 1$ mark concerns for status, meaning that citizens gain utility from being relatively better off than others in their reference group and lose utility from being worse off, in addition to gaining utility from absolute resources. Implementation of the housing project now involves a certain loss in status for W_i and a possible loss in status for N_i, whereas before the housing project meant, respectively. No change in utility or a positive gain W_i now always opposes implementation because it introduces a $\frac{-j}{n-1}$ loss in utility and offers no gains over the status quo. Likewise, N_i is more likely to oppose implementation than in the scenario in which she disregarded relative position. For instance, if $p = 0$—that is, if N_i has no chance of receiving one of the houses—she would now oppose implementation ($\frac{-w-j}{c-1} < \frac{-w}{c-1}$), whereas before she would have been indifferent. Likewise, if p is low, or if she weights losses more heavily than gains, then N_i will

politicians may perceive that citizens would rather that such policies not be implemented at all than become worse off compared to their neighbors and others like themselves. Where status motivations are salient and unmanaged, spending on policies that make only some people better off within their local reference groups should be difficult to implement, all else equal.[68]

South Africa is an analytically useful place to investigate these arguments, because it provides variation in the conditions under which I would expect status motivations to be politically salient. The end of apartheid ushered in a period of economic and social transition for black South Africans, for whom formal barriers to economic advancement were removed. However, the removal of these formal barriers did not entail in practice that all black South Africans benefited economically from the new system, and opportunities for black advancement were unevenly distributed across the country. Some areas of South Africa experienced dramatic, visible increases in black income inequality, while others did not.[69] Certain sectors (e.g., large tourism enterprises, fishing, mining sectors, low-skill enterprises) appear to have created opportunities more quickly than others.[70] Black South Africans who became

---

prefer that the project not be implemented; on loss aversion see Kahneman and Tversky. "Prospect theory: An analysis of decision under risk."

[68] These predictions are in keeping with findings in laboratory experiments. Subjects in laboratory experiments have found Pareto improvements (policies that make no one worse off and some people better off) unpalatable when they make some subjects better off than others. For instance, Sauermann and Kaiser found that participants viewed Pareto improvements unpalatable when they might make them worse off than others. Subjects were asked to vote on different policy options. The authors summarized, "New institutions that theoretically create Pareto improvements compared to a given status quo might fail in practice if the resulting distribution increases inequality": Jan Sauermann and André Kaiser. "Taking others into account: Self-interest and fairness in majority decision making." In *American Journal of Political Science* 54.3 (2010), pp. 667–685, 680.

[69] Inequality across groups remained much more constant. See Seekings and Nattrass. "Class, distribution and redistribution in post-apartheid South Africa."

[70] Christian M. Rogerson. "Tourism, small firm development and empowerment in post-apartheid South Africa." In *Small firms in tourism*. Ed. by Rhodri Thomas. New York, NY: Routledge, 2013, pp. 13–35; Stefano Ponte and Lance van Sittert. "The chimera of redistribution in post-apartheid South Africa: Black

better off in areas with these more open sectors did not necessarily move away from the towns and cities they lived in during apartheid, at least until the early to mid-2000s.[71] In some areas there were new, sudden increases in economic inequality among black South Africans that were not immediately diminished by residential sorting.[72]

In areas experiencing rapidly increasing black economic inequality, the social mechanisms for addressing envy and spite appear to have broken down.[73] On the one hand, anti-apartheid activists had fought for black advancement through years of struggle. It was not obvious that black South Africans now able to get ahead should hide or forgo their new advantages in order to prevent the envy of those left behind. Advancement was to be celebrated. On the other hand, since black economic advancement was uneven, it was not necessarily clear to those who were not advancing that they should be glad about others' successes: Were they being abandoned? What differentiated those who were getting ahead from those who were not? Shouldn't they have gotten

---

Economic Empowerment(BEE) in industrial fisheries." In *African Affairs* 106.424 (2007), pp. 437–462; S. C. Goudie, F. Khan, and D. Kilian. "Transforming tourism: Black empowerment, heritage and identity beyond apartheid." In *South African Geographical Journal* 81.1 (1999), pp. 22–31.

[71] Exceptions are in the largest cities, where neighborhoods are more spread out to begin with and separated to a greater degree by highways. There, newly upper-middle and upper-class black South Africans moved between 1994 and 2001 to neighborhoods far removed from the townships to which they were previously confined. See Amy Kracker Selzer and Patrick Heller. "The spatial dynamics of middle class formation in postapartheid South Africa: Enclavization and fragmentation in Johannesburg." In *Political Power and Social Theory* 21 (2010), pp. 171–208. Even in these big cities, the living patterns of newly middle-class blacks were remarkably static during this period. See Daniel Schensul. "Remaking an apartheid city: State-led spatial transformation in post-apartheid Durban, South Africa." PhD thesis. Brown University, 2009.

[72] I return to the possibility of geographic sorting in the 'Elaborations' chapter of the book.

[73] Adam Ashforth. *Witchcraft, violence, and democracy in South Africa*. Chicago, IL: University of Chicago Press, 2005, pp. 89, 93. Jonny Steinberg. *Sizwe's test: A young man's journey through Africa's AIDS epidemic*. New York, NY: Simon and Schuster, 2008.

ahead, too? In her ethnographic study, Dawson observed that there was "the very real fact that many South Africans [saw] people they know rise from relative poverty to wealth, which pose[d] a new set of questions about the desire to consume and what it represents."[74] As in the anecdotal example of funeral regulations in Chengdu, China, described earlier, it suddenly became unclear how to make sense of and respond to new disparities among coethnics and neighbors. Where these rapid within-group changes were happening, neighbors began to treat new interpersonal differences with more open, unmanaged resentment.[75] In a study in an area of Cape Town experiencing these changes, Seekings et al. observed, "Many believe their neighbours revel in their misfortunes, are envious or jealous of them."[76] The same study notes, "Jealousy occurred within as much as, and perhaps more than, across racial boundaries."[77] In other words, areas that experienced increasing within-group inequality exhibited unmanaged envy among neighbors

[74] Hannah Dawson. "Youth politics: Waiting and envy in a South African informal settlement." In *Journal of Southern African Studies* 40.4 (2014), pp. 861–882, 875.

[75] Ashforth offers an ethnographic study of envy and jealousy in Soweto during this time period and observes many social conventions that had previously regulated such emotions breaking down. Whereas people previously followed clear rules about how to behave in reaction to positive events (the birth of a child, an impending marriage, a new job), such conventions no longer assuaged others' resentment. Ashforth describes this period as one in which "procedures that previously served to hold jealousy and resentment in check decline[d] in effectiveness" as dramatic socioeconomic inequality presented "enormous problems of interpretation." "When those not enjoying the good life in Soweto ask themselves why, few ready answers present themselves... [Those advancing] ran a serious risk of being branded sellouts [whatever else they did]." Ashforth. *Witchcraft, violence, and democracy in South Africa*. For ethnographic and other field accounts of how changes in within-group inequality can raise these questions, see, also, Steinberg. *Sizwe's test: A young man's journey through Africa's AIDS epidemic*; Ramphele. *Steering by the stars: Being young in South Africa*; Dawson. "Youth politics: Waiting and envy in a South African informal settlement"; Frank Ellis. "We are all poor here: Economic difference, social divisiveness and targeting cash transfers in sub-saharan Africa." In *Journal of Development Studies* 48.2 (2012), pp. 201–214.

[76] Jeremy Seekings et al., *The social consequences of establishing mixed neighbourhoods*. Cape Town: Centre for Social Science Research, Cape Town, 2010, 96.

[77] Ibid., p. 142.

and coethnics.[78] The observable implications of status motivations are most likely to be evident in such places. Individually and household-targeted spending—which makes some neighbors and coethnics visibly better off than others—should be more difficult there.

South African politicians have reasons to be sensitive to the threat of envious and spiteful conflict in their constituencies. Each ward within a municipality[79] has a representative on the municipal council who is elected by plurality in a first-past-the-post race. These politicians may fear that implementing policies that are likely to exacerbate within-group disparities will threaten their chances of reelection. Ward representatives are also required to live permanently in their wards and deal regularly with interpersonal disputes. According to the 2006 Afrobarometer poll, local councillors ranked second only to religious leaders as the authority figure most often consulted on interpersonal conflicts.[80] Interpersonal disputes can escalate and even become violent. A ward representative in eThekwini mentioned to me that she encouraged a delay in one housing project because she had sensed in public meetings that those left behind might resort to vandalizing or burning down built houses. "I didn't want jealousy incidents," she said. At the very least, she wanted to prevent such incidents because she would have to deal with them personally. "I would like to avoid these things happening ... for my own sake," she said.[81] Whether she is correct in her prediction or not, concerns about envy could reasonably have influenced decisions about municipal

[78] By contrast, Steinberg describes how a young man in a village largely untouched by the economic and social transitions knew to hide his wealth and achievements; he knew the "silent rule: becoming a success in the midst of a generation that is failing is disallowed": Steinberg. *Sizwe's test: A young man's journey through Africa's AIDS epidemic*, p. 61.

[79] A given informal settlement is usually contained within a single ward.

[80] The percentages of respondents on the 2006 Afrobarometer who said they had contacted each type of leader at least once were: 22.4% for local councilors, 4.8% for members of parliament, 5.8% for government administrators, 14.3% for party officials, 14.8% for traditional leaders, and 31.4% for religious leaders.

[81] Interview, July 1, 2009.

spending. Many ethnographic accounts document that envious and spiteful dynamics became more intense and public among citizens during this period.[82] Connecting status motivations to government spending patterns requires only that politicians act *as if* they were responding to constituents, envy and spite. It does not necessarily require that citizens ever actively harm one another out of a concern for within-group status, or even that they make demands explicitly citing within-group status as a motivation.[83]

Indeed, local politicians do appear to be more sensitive to openly envious behavior among their constituents in places where intra-group inequality has strained social conventions managing status motivations. Evidence for this claim comes from a pen-and-paper survey others and I administered to locally elected politicians in parts of the Eastern Cape in 2009.[84] I included a question in this survey to assess whether politicians observe or worry about envious behavior among constituents. Councillors were asked to choose which of two statements they agreed with more when thinking about typical behavior in the constituency they were elected to represent.

---

[82] Ashforth. *Witchcraft, violence, and democracy in South Africa*; Steinberg. *Sizwe's test: A young man's journey through Africa's AIDS epidemic*; Dawson. "Youth politics: Waiting and envy in a South African informal settlement."

[83] I cannot entirely rule out the possibility here that politicians were using constituents' envy and spite as an excuse for underspending. However, as discussed above, accounts other than mine document an increase in publicly, conspicuous envy and spite among ordinary citizens during this period, especial in places where inequality was rapidly increasing.

[84] Evan S. Lieberman. "The perils of polycentric governance of infectious disease in South Africa." In *Social Science & Medicine* 73.5 (2011), pp. 676–684. Local councillors (n = 163) from ten municipalities in the Eastern Cape province responded to the survey. The survey contained over 150 questions soliciting basic demographic information and asking councillors about the main problems and risks facing their constituents, their policy preferences on a variety of issues, which government and nongovernmental actors they think should be responsible for dealing with policy problems, and their perceptions of their constituents' behavioral tendencies. Specific metros and smaller municipalities within the province were selected to maximize variation in characteristics like racial make-up, while holding geographic and provincial-level characteristics constant.

Statement A: When someone does well—makes money, earns good marks, lives in a nice house—it can cause jealousy and conflict.

Statement B: When someone does well—makes money, earns good marks, lives in a nice house—others always celebrate their successes.

In Ndlambe, one of the municipal case studies in which I argue that envy undermined the delivery of low-income housing, locally elected councillors reported observations of envious behavior at high rates. Two-thirds of councillors there agreed only with statement A, and every single Ndlambe councillor either agreed outright with that statement or said that both statements were true to some degree. No one agreed only with statement B. By contrast, in Makana, another case study I discuss below, in which I argue that envious behavior was less consequential for politics during this particular period, less than half of locally elected politicians agreed outright with statement A.[85] In other words, there is variation across space in the extent to which local politicians were concerned about status motivations. In places where dramatic increases in inequality had strained social conventions, local politicians noted the possibility of jealousy and conflict.

To examine whether places where status motivations were likely to be unmanaged also exhibited difficulties in implementing spending, I took both a quantitative and a qualitative approach. I conducted a statistical analysis to assess whether the main argument's observable implications hold *across* municipalities in South Africa. I also conducted case studies to look for observable implications *within* particular municipalities. Both approaches are observational, which makes strong causal claims difficult, but South Africa offers certain methodological advantages to that end. For instance, I am less concerned about the possibility of

---

[85] Note that the survey did not receive responses from councillors in the third case study municipality (Kou-Kamma) discussed below.

reverse causality because of when the municipal governments were established. The national dismantling of apartheid happened in the years following 1994, but new post-apartheid municipal governments were not created until 2001. Transitional Local Councils (TLCs) operated in smaller units between 1996 and 2001, but my understanding is that they had little power and were amalgamated into brand-new municipalities in 2001.[86] These facts lessen the possibility that municipal policy implementation led to different changes in inequality among black South Africans (rather than the other way around) during the 1996–2001 period, because the municipalities as such did not yet exist. I can examine how new municipal governments reacted to the changes in inequality in the prior period that were not of their making. This lessens the possibility that municipal spending shaped envy and spite dynamics rather than the other way around.[87]

Though imperfect, the statistical analysis provides preliminary evidence consistent with the main arguments. Municipalities that experienced increases in black income inequality after the dismantling of apartheid are the places where conventions around managing status motivations were likely to be in flux and where politicians reported sensitivity to jealousy and conflict among constituents in the pen-and-paper survey. The statistical analysis reported in table 2.8 then shows an association between increases in black income inequality and subsequent municipal underspending. As in the analysis for figure 2.6, I used the percentage of the allocated capital budget spent, averaged over four years after the new municipalities were created (2003–2006), as a dependent variable. I examined the percentage of capital expenditure, because status motivations should be triggered by *visible* interpersonal

---

[86] As the South African Local Government Association (SALGA) put it, "Because of their lack of constitutional status, [the TLCs] were creatures of statute.... [That statute] rendered all their actions, including the passing of by-laws, administrative actions, subject to judicial review. Municipalities, it can be said, thus existed at the mercy of the provinces." See http://www.salga.org.za/pages/Municipalities/About-Municipalities.

[87] I discuss additional concerns about omitted variable bias in the Elaborations chapter of the book.

differences. Such differences can be created by the uneven delivery of larger-scale targeted goods and services (e.g., toilets, houses); funding for such goods is provided in the capital budget in South Africa municipalities.[88] There are admittedly some oddities in the data. For instance, a few data points reported spending well over 200 percent of the allocated budget. I am not confident that these are reliable reports, so I excluded them from the main analysis but return to discuss them below. I also used a binary dependent variable indicating whether a municipality consistently spent less than 100 percent of its allocated capital budget in each of the four years.[89]

One might be concerned that the percent of allocated budget spent or consistent underspending might actually signal efficient policy implementation. But there is little evidence that this is the case. The provincial and national governments[90] tend to be conservative in allocating funding in the first place.[91] Scholars, policy analysts, and journalists in South Africa have all consistently focused on municipal budget underspending as an indicator of low levels of goods and service provision.[92]

---

[88] Using the percentage of the allocated budget rather than the total amount spent also takes into account the size of the grants received. The question is not why some governments receive or spend more money than others, but rather, given the funding municipalities receive, why do some spend it and others do not?

[89] The main results are strongest for 2003. The association remains in the same direction in 2004 and 2005, though statistically insignificant, and is close to zero on 2006. This pattern is consistent with the expectation that the effects of "unsettled" periods might diminish over time.

[90] My understanding is that the principal sources of capital financing are government grants, private or foreign donations (rarer for smaller municipalities), and public–private partnerships and loans, though interest rates are high in South Africa. Municipalities do collect service rates and property taxes, though these tend to fund operating budgets and smaller purchases, such as office furniture, rather than capital expenditures, and, as mentioned in the last section, are subject to review.

[91] Interviews with Municipal Liaison Officers, November 11 and 12, 2010. Interview with the provincial supervisor of housing delivery in Nelson Mandela Bay Metro, November 24, 2010. I return to the cases of outright overspending below.

[92] See, for instance, *Mail and Guardian* Staff. "State to spend R800bn on infrastructure." In *Mail and Guardian* (Feb. 2011); and Linda Ensor. "Municipal

The key independent variable is thus the percent change in black income inequality in each municipality from 1996 to 2001.[93] I used the percentage change in the decile dispersion ratio among black-headed households—that is, the change in the ratio of average household income of those in the top 10 percent to average household income of those in the bottom 10 percent, based on 1996 and 2001 census data, divided by the decile dispersion in 1996 and multiplied by 100.[94] I then controlled for the same variables included in the regression analysis for figure 2.6 to account for existing explanations.

Results from these regression analyses are presented in table 2.8. Consistent with the theory, the more black income inequality increased, the smaller the percentage of the capital budget spent on average (column 1). Skeptics might note that the coefficient in this first column is not large. A 1 percent increase in black income inequality is associated with a decrease of only 0.03 percentage points in average budget expenditure. Yet the goal here is to understand whether a theory of status motivations can help us understand more of the variation in spending rather than to establish that status concerns are the only (or main) explanation, and the explanation does this quite well.[95] It remains robust to the inclusion of these other control variables, and the magnitude of the association is substantively meaningful. A one-

---

leaders 'should account for underspending of grants.' " In *Business Day* (Oct. 2010).

[93] The same pattern holds if I use change in black income inequality and control for the level of black income inequality (decile dispersion) in 1996.

[94] The measure is generated using data on annual household income sorted by the race of the head of the household. Members of the geography unit at Statistics South Africa reformulated the 1996 data to reflect the new 2001 municipal demarcations so that the measures of decile dispersion in those two years would be geographically comparable even though new municipalities were created to begin work in 2001. On each census, household income was reported in 14 brackets. In calculating change in the black decile dispersion ratio, households were treated as having the average income in their respective brackets. Households in the highest income bracket (for which no upper bound was reported) were treated as earning 110% of the lower bound of the bracket.

[95] The r-squared statistic for this OLS regression excluding percent change in black inequality is 0.09; including it increases the r-squared statistic to 0.135.

TABLE 2.8 Relationship between Changes in Black Income Inequality and Municipal Budget Spending

	Avg % budget spent 2003–2006	Consistent underspending
Percent change in black inequality	−0.03**	0.14**
	(0.01)	(0.06)
% of pop in informal (2001)	−0.42	0.13*
	(0.52)	(0.07)
Log staff (2003)	−2.04	0.03
	(4.02)	(0.07)
Years of MM experience (2003)	−0.23	−0.01
	(0.38)	(0.05)
% HH black (2001)	−0.36	0.01
	(0.32)	(0.13)
Log HH (2001)	7.36*	−0.01
	(4.29)	(0.05)
ANC vote % (2000)	0.42*	−0.00
	(0.25)	(0.09)
	N = 147	N = 147

Notes: * $p<0.10$, ** $p<0.05$. Standard errors in parentheses. Province fixed effects included. OLS in first column, logistic regression in the second. The dependent variable in first column is the percentage of the budget spent, averaged over 2003–2006. The dependent variable in the last column is a binary variable indicating whether the municipality underspent in each of those years. That column presents changes in the predicted probabilities of being a consistent underspender associated with a one-standard-deviation change in the independent variables, holding others at their means. Municipalities missing values dropped.

standard-deviation change in the main measure of increasing black inequality corresponds to an 8.5 percentage point change in the capital budget spent.[96] For comparison, a one-standard-deviation change in the ANC's percent of the vote is associated with a 10.1 percentage point change in average capital expenditure, which is comparable.

I also find support for a status motivations explanation if I examine consistent underspending—that is, whether a municipality underspent its capital budget in each of the four years.

---

[96] There is quite a bit of variation in changes in black income inequality during this period: one standard deviation is a 341% change, around a mean of a 71% increase. Excluding outliers more than two standard deviations away from the mean does not change results.

Here, too, the more black income inequality increased just after apartheid, the more likely it is that a municipality subsequently underspent its budget every year. One standard deviation of percentage change in black income inequality is associated with a fourteen percentage point increase in the probability of being a consistent under spender. As one might expect, municipalities faced with higher levels of poverty (measured here by the percentage of houses that are informal) are also robustly more likely to be consistent underspenders. Other explanations fall short.

But if the pursuit of within-group status prompts concerns about exacerbating local within-group disparities, why not overspend rather than underspend? Skeptics might wonder why municipalities do not simply spend as much as possible, in order to distribute goods equally and simultaneously, and hope that the provincial or central government eventually agrees to cover the difference. But overspending is not as straightforward a strategy as it might seem. There is no guarantee that the difference will be covered. If it is not, the municipality may have to underspend on other things. Politicians and bureaucrats at the local level are often looking to move up to the provincial or local government later in their careers and may not want to risk relationships with higher-ups by flagrantly violating budget constraints.

As mentioned, there are examples in the municipal expenditure data of enormous overspending of capital budgets. These outliers may not be reliably measured, and when they are excluded, increasing black income inequality is consistently associated with underspending, which supports the theory. At the same time, these outliers may also be consistent with a status-based argument. The seven municipalities that consistently overspent in this vast way are generally those where the black decile dispersion increased greatly (by 112%, on average). This suggests that municipalities facing increasing within-group inequality may engage in one of two strategies. The more common (and less risky) strategy is to underspend rather than implement policies that would exacerbate local within-group disparities. The other strategy is to vastly overspend in order to try to deliver goods simultaneously to everyone who qualifies for them.

However, if status motivations help explain these patterns of government spending, an additional observable implication is that they should hold up as an explanation for spending on individually or household-targeted goods and not for spending on non-excludable public goods. Building low-income houses for only *some* of those who need them and delivering toilets to only *some* needy houses or corners of the neighborhood represent the kinds of visible expenditures that make some neighbors identifiably better off than others. By contrast, envy and spite should be less of a problem for spending on goods that create no such disparities among neighbors.

Table 2.9 offers partial support for this observable implication of the theory. It shows that percentage change in black inequality is *not* related to spending on roads, which are a non-excludable public good and should be less likely to create visible disparities among neighbors than the delivery of individually and household-targeted goods. Everyone should be able to use roads and benefit from improvements (paving, repairs) to them.[97] Spending on roads is accounted for by more standard explanations. The table presents the results of a logistic regression using an indicator for whether municipalities ever reported underspending on roads during the relevant time period as the dependent variable.[98] The percentage change in black income inequality is not significantly associated with spending on roads, while existing types of explanations (size of the bureaucratic staff, size of the municipality, political ties to the center) *are* related to whether a municipality

[97] Some might point out that construction of a road could create more disruption for some people (generating more noise for those who live closer, perhaps even displacing some people during construction). Yet, even if this is true, roads are *less* likely to provoke status concerns among neighbors than the delivery of individually- and household-targeted goods.

[98] In other words, the dependent variable is binary, indicating whether in 2003–2006 a municipality ever reported spending less than 100% of its allocated capital budget for roads. Unfortunately, fewer municipalities reported line items allocated for roads than reported the allocated capital budget overall and so using averages or consistent underspending indicators made less sense.

TABLE 2.9 Relationship between Changes in Black Income Inequality and Roads Spending

	Ever underspent on roads 2003–2006
Percent change in black inequality	0.02
	(0.05)
% of housing informal (2001)	−0.04
	(0.08)
Log staff (2003)	−0.17**
	(0.08)
Years of MM experience (2003)	0.11*
	(0.06)
% HH black (2001)	−0.03
	(0.14)
Log HH (2001)	0.15*
	(0.06)
ANC vote % (2000)	0.19*
	(0.11)
	N = 140

Notes: * $p < 0.10$, ** $p < 0.05$. Standard errors in parentheses. Province fixed effects included. The table presents changes in predicted probabilities of the dependent variable associated with a one-standard-deviation change in the independent variables.

ever reported underspending its road budget.

By contrast, status motivations should, for example, help explain the construction of low-income houses, which can make some neighbors quite visibly better off than others. This is particularly the case in South Africa, where the policy of low-income housing construction has, with very few exceptions, been to deliver RDP homes. If low-income houses are not built simultaneously for everyone in an area who qualifies, those who receive houses become identifiably better off than qualifying nonrecipients. I expect the politics of status motivations to play out around individually and household-targeted goods like these. Even when housing delivery poses no obvious material costs to anyone,[99] it makes *some* households better off than others. This dynamic should contribute

[99] It could be argued that underspending on low-income housing is particularly puzzling in South Africa because low-income housing there is often constructed on the same sites as existing informal settlements for the shack residents already living

to delays in the delivery of houses where social conventions around status motivations have broken down.

I found evidence for these claims in examinations of three municipalities. Unfortunately, the data on percentage spent of the budget allocated specifically for housing during these years is more unreliable than that for the roads line item.[100] However, closer examination of a few municipalities allowed me to assess observable implications of the theory in the absence of more reliable large sample size data on housing spending, and given missing or potentially unreliable observations in the capital budget spending mentioned earlier. This approach also allowed me to investigate the process linking "unsettled" times to patterns of spending on visible household-targeted goods. I was able to probe the views of some of the relevant actors as well as some parts of the municipal record relevant to housing construction.

These examinations combined "most similar" and "most different" case selection. Two of the cases (Makana and Ndlambe) provided a paired comparison of very similar municipalities across which there is variation in changes in black income inequality just before this period (increasing in Ndlambe, decreasing slightly in Makana). While several demographic characteristics of the third municipality (Kou-Kamma) were quite different from those of the other two, it demonstrated the same logic as in Ndlambe: increasing black inequality associated with underspending on housing.

All three municipalities share certain very basic similarities. For instance, they each lie within the same province (the Eastern Cape) and district (Cacadu), in areas officially designated white areas

---

there. On in-situ construction, see Schensul, "Remaking an apartheid city: State-led spatial transformation in post-apartheid Durban, South Africa." This approach to construction arguably benefits most (if not all) affected parties in some way. For instance, it increases the value of nearby formal properties, making "not in my backyard" (NIMBY) objections by neighbors less likely.

[100] This assessment departs from the dissertation on which this book is based, for which I tried to assemble data on this issue. Further probing left me insufficiently confident in the quality of the data across a number of municipalities during these years.

under apartheid even though all four were also home to a large number of black (Black and Coloured)[101] people throughout the same area. Many of the first black African residents of the area were refugees from colonial wars or labor recruited by the British to work on farms around their new garrison towns. Slums with a mix of formal houses and shacks were created in these areas by Black and coloured workers. In 2000 the National Demarcation Board amalgamated local areas in order to combine racial groups so that white, richer residents could provide a tax base for services supplied to lower-income residents from other race groups. All three municipalities examined here were constructed from an amalgamation of a core white area (previously administered by a white council with its own tax base), coloured and Black "locations" (previously funded by grants from the national government, though always underfunded), and surrounding agricultural areas (often previously administered by a district council that managed all surrounding white agricultural areas).

The formal housing implementation process seems to have been implemented fairly consistently across these municipalities. In my understanding, the provincial governments, which have formal responsibility for housing issues,[102] distribute funds earmarked for housing construction to be spent in each municipality. Provincial government housing directors then supervised local politicians and municipal bureaucrats, who often worked with community committees to identify the sites in need of in situ upgrading, the number of qualifying beneficiaries, and the number of units needed. Since the size of each house (in square meters) is nationally mandated, and houses are supposed to meet a uniform standard of quality, the number of houses that can be built with the allocated budget is fairly fixed. But

---

[101] Under apartheid, South Africa had four race categories by law: Black/African, Coloured, Asian, and White/European. I use the term black here to denote people of color (non-whites).

[102] South Africa has three main levels of government: national, provincial, and municipal. I selected case studies from the same province in order to ensure similar higher-level government management for each municipality.

the committee's investigation can reveal the extent to which the allocated funding provides for the number of qualifying families in that area. Steering committees are supposed to include residents of the areas in need of low-income housing (potential beneficiaries and their neighbors).[103]

These committees usually also contained one or two bureaucrats involved in housing policy in the municipalities as well as local politicians elected in the wards with informal settlements. Steering committees then held public meetings in informal settlement areas that needed to be upgraded to present the projects. The minutes of these public meetings and of the steering committee meetings were supposed to be submitted to the full municipal council (though they are sometimes paraphrased or partial, and often some records are missing), along with recommendations from the committee, before projects were implemented. The council then reviewed these reports and voted on whether to continue with the proposed housing projects or not. If the council voted to proceed, the provincial housing office reviewed the full list of qualifying beneficiaries and decided which families would receive the houses that could be built with the allocated funding.[104]

Despite these similarities, the delivery of low-income housing varied between Ndlambe and Makana in these years. Makana spent

---

[103] The process of selecting these individuals does not seem to be particularly transparent. One might worry that in municipalities with increasing black inequality, politically connected individuals are somehow better able to capture these committees, triggering opposition to housing delivery from ordinary people because of a concern for fairness rather than because of envy. I return to this possibility in the Elaborations chapter. I show that residents of municipalities with increasing black inequality are no more likely than others to perceive such types of municipal corruption.

[104] Preference ordering varies and is not particularly transparent; in theory it takes into account length of residence in the municipality, family size, and disabilities. Author interviews in Eastern Cape housing office, November 3, 2010; author interview with Cacadu district housing supervisor, November 4, 2010; author interviews in municipal offices in Makana, September 30, 2010, and in Ndlambe, November 14, 2010.

TABLE 2.10 Variation across Case Study Municipalities

	Ndlambe	Makana	Kou-Kamma
% households in informal housing (2001)	14%	13%	6%
Share of households Black (2001)	74%	78%	31%
Racial fractionalization (2001)	0.38	0.38	0.28
ANC vote share (2000)	0.75	0.82	0.48
ANC council seats share (2001)	0.76	0.83	0.63
Qual. evidence of infighting	Yes	Yes	No
FM with tertiary ed (2003)	Yes	Yes	Yes
Total population (2001)	55,479	74,540	34, 293
District	Cacadu	Cacadu	Cacadu

most of its allocated housing budgets during this time,[105] while Ndlambe did not.[106] According to a basic delivery index across the period from 2001 to 2007, both Makana and Ndlambe started out with approximately the same capacity to roll out services, including new housing, and thus with the same score on the index.[107] But Makana's score on basic service delivery rose by almost twice the amount that Ndlambe's did during this time.[108]

Existing explanations for these differences in spending are not particularly satisfying. In addition to the similarities discussed above, Ndlambe and Makana also shared a number of other characteristics that might be expected to shape housing delivery, such as the size of the informal housing problem they faced when amalgamated, their racial demographics, the makeup of their municipal councils (heavily dominated by the ANC), and the relative size and competence of their bureaucracies (see table 2.10).

[105] Interviews with treasury and human settlements offices in Makana in October 2010.

[106] Interviews with Ndlambe council and corporate services department in November 2010. For housing unit delivery numbers by province for this period, see Kate Tissington. *A resource guide to housing in South Africa 1994–2010*. Tech. rep. Socio-Economic Rights Institute of South Africa, 2011.

[107] Waldo Krugell, Hannelie Otto, and Jacky van der Merwe. "Local municipalities and progress with the delivery of basic services in South Africa." In *North-West University Working Paper No. 116* (2009).

[108] Makana's score rose from 0.365 in 2001 to 0.859 in 2007. Ndlambe's rose more modestly from 0.361 to 0.637.

Further qualitative probing confirmed that any differences in spending and implementation are not easily accounted for by bureaucratic competence. Both Ndlambe and Makana had fairly robust municipal staffs. In interviews the Cacadu District and provincial supervisors for housing projects in these municipalities at the time identified both as the better-staffed municipalities in the district. In Ndlambe the former town clerk of Alexandria, who had several prior years of experience as an administrator, served as municipal manager during the first several years of the new municipality's existence and was accompanied by former members of her staff. Investigators from the province in 2001 praised the general efficiency of the municipal management staff in Port Alfred.[109] There were concerns about some of the contractors hired to build the houses, but these were usually linked to concerns about the quality of the built structures rather than the efficiency of the roll-out.[110] Makana also assembled a full housing staff in these early years, with engineers and planners on staff who could work with the province. Clearly, spending did not necessarily follow from bureaucratic competence.

Nor are the differences easily accounted for by intra-elite political dynamics. There were certainly tensions within the governing ANC in Ndlambe during this time, though they appeared to be unrelated to constituent concerns about equitable policies. Instead, the dispute seemed to involve which parts of the municipality would be in charge following the amalgamation. The local newspaper documented a constant divide between ANC councillors from Port Alfred and ANC members from formerly independent Kenton and Alexandria.[111] One ANC councillor recalled, "Disagreements during this time were often about where we should hold meetings ... like, how far would people have to travel if they were coming from different parts of the

[109] "Local ANC and SANCO shake hands," *Talk of the Town*, September 25, 2001.
[110] See, for instance, "From the council chambers," *Talk of the Town*, March 30, 2002.
[111] See "From the council chambers," *Talk of the Town*, September 18, 2001, March 23, 2002, April 20, 2002, and May 4, 2002.

municipality... or about who would hold important positions."[112] In council meetings throughout 2001 and 2002, at least, ANC councillors openly voted against ANC proposals, particularly those involving the nomination of leaders (for mayor, committee chairs, etc.). The mayor made several open pleas during council meetings for councillors to work together.[113] Yet these divisions did not drive decisions about the housing projects. No reference I saw was made in the municipal record of housing disputes between the Port Alfred and Kenton/Alexandria factions of the ANC. Meanwhile, though it controlled a healthy share of the municipal vote, the ANC in Makana was not unified either. One councillor recalled infighting beginning in 2001 between the South African Communist Party (SACP) and the ANC, even though members of both were ostensibly ANC councillors. He recalled that in his first year as an opposition party (DA) councilor, he went to a funeral where the SACP ANC members asked him to give them a lift back to the township instead of getting in a car with their ANC counterparts. "I knew from then that something was going on between them," he said. Indeed, in 2001 and 2002 there was an open controversy about the selection of the mayor, with four councillors opposed to the ANC caucus nominee.[114] But, again, these internal disputes did not appear linked to discussions over housing projects.

What plausibly had some influence over policy implementation during this period was the perception that citizens did not want policies that would exacerbate relative local disparities. In Makana the implementation process during this time appears to have proceeded without hiccups due to perceived social opposition. By contrast, in Ndlambe potential beneficiaries and their neighbors objected (or were perceived by politicians to object) to housing projects that would have created new disparities among them.

[112] Interview, October 29, 2010.

[113] E.g., "From the council chambers," *Talk of the Town*, February 2, 2002.

[114] *Grocott's Mail*, August 8, 2002, p.3.

In the coastal town of Ndlambe, black African residents did not all face the same economic opportunities during and after the transition from apartheid. As new opportunities in business (particularly in the tourism and service sectors) opened up for some black Africans in the late 1990s, some black residents from the area secured employment in the tourism industry along the coast near Port Alfred as well as in the pineapple-growing agricultural areas near Bathurst. While most of the bed and breakfast and hotel establishments on the coast remained white owned, several businesses involved in organizing tours and recreational activities hired black individuals, particularly in order to appeal to the new black political elite in Johannesburg who started coming to the "Sunshine Coast" for vacations. In addition, a black-initiated project from Bathurst (*Siyazikhulisa*/"We are cultivating it") to boost pineapple sales won a grant from the central government in 1999 and focused on integrating black local residents into the business as managers.[115] Public officials in Ndlambe recalled that the mid- to late 1990s brought visible changes in the economic circumstances of some (but not all) black residents.[116]

By contrast, disparities among black residents were arguably not growing as rapidly or as visibly in Makana. Some of the social mobility within the black population in Makana was directed through the university, but this did not result in a newly visible accumulation of wealth in the hands of a local few. As one local councillor recalled, "It was a time of change, but most of the up-and-coming Africans in this town were going through Rhodes [University]. They were young, not yet established and they were moving up and moving out."[117] There were some larger houses in the townships of Makana, notably in Extensions 4 and 5, but these had been there since well before the transition and remained

---

[115] Matthew Gibb. "The 'global' and the 'local': A comparative study of development practices in three South African municipalities." PhD thesis. Rhodes University, 2006.

[116] Interviews, October 29, 2010.

[117] Interview, September 18, 2010.

relatively modest.[118] Car ownership also did not increase rapidly in the historically black areas of Makana until after 1999.[119] The local newspaper noted that Makana did not seem to be developing the same pockets of newly acquired black wealth as the quickly developing coastal towns.[120]

Where intra-group inequality was visibly increasing, the implementation of housing projects that could not accommodate all qualifying families were often delayed or halted altogether. For instance, during its first term, the municipal council in Ndlambe received funding from the provincial government for housing projects, but the implementation of those projects often met with resistance from steering committees. In February 2001 a steering committee submitted a memo to the new council questioning a project to build houses in Station Hill. The allocated funding was sufficient to build only 11 housing units, far short of the 113 that the committee had identified as needed. The memo allegedly argued that building should not go forward for the 11 units and that funding should either be returned to the province or transferred to another neighborhood project if it could round out the full number of units needed there. In the council meeting the following month, the council decided, on the recommendation of the Station Hill steering committee, not to implement the housing project, because there were not enough funds to build all the units required and because the Nemato neighborhood project, which had all the necessary funding, was already going forward.[121] There are records of similar steering committee and public meetings about projects planned in 2002, 2003, and 2004 that would serve only a fraction of the identified beneficiaries. Many of these projects were stalled, even though steering committee members likely knew that not spending the money might jeopardize future

[118] ISER. *Living in Rhini: Research report series*. Tech. rep. Institute of Social and Economic Research, 2007.

[119] Ibid.

[120] *Grocott's Mail.* January 19, 2001, vol. 132, no. 5.

[121] The council continued to apply for additional funding for the housing project in Station Hill, but as late as June 2001, the province continued to deny the request.

budgets. In April 2003 the full council meeting minutes noted a problem for a planned housing project in Wentzel Park, citing objections to the fact that the provincially granted funds could cover all four hundred beneficiaries in that neighborhood at the nationally mandated size of 40 square meters. Rather than build fewer units, the council proposed either seeking a waiver from the national government to build smaller units or using cheaper materials. In other words, rather than going forward with a project that would exacerbate local disparities, the council found it more politically palatable to treat beneficiaries equally but to give them less.

By contrast, these kinds of concerns do not appear to have arisen in Makana during this time. Soon after its inauguration in 2001, the new council in Makana executed new housing projects bit by bit, continuing a project that built just 55 RDP (Reconstruction and Development Programme) houses in Ndancama and Newtown.[122] No debates over the number of units appear to have arisen in the steering committee recommendations or council records, even though it was clear that at least 150 families in these areas qualified for low-income housing at the time.[123] Indeed, when the province failed to select a contractor right away, the mayor took a council vote to decide on a stronger role for the municipality in the project so that it could go forward.[124] The municipal records between 2001 and 2006 that I saw showed no concerns about the implementation of housing projects or

[122] ISER. *Living in Rhini: Research report series.*

[123] A dispute arose between the ANC and the Democratic Alliance in 2001 over how closely to cooperate with provincial housing supervisors on the Mayfield Housing Project, but the question of whether enough units were being built does not appear to have been raised by the steering committee or other community advisors even though only half of the qualified beneficiaries on the list for Mayfield would be serviced by the new development. Dumile Meintjies. "Big buzz as Mayfield gets going," *Makana Voice*, February 6, 2001. On another housing project, see Adrienne Carlisle. "All systems go for Vukani," *Grocott's Mail*, March 9, 2001, vol. 132, no. 19.

[124] Richard Buckland. "Makana council goes it alone," *Grocott's Mail*, August 31, 2001, vol. 132, no. 37.

the possibility of social instability should all beneficiaries not be accommodated. Housing projects continued in all parts of the municipality with the recorded support of potential recipients and those who lived nearby. By the end of 2003, the province recognized Makana as the "top achiever in housing" in the Eastern Cape.[125]

The contrast between the experiences of Ndlambe and Makana thus casts additional doubt on the adequacy of existing explanations of municipal spending and underscores the potential analytic usefulness of status motivations. In addition, I looked at policy implementation in Kou-Kamma during this period, because it is very different on a number of scores but, like Ndlambe, it underspent during this period.[126] Kou-Kamma is a smaller town—50–60 percent the size of the other two municipalities. It is more racially diverse because a smaller share of its population is black/African. It faced an informal housing problem on a much smaller scale at the start, and it operated at the time under a divided, rather than ANC-dominated, government.

Closer examination suggests that despite these differences, the logic in Ndlambe may also have been playing out in Kou-Kamma during this time. There were emerging pockets of inequality in Kou-Kamma. The coastal tourist businesses nearby opened up opportunities for some black residents,[127] while many remained farmworkers or unemployed.[128] Councillors remember that larger houses with new owners had popped up near those coastal areas

---

[125] *Makana News*, vol. 1, no. 4, December 2003, p. 1. See, also, "RDP projects in the country are not working—except in Grahamstown," *Grocott's Mail*, September 6, 2002, p. 2.

[126] Kou-Kamma's share of the population in informal housing barely budged from 2001 to 2007, from 5.9% to 6.1% of households. Kou-Kamma's score on basic service delivery decreased by about 40% during this period: Krugell, Otto, and Merwe. "Local municipalities and progress with the delivery of basic services in South Africa."

[127] Gibb. "The 'global' and the 'local': A comparative study of development practices in three South African municipalities."

[128] Kou-Kamma municipality was created in 2000 by joining the towns of Joubertina and Kareedow—both the commercial centers for surrounding farmland—a coastal area with tourist attractions (game parks) and other rural areas.

and just outside the major towns even by the late 1990s. The case of Kou-Kamma also points to real or perceived citizen concerns over neighborhood dynamics if every qualifying beneficiary could not receive a house. In September 2000 there was a recorded council meeting to approve 484 units as part of the Mbabala project. The council did not approve the project, however; the relevant steering committee did not reach a consensus as to whether enough units had been provided. In October 2000 the council identified an area in Mountain View for a new housing project, but there were concerns that the location was too small to build enough units for all qualified beneficiaries to get a house right away. In May 2001, a steering committee wrote a memo to the Kou-Kamma municipality stating that the committee had determined that they needed 600 housing units but understood from the council that only enough money for 300 units had been received from the Provincial Housing Development Board. The committee recommended an additional public meeting. Based on the consensus of this meeting, the Joubertina committee proposed to the council that it either purchase more land or cancel the project—that is, that it not proceed with the construction of 300 units. The committee reportedly decided it would wait for more money rather than continue with the original plan, though this may have jeopardized future funding. In June of that year the council agreed to pursue new tactics in order to build more units, but in November it concluded that it could not secure enough land. The following month the council recorded in its meeting minutes that money for the housing project could not be spent until more land or money had been secured for more units. Some housing projects met long delays or never began.

Status motivations are thus consistent with the inhibited distribution of individually and household-targeted goods that would have benefited many but would also have made some better off than others. In the wake of the transition from apartheid, some places in South Africa immediately experienced growing within-group inequality that disturbed social conventions designed to manage conflict around interpersonal economic disparities. In these places, politicians were more likely to observe and report in a survey the threat of envy and spite exacerbated local within-group economic disparities. Policies designed to deliver single-family houses to only some recipients who needed them would have made some neighbors visibly better off than others and were thus treated as worrisome. Steering committees and municipal councils reacted more cautiously to plans to deliver houses in a piecemeal fashion, erring on the side of not implementing the project at all rather than providing for some qualifying beneficiaries and not others. In a few cases, municipal governments facing these circumstances appear to have vastly overspent their budgets, which is consistent with a riskier strategy of trying to provide goods simultaneously and equally so as to avoid exacerbating local inequalities. Status motivations have observable implications consistent with these puzzling instances of under- and overspending.

More generally, these patterns raise the possibility that it is more difficult to make things better for anyone when status motivations become politically salient, unless governments are willing to take extraordinary steps.[129] To move forward, policies might have to not only be materially beneficial; they may also have to avoid exacerbating status differences. When unmanaged, envy and spite (whether real or perceived) make the implementation of local distributive policies more difficult. Thus, status motivations have implications for explaining variation not only in individual-level political attitudes but also in policy outcomes.

Since the account here has been largely focused on citizens (rather than elites), one might be concerned that my treatment of underspending unfairly blames the victims for policy failures. I am sympathetic to this concern but would point out two considerations. First, many of my claims in explaining patterns of underspending do not require (or even establish) actual conflict among citizens over status. They simply require that politicians and policy makers perceive that such dynamics might occur. The

---

[129] Carles Boix. "Origins and persistence of economic inequality." In *Annual Review of Political Science* 13 (2010), pp. 489–516. Boix speculates that envy may make it difficult to move away from the status quo.

proverbial "buck" thus does not pass over elites by any means. In fact, in some ways it stops with elites' decisions about how to assess and respond to citizens' preferences. Perhaps if elites were to direct more resources to communities where envy is perceived to be highly salient—such that similarly positioned families in a particular neighborhood could all benefit at the same time— concerns about opposition to policy implementation or social conflict would prove less pressing. Second, as in most social science studies, the explanations offered here are partial at best. Status motivations help explain puzzling variation in policy implementation, but other factors—for example, elite incompetence and corruption—also contribute to these patterns. Both in South Africa and around the world, elites are certainly responsible for the redress of problems like corruption and incompetence. This book discusses the actual and perceived behavior of citizens as they are, and it does not intend to apportion blame. However, to the extent that the implications of the argument could point fingers, they do not point them only at ordinary citizens.

Mobilization of Collective Action

From protests in the Middle East[130] to participation in the US civil rights movement,[131] from demonstrations against the Soviet Union[132] to mass protests in various parts of Sub-Saharan Africa,[133] understanding the occurrence of "contentious politics"[134]—of

---

[130] Lisa Anderson. "Demystifying the Arab spring." In *Foreign Affairs* 90.3 (2011), pp. 2–7.

[131] Dennis Chong. *Collective action and the Civil Rights movement*. Chicago, IL: University of Chicago Press, 1991.

[132] Mark R. Beissinger. *Nationalist mobilization and the collapse of the Soviet state*. New York, NY: Cambridge University Press, 2002.

[133] Peter Alexander. "Rebellion of the poor: South Africa's service delivery protests—a preliminary analysis." In *Review of African Political Economy* 37.123 (2010), pp. 25–40; Michael Bratton and Nicolas van de Walle. "Popular protest and political reform in Africa." In *Comparative Politics* 24.4 (1992), pp. 419–442.

[134] Contentious politics are "episodic, public, collective interaction[s] among makers of claims and their objects when (a) at least one government is a claimant,

protests, demonstrations, rebellions, riots, and social movements —has long been of interest to political scientists. Some researchers focus on the structural conditions and dynamic processes that lead to the occurrence of such events.[135] Yet implicit or explicit in these macro-level theories are questions about the factors that motivate individuals to take part in political forms of collective action.

When (and why) does an ordinary citizen decide to take part? Who participates, and who does not? From the perspective of material self-interest, each individual should stay at home, because she stands to benefit most from not participating—from "free-riding" off the efforts of others.[136] To participate she would have to take on material costs, but these costs are not worthwhile, since her participation is not uniquely necessary and since she cannot be excluded from the public benefits of a successful collective action effort if she abstains. In this sense, the puzzle resembles those discussed earlier in the book. Why do individuals undertake action that is materially costly to them when it is not clear that the material benefits outweigh those costs?

Status motivations can help us make more sense of participation in collective action, especially if we consider status motivations from a slightly different angle: through people's desire for admiration. As I discussed in the introduction, within-group status is not just about economic disparities. It also involves disparities in esteem.[137] I have thus far focused mostly on the influence of desires

---

an object of claims or a party to the claims and (b) the claims would, if realized, affect the interests of at least one of the claimants": Doug McAdam, Sidney Tarrow, and Charles Tilly. *Dynamics of contention*. New York, NY: Cambridge University Press, 2001, p. 5.

[135] Bratton and Walle. "Popular protest and political reform in Africa;" Steven I. Wilkinson. *Votes and violence: Electoral competition and ethnic riots in India*. New York, NY: Cambridge University Press, 2006; Beissinger, *Nationalist mobilization and the collapse of the Soviet State*; Sidney G. Tarrow. *Power in movement: Social movements, collective action and politics*. New York, NY: Cambridge University Press, 1994.

[136] Mancur Olson. *The logic of collective action*. Cambridge, MA: Harvard University Press, 1965.

[137] I treat esteem of others and admiration of others as the same thing—that is, as the positive assessment by others that one has met and exceeded social standards

for within-group status along economic dimensions—in income and material assets. This lens has proved analytically useful. The previous two empirical applications examined ways that status concerns on economic dimensions influence how people evaluate public policies, and how the government acts on an assessment (right or wrong) of people's policy preferences. But leaving the discussion there would do the concept of within-group status a disservice. It would leave out the desire for esteem altogether,[138] a desire that John Adams called "as real a want of nature as hunger." If status operates according to both tangible metrics (income, assets) and intangible ones (others' high regard), can we also leverage pursuit of the latter to account for political behavior that deviates from material self-interest?

Participation in collective action is one political domain in which the pursuit of admiration can help us to better understand political behavior that diverges from concerns for material interest. Admiration is a positive reaction to upward comparisons that conveys the admired person's higher relative position.[139] We know from behavioral economics experiments that people desire admiration from in-group members for its own sake and are even willing to sacrifice money to have it. Huberman et al. found in their experiment that participants reduced their own expected

---

for behavior and/or achievement and therefore occupies a higher status within the group. Others use a slightly different definition of admiration and distinguish the two concepts: see Brennan and Pettit. *The economy of esteem: An essay on civil and political society.*

[138] As mentioned in the introduction, in taking a first cut at the implications of status motivations for comparative political behavior, I treat income and admiration as independent dimensions for simplicity. However, in some contexts, higher levels of income may denote competence and thus also bestow admiration upon an individual, or the pursuit of relative income and the pursuit of admiration may be linked. In the most materialist societies, economic and esteem dimensions of status may collapse.

[139] Cuddy et al., "Stereotype content model across cultures: Towards universal similarities and some differences"; Mary Helen Immordino-Yang et al., "Neural correlates of admiration and compassion." In *Proceedings of the National Academy of Sciences* 106.19 (2009), pp. 8021–8026.

earnings in order to win high status.[140] Willer found in his lab that individuals who received positive feedback from others about their past contributions to a collective endeavor were more likely to participate in public goods provision in subsequent rounds than were participants who received negative feedback from others.[141] These findings would not surprise political theorists. As mentioned in the introduction, Adam Smith wrote eloquently of the desire for admiration as an end in itself:

> Nature, when she formed man for society, ...taught him to feel pleasure in their favourable, and pain in their unfavourable regard. She rendered their approbation most flattering and most agreeable to him *for its own sake.*[142]

People make real sacrifices of time, money, and effort in order to win the high regard of their peers. Status is a personal benefit that, if given in exchange for participation in collective action, could act as a meaningful selective incentive not to free-ride.

Participation in collective action is a domain of behavior in which within-group status is often at stake. It is not uncommon for participation in collective action to be viewed as morally "good" behavior.[143] Participation is a prosocial act—personally costly but beneficial to a larger group. Because of the sacrifice they have made, individuals who take part in collective action are often viewed as heroes within the group—as worthy of deference and respect from those who do not contribute to the collective endeavor.[144] However, the possibility of winning admiration is

---

[140] Huberman, Loch, and Önçüler. "Status as a valued resource."

[141] Robb Willer. "Groups reward individual sacrifice: The status solution to the collective action problem." In *American Sociological Review* 74.1 (2009), pp. 23–43.

[142] Smith. *The theory of moral sentiments*, p.116, emphasis added.

[143] Willer. "Groups reward individual sacrifice: The status solution to the collective action problem."

[144] Simon Gächter and Ernst Fehr. "Collective action as a social exchange." In *Journal of Economic Behavior & Organization* 39.4 (1999), pp. 341–369.

not guaranteed in all collective action settings. When participation is compulsory, or when other selective incentives are so prevalent that almost all group members are expected to join in, then potential participants will not expect participation to distinguish them within the group. Furthermore, scholars have shown that in some settings, group members actually punish those who "show off" by contributing to collective endeavors.[145] For instance, in a series of experiments across European, US, Asian, and Middle Eastern cities, Hermann et al. demonstrate that this kind of behavior—what they call "antisocial punishment"— is not as rare as one might think; it appeared frequently in at least eight of the sixteen cities they examine.[146] In other words, participation in collective action could offer the possibility of higher status, no change in status, or even envious punishment, depending on the social context and how the action is framed by elites.

When it comes to protests, demonstrations, rallies, and other forms of political collective action, individuals should be more likely to participate if they anticipate winning higher withingroup status through in-group admiration, all else being equal. If potential participants anticipate higher esteem from joining the fray, then this prospect should serve as a selective incentive to take action,[147] despite the material costs. Whether potential participants see some prospect of status rewards could be shaped by common knowledge about the social valuing of protests within the group.[148] Alternatively, organizers might explicitly offer promises of admiration for participation. If credible, such elite promises of increased status could draw more individuals into contentious political action.

---

[145] James A. Kitts. "Collective action, rival incentives, and the emergence of antisocial norms." In *American Sociological Review* 71.2 (2006), pp. 235–259.

[146] Herrmann, Thöni, and Gächter. "Antisocial punishment across societies."

[147] Olson. *The logic of collective action*.

[148] See the compelling account of how a culture of honor can stoke status-related emotions in Richard E. Nisbett and Dov Cohen. *Culture of honor: The psychology of violence in the South*. Boulder, CO: Westview Press, 1996.

As in the previous empirical applications in this book, I do not claim that status motivations are the only explanation of the puzzling political behavior in question. There are many forms of selective incentives, both material and social. Individuals might be paid to participate,[149] or they might believe that participating provides them with, needed physical security.[150] Participation might also be fun or provide a needed catharsis[151] or sense of purpose and belonging.[152] My claim is that status motivations can also drive political participations.[153]

As in other applications in this book, the literature discussing this puzzle is dense, both because it is a genuine puzzle and because it is a core domain of politics. Joining a strong tradition within the contentious politics literature, this essay does not attempt to override these other theories but rather seeks to "pluralize understandings of the microfoundations of contentious politics."[154] This book aims to parse the promise of status rewards from other selective incentives in order to explore whether status motivations might be an important overlooked part of the story of contentious political participation, and to discuss what we learn from status motivations about which groups and situations are conducive to the mobilization of collective action.

---

[149] Material selective incentives need not be as blatant as direct monetary payments. The Student Nonviolent Coordination Committee of the U.S. civil rights movement, for instance, offered to do chores for Mississippians who participated in marches and sit-ins: Clayborne Carson. *In struggle: SNCC and the black awakening of the 1960s.* Cambridge, MA: Harvard University Press, 1981, 79–80.

[150] Alexandra Scacco. "Anatomy of a riot: Participation in ethnic violence in Nigeria." In Book Manuscript, New York University (2012).

[151] David Keen. *The economic functions of violence in civil wars.* New York, NY: Routledge, 2005.

[152] Chong. *Collective action and the Civil Rights movement.*

[153] I should underscore, as I do in the introduction, that even as I pay attention to status motivations as selective incentives, I bracket the ways status emotions, and other emotions, might influence participation in contentious politics through noninstrumental means. For instance, the experience of pride by potential participants might reduce their risk aversion, thus enabling further participation in contentious politics. Wendy Pearlman. "Emotions and the microfoundations of the Arab Uprisings." In *Perspectives on Politics* 11.02 (2013), pp. 387–409.

[154] Ibid., p. 388.

Engaging in this inquiry deepens our understanding of the role of social ties in collective mobilization, which has been a central focus in the literature on contentious politics. Researchers have repeatedly found that the most likely participants in protests and demonstrations are people who know other participants.[155] Yet the link between social ties and participation could operate in theory through at least three different mechanisms: (1) the provision of information, (2) the construction of grievances and identity commitments, or (3) the promise of social esteem. Regarding the first, when embedded in a social network, an individual has a better sense of who else and how many others might participate; she also has access to accurate information about when and where the event will take place, so social ties might facilitate collective mobilization through the provision of information.[156] Second, social ties might help to build a sense of shared identity, commitment, and purpose.[157] According to this mechanism, social networks function "as workshop[s] where grievances, identities and strategies of resistance are constructed."[158] Or, third, social networks and relationships might spur individuals to participate because they care about their social standing within those groups. To my knowledge, prior to this experiment, researchers had not rigorously tested whether any of these mechanisms operate to

---

[155] Susanne Lohmann. "A signaling model of informative and manipulative political action." In *American Political Science Review* 87.02 (1993), pp. 319–333; Karl-Dieter Opp and Bernhard Kittel. "The dynamics of political protest: Feedback effects and interdependence in the explanation of protest participation." In *European Sociological Review* (2009), pp. 97–109.

[156] Jennifer M. Larson and Janet I. Lewis. "Ethnic networks." In *American Journal of Political Science* 61.2 (2017), pp. 350–364.

[157] Bert Klandermans. "How group identification helps to overcome the dilemma of collective action." In *American Behavioral Scientist* 45.5 (2002), pp. 887–900; Jocelyn Viterna. *Women in war: The micro-processes of mobilization in El Salvador.* Oxford, UK: Oxford University Press, 2013.

[158] James Kitts. "Mobilizing in black boxes: Social networks and participation in social movement organizations." In *Mobilization: An International Quarterly* 5.2 (2000), 241.

connect social ties to contentious mobilization.[159] The study thus offers a proof of concept of the mechanism that social ties might be connected to contentious mobilization through the promise of status rewards.

Observational research has drawn attention to the possible role of status motivations in mobilizing various forms of contentious political action. For instance, Carpenter argues that some sixteenth, seventeenth and nineteenth century petitioning efforts targeted high-status individuals as early signers so that seeing their names would entice others to join for the status benefits.[160] In a study of US social media users, Park et al. found that users report attending offline political meetings and events because subsequently posting about them online won them esteem from their peers.[161] Evidence of similar motivations shows up in work on extremely dangerous forms of contentious political participation as well. Einwohner argues in her seminal study of the Warsaw ghetto uprising that some people participated, even though the prospects of success were nil, because doing so would give them hero status within their community, as well as elevate the honor and dignity of the entire group.[162] Guha argues that the desire for both self-respect and prestige was a more important motivator for participants in peasant rebellions in colonial India than considerations of material gains.[163] As Viterna illustrates in her study

---

[159] For a recent, innovative effort to test the spread of information through social networks to encourage participation in a collective meeting, see Larson and Lewis. "Ethnic networks."

[160] Daniel Carpenter. "Recruitment by petition: American antislavery, French Protestantism, English suppression." In *Perspectives on Politics* 14.03 (2016), pp. 700–723.

[161] Namsu Park, Kerk F. Kee, and Sebastián Valenzuela. "Being immersed in social networking environment: Facebook groups, uses and gratifications, and social outcomes." In *Cyber Psychology & Behavior* 12.6 (2009), pp. 729–733.

[162] Rachel L. Einwohner. "Opportunity, honor, and action in the Warsaw ghetto uprising of 1943." In *American Journal of Sociology* 109.3 (2003), pp. 650–675.

[163] "It was this fight for prestige that was at the very heart of insurgency": Ranajit Guha. *Elementary aspects of peasant insurgency in colonial India*. Durham, NC: Duke University Press, 1999, 75.

of female guerilla fighters in El Salvador, prestige is sometimes awarded not just to participants (over nonparticipants) but also at different levels *among* participants, depending on the kinds of tasks they perform in the movement and the intensity with which they participate.[164]

However, it is difficult to test the argument that within-group status can act as a selective incentive to participate in contentious politics.[165] People's relative positions on nonmaterial dimensions, such as esteem, are often difficult to gauge. Unlike in the previous applications, we cannot measure a person's relative disparity in esteem as easily as we can measure her relative position in income or assets. Disparities in esteem are communicated through body language, attention, and deference but are often subtle or are misreported if individuals are asked directly.[166] It is often more straightforward to observe the *promise* of admiration for a particular action if it is explicitly articulated by the organizers of a demonstration or protest. However, if this promise is offered to all potential participants, we cannot easily approximate the counterfactual of how individuals would have behaved had they not been offered the promise of esteem for participating.

To overcome these methodological challenges, I conducted a field experiment in which the promise of within-group esteem for participation in contentious politics was randomly assigned to some potential participants but not to others. The people studied in the experiment were members of a lesbian, gay, bisexual, and transgender (LGBT) advocacy and support organization in New Jersey (hereinafter "the cooperating organization"). In 2011 the cooperating organization coordinated a political event that included a rally and march intended to celebrate the LGBT community,

[164] Viterna. *Women in war: The micro-processes of mobilization in El Salvador.*

[165] Olson expresses skepticism that social incentives are powerful enough, particularly within large groups, to sustain collective action.

[166] For an interesting effort to document status conferral observationally by examining funeral attendance across a collection of villages in Zimbabwe, see A. Barr and M. Stein. "Status and egalitarianism in traditional communities: An analysis of funeral attendance in six Zimbabwean villages." In *Mimeograph* (2008).

to recognize the repeal of the Clinton-era "Don't Ask Don't Tell" policy, and to demonstrate support for marriage equality in the state. The experiment sought to identify whether the promise of within-group admiration could induce higher rates of participation in the event. Each of the 3,651 potential participants was thus randomly assigned to one of three conditions. In two of those conditions, people were invited to participate in the event with an explicit promise of admiration from other members of the LGBT community. In a third condition, participants were given only information about the timing, purpose, and location of the event. Because of the random assignment, priming of within-group status rewards for participation is orthogonal to the unobservable individual costs of participating as well as to unobservable inclinations to participate (e.g., the extent to which individuals feel an intrinsic obligation to help others in the group or to stand up for a cause). As a result, I can more reasonably infer that any effect of promised in-group admiration on individual participation is due to that treatment and not due to differences in altruism, attachment to the goals of the event, information, or material costs.

I examined this particular collective action event because it took place in a physically safe environment but still involved contentious issues.[167] The nature of the group and the mode of communication were also important. The group's members share a commitment to a social identity category of "similar" others and were likely to care about their standing within the LGBT community. Yet the group was largely delineated by membership in an organization's online Listserv. For the most part, its members did not have close personal relationships with one another.

---

[167] A safe environment was important so that the cooperating organization and I could be sure that we were not inducing people to take on more than minimal risk. The issue was nevertheless contentious at the time: Marriage of same-sex couples was not legal in New Jersey at the time of the experiment, and, despite then-recent changes in the neighboring state of New York, New Jersey did not recognize same-sex marriages performed elsewhere. The governor was quite vocally opposed to legalization and vetoed a marriage equality bill in February 2012.

Potential participants were unlikely to have strong informal ways of managing social comparison emotions within the group, absent mechanisms offered by the organizers. In this context the explicit promise of admiration for participation could be expected to have consequences for political behavior.

The cooperating organization sent out email invitations a week before the event, using an online Listserv management program.[168] Three types of email invitations were sent out. In one (the Information-only condition), individuals were told the goals of the event and told when and where they should go to participate. The second email (the Newsletter condition) contained the same content as the first but also told the recipient that participants were worthy of admiration and that their names would be listed in the monthly newsletter if they attended so that their attendance could be "celebrated" by other members of the organization. A third version of the email (the Facebook condition) mimicked the second, but rather than promising that participants' names would be circulated in the newsletter, it invited participants to post photos from the event to the group's Facebook page so that other group members could express admiration by "liking" the photos. The second two treatments offered the promise of admiration through different mechanisms.

Email Text

From: [cooperating organization]
Subject: Rally for Marriage Equality on October [date]

Join us on October [date] and support marriage equality. *We have the greatest admiration for anyone who takes the time to support LGBT causes, [so we will be listing the names of people*

---

[168] Because the online program keeps track of any email addresses to which mail is undeliverable and because the cooperating organization regularly sends out emails, the list of email addresses is kept up to date. In the case of this experiment, only four emails were undeliverable: these four addresses were dropped from subsequent analysis.

who attend in our monthly newsletter, to be shared with and celebrated by all of our supporters.]*/[so we invite you to post your photos from the event on our Facebook page so that friends can show their support for attendees by "Liking" the posts.]**
When: [date]
Where: [location]

At the entrance... you will get FREE raffle tickets to win an iPad2 when you present the following code: [ ].

An Evite will follow immediately. We need to know how many people to expect, so please RSVP.

Notes: Italicized words were not included in emails to Information-only subjects. *This clause in brackets as well as the preceding italicized phrase were included in emails to subjects in the Newsletter condition. **This clause in brackets as well as the phrase "We have the greatest admiration..." were included in emails to subjects in the Facebook condition.[169]

Individuals in all three conditions were also told that by presenting a code (provided in the email and different for each experimental condition) at the entrance to the site, they could obtain free tickets for a raffle to win an iPad2. This detail meant that we could count the number of individuals who showed each code and match the attendees' names, which they wrote on the raffle ticket stubs, to the cooperating organization's Listserv. The cooperating organization had previously conducted raffles as part of its public advocacy events, thus providing a mechanism for keeping a record of attendees that was unlikely to introduce novelty effects.[170]

[169] Steps have been taken to anonymize the email text while still conveying the content of the treatments.

[170] The raffle codes may also have reduced email forwarding because recipients believed that the codes were personal and could not be used by others, or because they did not want to reduce their chances of winning by having others enter the

The experiment measured participation in the rally in three ways. Unlike other forms of political participation (voting, campaign donations), individual participation in contentious politics is rarely systematically and publicly documented. Previous studies have thus looked at self-reports of intent to participate[171] or at reported past participation,[172] but these measures are subject to recall error or to subjects' changing their minds. To my knowledge, few if any studies measure real-time participation alongside intentions to participate and reported participation. This study measured all three. First, email recipients were asked to RSVP and directed to an Evite site, thus generating a measure of intent to participate.[173] Second, actual participation at the event was measured using raffle tickets. Attendees presented the code from their email invitation to volunteers at the event who did not know which code corresponded to which condition. The code each individual presented was written on the back of the ticket stub along with her name and email address so that she could be contacted were she to win. Each participant had her hand stamped so she could not present a code twice. Third, an online survey was sent to all Listserv members a week after the event and asked respondents if they attended.[174] Although only a small portion of the Listserv elected to participate in the online survey, this mechanism generated a measure of reported participation.

The results of the experiment demonstrate that the promise of admiration motivated participation in the rally. I first

---

raffle. However, any sharing of messages across treatment conditions would likely have led to underestimates of the true treatment effects.

[171] Klandermans. "How group identification helps to overcome the dilemma of collective action."

[172] Mark R. Beissinger. "The semblance of democratic revolution: Coalitions in Ukraine's Orange Revolution." In *American Political Science Review* 107.03 (2013), pp. 574–592; Scacco. "Anatomy of a riot: Participation in ethnic violence in Nigeria."

[173] I set up a website for each condition. Each repeated the text from the respective email message.

[174] All respondents viewed identical surveys but arrived at the survey questions through a link corresponding to their assigned treatment condition. Respondents were entered into lotteries for gift cards.

TABLE 2.11 Differences in Rates of Intended and Actual Participation

	Intent to participate	Actual participation
Effect of newsletter treatment		
Newsletter	6.08%	3.04%
	N = 1217	N = 1217
Information-only	3.53%	1.72%
	N = 1217	N = 1217
Difference	**2.55**	**1.32**
(S.E.)	**(0.867)**	**(0.618)**
p-value (two-sided Welch)	**0.003**	**0.034**
Effect of Facebook treatment		
Facebook	5.93%	2.96%
	N = 1213	N = 1213
Information-only	3.53%	1.72%
	N = 1217	N = 1217
Difference	**2.40**	**1.24**
(S.E.)	**(0.860)**	**(0.614)**
p-value (two-sided Welch)	**0.005**	**0.043**
Pooled results		
Newsletter and Facebook	6.01%	3.00%
	N = 2430	N = 2430
Information-only	3.53%	1.72%
	N = 1217	N = 1217
Difference	**2.48**	**1.28**
(S.E.)	**(0.720)**	**(0.509)**
p-value (two-sided Welch)	**0.000**	**0.012**

considered two of the outcome measures: intended participation (coded 1 for a "yes" RSVP on the Evite and 0 otherwise) and actual participation (coded 1 when a subject picked up a ticket at the entrance to the event and 0 otherwise). Table 2.11 shows differences in mean rates of participation between the Newsletter treatment group and the Information-only group and then between the Facebook treatment group and the Information-only group, and then the pooled results.[175] For both the Newsletter and Facebook treatments, assignment to that condition led to a positive and statistically significant increase in participation relative

[175] Because of randomization, consistent estimates of the effects of assignment to different email messages, or the intent-to-treat effects, can be calculated as the mean outcome for a treatment message (either Newsletter or Facebook) minus the average outcome for the Information-only group.

to the Information-only group. The Newsletter email produced a 2.55 percentage point increase in intended participation and a 1.32 percentage point increase in actual participation compared to the Information-only email. Similarly, the Facebook email induced a 2.40 percentage point increase in intended participation and a 1.24 percentage point increase in actual participation.[176] These numbers might seem small, but they are substantively large. Base actual participation in the Information-only condition was only 1.72 percent, or twenty-one people. The effect of assignment to the Newsletter treatment therefore represented a 76 percent increase in actual participation relative to the Information-only condition. For the leaders of the organization, this is a meaningful increase in participation.

But did people even read the emails? The organization's online management system keeps track of recipients who click on an icon within the email in order to "display images below." When this action is observed, I can be fairly certain that a human being opened the email and attempted to read it closely. Thus, to estimate the effect of closely reading the treatment emails (as opposed to simply being assigned to receive them), I used an instrumental variable (IV) approach, where random assignment to one of the two admiration emails is an instrument for reading the admiration emails, as measured by tracking who clicked "display images below" within the email messages.[177] Table 2.12 shows the estimates of the effects of closely reading an admiration-promising email on both intent

---

[176] A difference-in-differences estimation does not reveal a statistically significant difference between the size of the effect from assignment to the Newsletter treatment (relative to the Information-only condition) and the size of the effect from assignment to the Facebook treatment (relative to the Information-only condition).

[177] Actually reading an email is not randomly assigned, and may be driven by factors related to the outcome (political participation). People who are more inclined to be politically active may be more likely to read the email. The factor I *know* is randomly assigned is treatment, which is why I use this approach rather than simply comparing mean participation rates across treatment conditions among those who read the emails.

TABLE 2.12 Effect of Closely Reading Admiration Emails on Participation

	DV = intent	DV = actual participation
Closely reading an admiration email	0.315	0.163
(Bootstrapped SE)	(0.090)	(0.063)
Constant	0.035	0.017
(Bootstrapped SE)	(0.005)	(0.004)
Number of observations	3,647	3,647
R-squared	0.079	0.108

Notes: 2SLS instrumented: closely read an admiration email. Instrument: assigned to receive admiration emails (either Newsletter or Facebook).

to participate and actual participation.[178] The effects are much larger than the corresponding intent-to-treat (ITT) estimates in table 2.11. The effect of closely reading an admiration-promising email on actual participation, for instance, is more than twelve times greater than the corresponding ITT effect (16.3 percentage points versus 1.3 percentage points). This measure of actually reading the email is not perfect. Other individuals may have read the emails closely but happen to have email clients that automatically display images within emails or display emails in text format only. But between the ITT estimates in table 2.11 and the estimates in table 2.12, we can be fairly confident that the promise of admiration increased intended and actual participation.

The promise of admiration also increased reported participation. Unfortunately, I have measures of this outcome only for individuals who responded to the post-experiment survey (298 people). This is not a representative sample of the overall subject pool. Because they chose to participate in the online survey, they are likely to be the more active people within the group. (And, indeed, the rate of reported participation within this group is higher than the rate of actual or intended participation in the larger subject pool.) Nevertheless, I cannot reject the null hypothesis that survey response rates were the same across

[178] The first stage of the IV estimation confirmed that assignment to the Newsletter/Facebook treatments is not a weak treatment, with an F-statistic of 104.

TABLE 2.13   Differences in Rates of Reported Participation

Newsletter	61.00% N=100	Facebook	59.79% N=97	Newsletter and Facebook	60.40% N=197
Info-only	45.54% N=101	Info-only	45.54% N=101	Info-only	45.54% N=101
Difference (S.E.) p-value	**15.46** **(6.99)** **0.028**	Difference (S.E.) p-value	**14.25** **(7.06)** **0.045**	Difference (S.E.) p-value	**14.86** **(6.08)** **0.015**

treatment conditions.[179] Table 2.13 shows differences in rates of reported participation across conditions among survey respondents. The estimated differences here are also statistically significant and substantively large. Assignment to the Newsletter treatment is estimated to boost the rate of reported participation by 15.46 percentage points relative to assignment to the Information-only condition. Assignment to the Facebook treatment is estimated to boost the rate of reported participation by 14.25 percentage points. The pooled effect on reported participation from assignment to the Newsletter or Facebook condition is 14.86 percentage points.

Skeptics might worry that the effects on actual participation could have been due to Information-only people's being less likely to make their presence known at the rally (even if they did show up). But there is little evidence to support this concern. To test for this possibility, I created the dummy variable "no pickup" with a value of 1 for individuals who reported on the post-experiment survey that they attended the event but who did not appear in the data as having attended. This dummy variable was coded 0 for all other individuals who responded to the survey. I could not reject the null hypothesis that "no pickup" rates were the same across experimental conditions. If anything, more people assigned to the two admiration conditions (38 out of 100 in the Newsletter condition, 36 out of 97 in the Facebook condition) failed to pick up their tickets at the event but reported that they attended in

[179] 100 people from the Newsletter treatment, 97 people from the Facebook treatment, and 101 people from the Information-only condition responded, and the Pearson chi-square statistic from a 2×3 table is 0.08 (p-value $= 0.96$).

the survey, compared to those assigned to the Information-only condition (30 out of 101).[180] These numbers certainly indicate that there was slippage between measures of reported participation and actual participation in this study. But while the correlation between the two measures was not perfect, I cannot reject the hypothesis that any mismatch did not differ systematically across treatment conditions.

Skeptics might also worry that the Newsletter and Facebook treatments primed some motivation other than a desire for admiration. Perhaps, for instance, because they were slightly longer emails than the Information-only email, the treatment emails primed the importance of the event or triggered subjects' intrinsic concern for LGBT causes. Perhaps by mentioning other members and social networking sites, they reminded subjects of the social nature of the event and made them think it would be more fun or that they would meet people. I tested for this possibility by looking for evidence of these patterns in follow-up questions on the post-experiment survey. Survey respondents were asked *why* they chose to participate or not. For those who reported participating, the question was:

For which of the following reasons, if any, did you attend on October [date]? (Choose all that apply.)

- I went to promote a cause I care about;
- I went for camaraderie, to meet people or to hang out with friends;
- I went to have fun;
- I went because I had time and/or it was easy for me to get there;
- I went because people in my community would think highly of people who attend;
- I went because I am interested in a leadership position with [the cooperating organization].

[180] The Pearson chi-square statistic for the 2 × 3 table is 2.08 (p = 0.35). The corresponding p-value from a Fisher Exact Test is 0.34.

- I went because it was an important event for [the cooperating organization].

The fifth option listed here indicates that participation promised admiration ("I went because people in my community would think highly of people who attend"). If the treatments primed admiration, one would expect mean selection of this option to be higher among attendees assigned to the Newsletter or Facebook conditions than among those assigned to the Information-only condition. The results in table 2.14 show that this is the case. By contrast, the frequency of reporting other motivations did not differ across the admiration-promising and information-only conditions among those who attended.

A similar pattern holds among people who reported not attending. For those who reported not attending, the question was:

For which of the following reasons, if any, did you not attend on October [date]? (Choose all that apply.)

- I did not think the cause was that important;
- I did not know anyone else who was going;
- I did not think it would be fun;
- I did not have time and/or it was too difficult for me to get there;
- I did not feel that my participation would be admired by people in my community;
- I am not interested in a leadership position with [the cooperating organization];
- I did not think it was an important event for [the cooperating organization].

Again, the fifth option indicates that participation does not promise admiration. If the treatments primed the promise of admiration, I would expect that individuals assigned to the admiration condition would choose this fifth option less frequently to explain their lack of participation than individuals assigned to the Information-only condition would. Table 2.14 shows that this is

TABLE 2.14   Differences in Mean Rates of Choosing a Reason for Participation Behavior

	Admiration	Information	Difference (SE)
Attendees			
I went to promote a cause I care about	0.521	0.543	0.022 (0.087)
I went for camaraderie, to meet people	0.520	0.630	0.109 (0.085)
I went to have fun	0.294	0.369	0.075 (0.083)
I went because I had time	0.286	0.261	0.025 (0.078)
I went because... highly of people who attend	**0.672**	**0.217**	**−0.455 (0.075)**
I went because... a leadership position	0.521	0.500	−0.021 (0.089)
I went because it was an important event	0.336	0.369	0.033 (0.084)
Non-attendees			
I did not think the cause was that important	0.013	0.055	0.042 (0.033)
I did not know anyone else who was going	0.205	0.218	0.013 (0.073)
I did not think it would be fun	0.962	0.964	0.002 (0.044)
I did not have time	0.462	0.509	0.047 (0.089)
I did not feel that... would be admired	**0.000**	**0.309**	**0.309 (0.062)**
I am not interested in a leadership position	0.808	0.800	−0.008 (0.071)
I did not think it was an important event	0.642	0.710	0.068 (0.083)

also the case. None of the respondents who had been assigned to one of the admiration conditions and who did not attend chose the fifth option. By contrast, 30 percent of respondents assigned to the Information-only condition who did not attend chose that option. While not definitive, these numbers suggest that, on average, the difference between those assigned to the admiration conditions and those assigned to the Information-only condition among both attendees and non-attendees was their perception that participation in the event would win them admiration and not other elements of their reasoning about the event.

From a practical standpoint, conducting a field experiment around contentious politics is not easy, and, to my knowledge, this study is the first field experiment that measures real-time participation in contentious politics. Unlike voter turnout or campaign donations, participation in contentious politics is not systematically and publicly documented at the individual level as a matter of course, so researchers have to find a way to measure individual-level attendance without introducing too much novelty and without putting participants at risk. In addition, contentious political events are rarely planned with a lot of advance warning (unlike, for instance, elections), such that researchers may have difficulty coordinating treatment content and assignment before the event takes place. Because of my partnership with this LGBT advocacy organization, and because of their regular use of raffles at their events (which provided a mechanism for systematically documenting individual-level real-time participation), this experiment was able to overcome such challenges.

For researchers who might conduct experimental research on contentious politics in the future, the study underscores the importance of partnerships between researchers and practitioners and of paying attention to existing activities and mechanisms when measuring individual-level participation. Mechanisms that mobilizers already use to document attendance (e.g., sign-in sheets, group pictures, color-coded wrist bands, or T-shirts) can be used by researchers to systematically record individual outcomes without introducing novelty effects. For instance, Young recently conducted an experiment in Zimbabwe in which she used social media (WhatsApp) communications to track different forms of participation, since this was a platform regularly used by the partner organization.[181] Preexisting measurement devices are also unlikely to raise ethical concerns, since potential participants expect that these mechanisms will be employed even in the absence of a research project. The researcher is not exposing participants to more than minimal risk by introducing a brand-new way of observing participation. Within these bounds, future researchers might also consider whether there are existing ways to measure variation in intensity of participation. This study measured participation only in a binary way, but some organizations might provide ways to observe how long participants stay at the event and the kinds of activities they engage in while there.

From a theoretical standpoint, the experiment provides evidence that status motivations can help explain patterns of

---

[181] Lauren E. Young. "Mobilization under threat." In Working Paper, Columbia University (2016).

participation in contentious politics. Even though such actions are materially costly, people are more likely to participate if they know that their political participation will be observed and admired by in-group members—that is, if they know they can boost their in-group status. The experiment demonstrates these effects in a real-world setting within a social identity group whose members were connected via weak ties. Evidence from the post-experiment survey suggests that receiving the promise of in-group admiration was associated with increased attention to the status rewards of participating, and not with increased attention to other possible reasons to participate.

The experiment underscores that we should pay attention to status motivations in their various manifestations and when studying many domains of political behavior. Concerns about within-group relative position, which can trump material costs, help explain not only variation in citizens' policy preferences and governments' responses to those preferences, as in the previous empirical applications. Within-group status motivations also help us understand why (and under what conditions) citizens take politics to the streets. Furthermore, whereas in the previous two application essays I investigated the observable implications of people's concern about their relative economic position within groups, this application shows that people's concern for relative position in more intangible terms—that is, their desire for the high regard of other group members—has concrete implications for their political behavior. This means that the implications of status motivations go beyond issues of material distribution. Indeed, they potentially extend to any area of political behavior where group members understand that they can achieve within-group distinction through political action.

This study not only expands our view of the range of domains in which status motivations might influence political behavior; it also advances our understanding of long-standing theoretical puzzles about contentious politics. It addresses the collective action dilemma by demonstrating that in-group status can indeed operate like a selective incentive. It also addresses the robust finding that social ties are a tight correlate of participation in contentious politics by isolating one of the mechanisms that could be behind that pattern. In addition, the study demonstrates connections between the arguments in this book about status motivations and the literature on "social pressure" and voting. Studies of voter turnout have argued that social pressure from peers can encourage people to engage politically.[182] Social pressure typically means telling people that their behavior will be publicized to others in their neighborhoods and social identity groups and that it will be revealed whether they are conforming to, exceeding, or falling short of a standard of behavior valued by that reference group.[183] The field experiment here suggests that it is not just a need to conform to a social norm but also a desire for positive distinction within groups that can drive costly political participation.

Would we be likely to find similar influences of the promise of status motivations on contentious political participation in other settings and groups? Although I cannot say so definitively on the basis of this experiment alone, observational research has certainly drawn attention to the possible role of status rewards

[182] Gerber, Green, and Larimer. "Social pressure and voter turnout: Evidence from a large-scale field experiment"; Patricia Funk. "Social incentives and voter turnout: Evidence from the Swiss mail ballot system." In *Journal of the European Economic Association* 8.5 (2010), pp. 1077–1103; Panagopoulos. "Affect, social pressure and prosocial motivation: Field experimental evidence of the mobilizing effects of pride, shame and publicizing voting behavior"; Betsy Sinclair. *The social citizen: Peer networks and political behavior.* Chicago, IL: University of Chicago Press, 2012. There is also relevant literature on the effects of social comparison information on charitable giving and energy conservation: Stefano DellaVigna, John List, and Ulrike Malmendier. "Testing for altruism and social pressure in charitable giving." In *Quarterly Journal of Economics* 127.1 (2012), pp. 1–56; Adriaan R. Soetevent. "Anonymity in giving in a natural context: A field experiment in 30 churches." In *Journal of Public Economics* 89.11 (2005), pp. 2301–2323; Robert B. Cialdini, Raymond R. Reno, and Carl A. Kallgren. "A focus theory of normative conduct: Recycling the concept of norms to reduce littering in public places." In *Journal of Personality and Social Psychology* 58.6 (1990), pp. 1015–1026.

[183] E.g., Gerber, Green, and Larimer. "Social pressure and voter turnout: Evidence from a large-scale field experiment"; Panagopoulos, "Affect, social pressure and prosocial motivation: Field experimental evidence of the mobilizing effects of pride, shame and publicizing voting behavior."

in the mobilizations of all forms of contentious politics, from petitioning[184] to social media organizing[185] to insurgency.[186] The promise of status rewards does not require vast material resources, or even centralized organization, so it is quite plausible that it could be used across different contexts and groups to facilitate mobilization. The highest-status distinctions, such as that of hero, may be most likely to be earned when the material costs of participating are high,[187] so the findings in this experiment are unlikely to be limited to safe physical environments.[188] Authors who draw attention to the role of prestige motivations in insurgency often describe opportunities that promise enhancement both of one's own personal status and of the status of one's group as the political opportunities most conducive to collective mobilization.[189] In this experiment all potential participants knew that the rally was intended to call for greater dignity and recognition of LGBTs as a group. The treatments added the promise of enhanced personal status for joining that effort. As discussed in the next chapter, these observations point to the need to further investigate the intersection of within- and between-group status motivations. Participation in contentious politics may be most likely when the two motivations point people in the same direction.

[184] Carpenter. "Recruitment by petition: American antislavery, French Protestantism, English suppression."

[185] Park, Kee, and Valenzuela. "Being immersed in social networking environment: Facebook groups, uses and gratifications, and social outcomes."

[186] Guha. *Elementary aspects of peasant insurgency in colonial India*.

[187] Willer. "Groups reward individual sacrifice: The status solution to the collective action problem"; Einwohner. "Opportunity, Honor, and Action in the Warsaw ghetto uprising of 1943."

[188] Einwohner. "Opportunity, honor, and action in the Warsaw ghetto uprising of 1943," argues that it is precisely *because* those involved in the Warsaw uprising knew that they would almost certainly die that the goals of lifting their own personal status (honor, heroism) and the status of the group as a whole became highly salient.

[189] Guha. *Elementary aspects of peasant insurgency in colonial India*; Elisabeth Wood. "The emotional benefits of insurgency in El Salvador." In *The social movements reader: Cases and concept.* Ed. by Jeff Goodwin and James M. Jasper. John Wiley and Sons, 2001, pp. 143–152; Viterna. *Women in war: The micro-processes of mobilization in El Salvador.*

Does this experiment teach us anything about the macro variables that explain contentious political activity? That is, can we learn something from this experiment about the conditions or group structures under which we are likely to observe rallies or other contentious political activity?

In my view, there are several possible implications related both to the types of groups that might use status motivations to mobilize collective action and to the conditions under which we might observe status motivations being primed to incentivize collective action. First, the results of this experiment point to features of groups that might make them more or less successful in mobilizing collective action, or more or less likely to mobilize in particular ways. For instance, the experiment shows that groups with weak intra-group ties can mobilize participation with the aid of status rewards for political action. Members of groups with weak ties may have access to fewer nonpolitical mechanisms for preserving and enhancing their status. They may thus find promises of status rewards for political action particularly appealing. To be sure, this experiment does not contrast the effects of status appeals in a group with weak ties with the effects of status appeals in a group with strong ties, so the proposition that status rewards are particularly salient within weakly linked groups would have to be further tested. But the experiment does show that promises of in-group status rewards are quite powerful within a group connected loosely through a Listserv. Olson cautioned that the collective action dilemma would present problems for large groups, and he worried that social incentives might not work particularly well within large groups, because individual members interact with each other less and are not as intimately connected.[190] Yet the results of this experiment suggest that large, loosely connected groups may nevertheless be quite effective at mobilizing turnout through appeals to status motivations. In fact, achieving status through political action is particularly appealing within large, weakly interconnected groups, since other social mechanisms for

[190] Olson. *The logic of collective action.*

achieving status may not be available. Status motivations provide one way to understand how large, loosely connected groups—students, non-unionized workers, urban populations connected only through the internet[191]—mobilize protests relatively frequently.

This experiment also points to other group features that are worthy of further exploration. For instance, the results suggest that the rigidity of a group's hierarchy should affect how it mobilizes collective action. In order for promises of status rewards to be credible, the status hierarchy within the group also has to be somewhat flexible. If the hierarchy is too rigid, any promises of an increase in status will wisely be ignored, as there is no hope for actually gaining higher status simply by showing up. Rigidly hierarchical groups might be more likely to use coercion or material selective incentives to induce participation. By contrast, more horizontal, fluid social movements—such as Occupy Wall Street in the United States and Fees Must Fall in South Africa—might be more likely to use appeals to status motivations to mobilize protest. Finally, groups that regularly utilize mechanisms to make participation more visible and identifiable at the individual level (lists of participants, profiles of active members, recognition ceremonies) are the ones that can distribute status rewards more easily. Some groups do not realize the benefits of these kinds of mechanisms. Others may be constrained in their ability to deploy them. In either case, the ability to use mechanisms to render participation visible and celebrated may correlate with the occurrence and manner of contentious political mobilization. Taken together, the results of this experiment suggest that the *nature of the ties* within a group, the *rigidity of the hierarchy* within the group, and the *availability of mechanisms to render participation visible* all have implications for whether and how groups mobilize collective action. Future research should test these possibilities more systematically.

---

[191] Beissinger notes that urban civic revolutions, made up of loosely connected urban dwellers mobilized through internet rather than in-person connections, are now the more frequent form of contentious politics: Beissinger. "The semblance of democratic revolution: coalitions in ukraine's orange revolution."

The findings from this experiment also raise interesting possibilities for explaining the clustering of contentious political
activity in particular places and within particular groups over
time. As mentioned earlier, it is not always the case that participation in collective action earns people within-group esteem.[192]
But once the promise of within-group status for participation in
contentious politics has been credibly made, it may become an
established social mechanism for allocating in-group status and
reinforce itself over time. Where earlier generations of activists
have won high in-group social status (e.g., in South Africa, where
the generations most involved in contentious efforts to resist
apartheid earned "struggle credentials"), subsequent generations
may be repeatedly drawn to contentious political participation
in part for its established status rewards (as well as for other
reasons), knowing that this is a socially valued type of behavior
through which one can earn distinction.[193] Some observers have
suggested that participants in recent student protests on South
African university campuses may, among many other goals, be
seeking to earn social status by proving that they, like their parents
and predecessors, can engage in confrontation with the state.[194]
A status-rewards mechanism could help some groups and societies
develop repertoires of contention over time.[195]

Status motivations also have interesting possible implications
for the intensity of participation in contentious politics, which, as
I mentioned above, future researchers might consider measuring.
Theoretical expectations about the influence of status motivations
on participation intensity point in two possible directions, both
of which have important implications. On the one hand, priming
status rewards for participation might lead people to show up

[192] Kitts. "Collective action, rival incentives, and the emergence of antisocial
norms"; Herrmann, Thöni, and Gächter. "Antisocial punishment across societies."
[193] I thank Sarah Lockwood for this suggestion.
[194] E.g., Eve Fairbanks. "Why South African students have turned on their
parents' generation." In *Guardian* (2015). The suggestions are subtle and much
more work would have to be done to probe these possibilities.
[195] Donatella Della Porta and Mario Diani. *The Oxford handbook of social
movements*. Oxford, UK: Oxford University Press, 2015.

and exert no additional effort. People might do just enough (no more, no less) to distinguish themselves from non-attendees, especially if the promise is that admiration will be bestowed on all attendees. They might participate but in the most minimal ways. On the other hand, people may be moved to further distinguish themselves from other attendees (and not just from non-attendees) once at the event. If driven by the promise of status to participate in the first place, people may see the possibility of additional status gains if they then demonstrate an intense commitment to the event. They may stay longer, chant louder, donate more money, or make future time commitments to the cause; they may even engage in risky behavior at the event to demonstrate their special level of participation. These two possibilities have distinct implications. If the first proves true, then priming status motivations fosters only shallow forms of contentious political participation; if the second proves true, priming status motivations prompts participation that then escalates. I suspect that the second is more likely. If so, the finding would illustrate how participation can beget participation.[196]

One might worry that the results of this experiment are limited to contexts and groups with low baseline rates of participation. In the Information-only group in this study, less than 2 percent of group members attended the rally. It makes sense that the promise of admiration would motivate participation in a context like this one. With low baseline rates of participation, the promise that showing up to the event would make a person stand out from the group is quite credible, because almost no one engages in this type of behavior as a matter of course. If we assume that showing up does not make the participant a "chump" and the target of shame—as the message used by the organizers in this study makes clear it will not—low baseline participation rates likely enhance the power of status motivations.

---

[196] Daniel Carpenter and Colin D. Moore. "When canvassers became activists: Antislavery petitioning and the political mobilization of American women." In *American Political Science Review* 108.03 (2014), pp. 479–498.

TABLE 2.15   Assurance Game for Participation

	Participate	Don't participate
Participate	a, a	c, b
Don't participate	b, c	d,d

The latter insight offers new suggestions for why participation in collective action is much more common than the literature on the dilemmas of collective action[197] predict.[198] Consider, for example, Chong's discussion of social incentives in the context of collective action.[199] Chong argues that there are selective social rewards for participation in collective action but that they are all contingent upon the participation of others. That is, he argues that the expressive benefits (joy, catharsis) and social benefits (a sense of belonging and collective purpose) of participating are realized *only if others participate as well*. He thus describes the collective action problem as an assurance game, in which individuals want to participate only if they believe that others will participate as well. Participating is the payoff-dominant strategy, whereas not participating is the risk-dominant strategy. An implication of this characterization is that we should see collective action increase when the costs of coordination are lowered and where individuals believe that others will also participate. The set-up of this assurance game is in table 2.15, where $a > b = d$ and $b > c$.

However, the importance of status motivations changes the game. Status motivations are about achieving distinction from others. In other words, unlike the social selective incentives Chong focuses on, status rewards are earned only if most other people do not show up. If individuals care only about status,

---

[197] Olson. *The logic of collective action*.

[198] The subsequent discussion notwithstanding, I would note that, in contexts in which levels of baseline participation are very high, status concerns may still influence decisions about whether to participate but may do so through the promise of shame for *not* participating rather than the promise of admiration for participation. Status motivations are at play in either case, but this means that there should be a tipping point somewhere in between, at which point the relevant status concern turns from one of winning admiration to one of avoiding shame.

[199] Chong. *Collective action and the Civil Rights movement*.

then the promise of status motivations transforms the decision about whether to participate into a prisoner's dilemma game: the individual gains status only if the other does not participate. Under this scenario, we might actually expect to observe collective action when there is an expectation that few people will show up. Furthermore, if we allow that individuals care about status and about other social benefits from participating alongside others, then the promise of status motivations from participation may mean the drop in payoffs between the top left and top right quadrants in table 2.15 is not steep. In fact, there might not be any drop-off. This would mean that while individuals anticipate some social and psychological benefits from participating when everyone else does, they also understand that in the event that others do not show up in large numbers, they will get a status benefit instead. Thus collective action may arise even when there is a low probability that many others will show up.[200]

Whether or not these macro implications hold up in future research, an important takeaway from this discussion is that it is helpful to think about status motivations as one set of considerations among many. Rather than muddying the waters, an approach that encompasses the complexity of the human mind can actually help us make sense of puzzling patterns. For instance, acknowledging that people care both about reaping social rewards that come from being part of a crowd and about individual distinction makes it less surprising that collective action occurs as often as it does. I further discuss interactions across motivations in the conclusion.

Finally, before turning to further elaborations on the general insights in this book, I should briefly comment on the normative valence of this essay, as I did briefly in earlier essays. My principal aim, as in the other applications in this book, is to describe and

---

[200] Again, I assume here that showing up alone or in small numbers would not *reduce* one's status. I think this possibility unlikely, especially in cases where the goals of collective action are viewed as highly important by all members. In these cases, those who show up even when others stay home are more likely to be viewed as heroes than as suckers.

explore the microfoundations of political behavior as they are rather than as they should be. It might seem as if this exploration of admiration and collective action provides a rosier account of the influence of status motivations on political outcomes than the applications to preferences over redistribution and underspending did. After all, even if we do not always openly admit to our desires for others' esteem,[201] the pursuit of admiration is less reviled than its cousins, envy and spite. It may seem also to be a positive result that priming a promise of within-group admiration increased turnout at an event aimed at raising concerns about the rights of a minority group. However, these reactions depend on our normative evaluations of the purposes and consequences of the particular contentious event and could easily run in the other direction. For instance, Petersen has argued that elites stoke the desire for esteem (in his discussion the desire for the esteem of one ethnic group over another) in order to mobilize inter-ethnic violence.[202] In other words, since collective action can take place in service of both "good" and "bad" goals, and can take both nonviolent and violent forms, the argument that status motivations are a driver of participation in collective action does not have an obvious normative valence, in my view.

~

Taken together, examinations of these three puzzles point to the important effects of status motivations, in their various manifestations, across disparate domains of political behavior. People support redistributive policies that hurt their pocketbooks when those policies would improve their relative position compared to that of coethnic neighbors. Politicians underspend on individually targeted goods for the poor when they (reportedly) perceive that citizens prefer that policies not go forward if such policies will make some neighbors visibly better off than others. People's

[201] Brennan and Pettit. *The economy of esteem: An essay on civil and political society.*
[202] Petersen. *Understanding ethnic violence: Fear, hatred, and resentment in twentieth-century Eastern Europe.*

decisions to participate in collective political action are swayed by whether they expect other group members to admire them. Prior to this book, there was evidence from behavioral economics and psychology experiments that status motivations influence behavior in the lab. There was evidence from anthropology that concerns for status shape social (though not necessarily political) behavior. There were anecdotal accounts, like the regulations on elaborate funerals in Chengdu, China, that politicians' concerns about citizens' status motivations can have an impact on policy. Here I have offered systematic evidence that status motivations can help us understand real-world political behavior.

The three essays span puzzles (about preferences over redistribution, government spending, and political participation) that might not otherwise be considered in tandem, and use different methods of investigation (surveys, case studies, experiments) depending on the puzzle and research context. My hope is that, rather than make definitive claims, the essays pique readers' interests in the disparate domains in which status motivations can influence politics, and that they convince readers that the use of status motivations to explain political behavior need not be methodologically specific. Status motivations have observable implications that are distinct from the observable implications of other psychological drivers of human behavior: self-interest, in-group bias, fairness, and altruism. These observable implications include that people make sacrifices (of time, money, goods and services, group welfare, the welfare of others) when as a result they could become relatively better off in income or esteem. They also include that people's political decisions are tightly tied not just to local conditions[203] but specifically to their own positions within local areas and groups. Both of the latter patterns (willingness to sacrifice and harm, and sensitivity to relative local position) occur under certain conditions: when elites explicitly prime status rewards and/or when social conventions for managing status motivations are weak or absent.

---

[203] Ansolabehere, Meredith, and Snowberg. "Mecro-economic voting: Local information and micro-perceptions of the macro-economy."

Both observational and experimental methods can detect these observable implications. My claim is not that within-group status motivations are the exclusive or primary driver of political behavior. However, they are important components of human psychology, and with attention to their distinct observable implications, they can help us understand more about puzzling variation in political behavior.

THREE

Elaborations on the Main
Arguments

I have explored several specific empirical applications of the
argument that status motivations influence political preferences and behavior. By examining several disparate puzzles,
and by examining different manifestations of status concerns, the
priority has been breadth rather than depth, diversity rather than
perfect cohesion. I have explored whether the observable implications of status motivations could give us leverage over many areas
of political behavior and tried to take into account that people
pursue status along both tangible and intangible dimensions.

Next I take a step back and consider some general issues related
to the analytic usefulness of arguments based on within-group
status concerns. For instance, even after seeing the empirical
applications, one might ask whether such status motivations are
really new, conceptually. Do closely related concepts—inequality
aversion, relative deprivation, fairness concerns—not cover the
same ground? Similarly, one might wonder about alternative
explanations that might account for the observable implications of
status motivations, regardless of the political puzzle one examines.
For example, can we simply boil status motivations down to the
pursuit of long-term self-interest? Do people not self-select into
(and out of) reference groups, and, if so, might compositional
changes better account for the observable implications of status
motivations? One might wonder about alternative approaches:
Why not focus on dispositional differences in within-status concerns rather than on situations that intensify status conflict?
Why focus on within- rather than between-group status concerns?

Finally, one might ask about the normative implications of drawing attention to status motivations. Is drawing attention to citizens' sometimes unsavory psychological goals an appropriate way to explain political puzzles? What, if any, policy implications should we draw?

I consider these general issues here rather than in the discussions of individual puzzles, because these issues extend across empirical applications. Consideration of these issues can inform our thinking not just about the three puzzles considered in this book but also about any future application of status motivations to other political puzzles. I will occasionally revisit parts of specific empirical applications for the purposes of illustration, but I largely discuss these issues in general terms to allow the reader to consider whether she would find it useful to use status motivations in her own work.

Related Concepts

How—and to what extent—are status motivations different from the simple dislike of inequality, or from principles of fairness? How do they relate to relative deprivation, status anxiety, and the tunnel effect, concepts used in an older political science literature? In considering these conceptual distinctions, it is worth bearing in mind that status motivations are concerned about what others have but only for the purposes of assessing one's own relative position. They are about bettering one's own within-group status and thus have different observable implications than helping others, reducing all inequities, or adhering to universal principles.

INEQUALITY AVERSION

How do status motivations differ from a simple dislike of inequality? Status motivations are certainly attuned to inequality, but an envious person feels bad specifically because of the difference between what she has and what others have, not because of

TABLE 3.1 Stylized Choices Involving Inequity Aversion, Altruism, and Status Concerns

	Option 1	Option 2	Option 3
Person A	10	7	6
Person B	8	7	6
Person C	5	2	6
Total	23	16	18

inequality writ large. Status motivations thus differ from general inequality aversion, which Fehr and Schmidt define as the willingness "to give up some material payoff to move in the direction of more equitable outcomes."[1] When envious, a person is willing to pay a cost to make herself relatively better off, not to move toward more equitable outcomes in general. When spiteful, a person prefers that there be greater inequity, if that inequity benefits her. When someone seeks distinction within a social group, she is seeking to avoid inequality that disadvantages her while at the same time seeking to preserve or increase inequality that advantages her. Status motivations thus differ from inequity aversion and from other types of interdependent preferences in their self-centeredness. Altruism, for instance, is an interdependent preference, but it means that an individual is moved to help other people become better off, not to distinguish herself from them.

Table 3.1 outlines a stylized example of three policy options that would yield material payoffs to three people: A, B, and C. Each policy has different consequences for the status and absolute welfare of each person, as well as for the level of inequality among the three. Consider Person B.

If Person B cares about his relative position, he will choose Option 2. He receives more absolute points in Option 1 than in Option 2, but in Option 1 he is worse off than Person A and better off than Person C by only 3 points. Under Option 2, no one else is better off than B and B is better off than C by 5 points.

[1] Ernst Fehr and Klaus M. Schmidt. "A theory of fairness, competition, and cooperation." In *Quarterly Journal of Economics* (1999), pp. 817–868, 819.

Notice that if B wanted to minimize inequality per se, he should instead choose Option 3, in which everyone is strictly equal. He would also choose Option 3 if he cared altruistically about making the least well-off person the most well off,[2] because Option 3 gives Person C 6 points instead of only 5 or 2. Inequality, altruism, and Rawls's, difference principle lead to different observable implications than status motivations. Pursuing a better relative position means maximizing the distance between oneself and those worse off rather than minimizing overall inequality or improving the absolute welfare of those worse off than oneself. In this example, the pursuit of relative position for Person B also diverges from the pursuit of aggregate group welfare, for if B wanted to maximize the number of points distributed to the whole group, he would choose Option 1, which yields 23 points rather than 16 or 18.

Notice also that in this example relative position concerns also create more conflict among the three persons than the other motivations. If all three persons (A, B, and C) care about minimizing inequality, about the difference principle, or about maximizing overall welfare, they will agree on the best option. If all three persons seek to maximize their own absolute welfare, Persons A and B will prefer Option 1 and Person C will prefer Option 3. At least by majority rules, the group would reach a decision. However, if all three persons care about their own relative position, then Person A will prefer Option 1, Person B will prefer Option 2, and Person C will prefer Option 3. For Person A, Option 1 gives him a utility of 13.5.[3] Option 2 gives him a utility of 9.5, and Option 3 gives

---

[2] Rawls argues that we should choose an allocation that makes those worst off in a society the best off that they can be. This principle is justified in two ways. First, if each member of society has an equal claim on the goods provided in that society, then inequality is permissible only if it benefits the least well off. Second, if we were to choose the allocation before knowing which position we would each occupy in the distribution of wealth, we would all foresee the possibility of occupying the position of the least well off and would therefore choose the allocation that follows the difference principle: see John Rawls. *A theory of justice*.

[3] I calculate utility using the following set-up. Assume that any person A's reference group consists of *n* people (including A), and assume that A cares about both her ordinal and her cardinal relative positions within that reference group. Let

him a utility of 6. Meanwhile, for Person C, Option 1 gives him a utility of 1, Option 2 gives him a utility of −3, and Option 3 gives him a utility of 6. Each person has a distinct preferential ordering of the three options, and a decision by either majority voting or consensus cannot be reached. This is not to say that status motivations will always make cooperation more difficult. But, as Grant suggested, one can see how they can lead to conflict unexplained by these other motivations.[4]

FAIRNESS

Even if status motivations can be distinguished from inequity aversion and altruism, can they also be differentiated from fairness concerns? Because antisocial status motivations like envy and spite are socially undesirable, people may use concerns for fairness as a way to talk about unhappiness with their own status. When asked why she would rather not be worse off than her neighbor, an individual might say "Because it is unfair" rather than "It makes me envious." Certainly children are quick to protest something as "unfair" when it disadvantages them,[5] and the same can be said of adults. The lack of clarity in self-reports can make the analytic distinctions between fairness and status motivations seem difficult.

In the introduction, I addressed some of the ways behavioral economists have empirically distinguished envy and spite from

---

the index of points earned be $x = x_1, \ldots, x_n$. Following Fehr and Schmidt, while specifying positive utility from being better off than others in the group, we can define A's utility function if he is concerned about within-group relative position as follows: $U_A(x) = x_A - \alpha_A \frac{1}{n-1} \sum_{j \neq A} max\{x_j - x_A, 0\} + \beta_A \frac{1}{n-1} \sum_{A \neq j} max\{x_A - x_j, 0\} + \epsilon_A$, where α_A and $\beta_A > 0$. For simplicity, assume $\alpha, \beta = 1$ for all players: Ernst Fehr and Schmidt. "A theory of fairness, competition, and cooperation."

[4] Grant. "Passions and interests revisited: The psychological foundations of economics and politics."

[5] Mark Sheskin, Paul Bloom, and Karen Wynn. "Anti-equality: Social comparison in young children." In *Cognition* 130.2 (2014), pp. 152–156. While young children consistently protest the fairness of *personally* disadvantageous allocations, they do not protest when others are left less well off than they are.

fairness. Before addressing the empirical distinctions further, it is important to note that "fairness" is a very broad concept. Individuals frequently label states of the world as "fair" or "unfair" without much precision or consistency.[6] Fischer has documented at least seven distinct and contradictory fairness principles used regularly in political discourse in the United States and New Zealand alone.[7] Hochschild, working in the United States, and Fischer both found that citizens and politicians articulate a whole range of colloquial notions of fairness, including principles of strict equality (all people should receive the same amount regardless of their individual characteristics), requisites (resources should be allocated according to people's needs), investment (people should receive resources according to the amount of effort they put into obtaining them), results (people should receive according to the quality of their outputs), and many others.[8] The English word "fair," comes from the Gothic *fagrs* ("pleasing to behold") and from an Indo-European word meaning "to be content," and was historically used in sports contests and tribal battles simply to refer to settlements that are "pleasing" to both sides. This etymology meant that a great many arrangements could be labeled "fair," including those that were simply displeasing to people because they left them personally at a relative disadvantage. Fischer writes, "Fairness was an abstract idea of right conduct that could be applied in different ways, depending on the situation."[9] Identifying that someone perceives an allocation as unfair often tells us little about the specific principle that underlies that perception, and it often tells us little about what the person would prefer instead.

But there are many allocation principles from which status motivations are clearly empirically distinct. As already discussed, status motivations are self-centered rather than based on universal

---

[6] Hochschild. *What's fair? American beliefs about distributive justice.*

[7] David Hackett Fischer. *Fairness and freedom: A history of two open societies, New Zealand and the United States.* New York, NY: Oxford University Press, 2012.

[8] Hochschild. *What's fair? American beliefs about distributive justice.*

[9] Fischer. *Fairness and freedom: A history of two open societies, New Zealand and the United States.* p. 16.

principles. Notions of fairness that seek to apply the same distributive principles to everyone—such as strict equality, compensatory justice, or distribution based on need, investment, or results—do not have the same observable implications as the pursuit of status. They are not dependent on one's *own* position in the economic hierarchy.[10] As Corneo and Grüner point out, these notions of fairness refer to general, abstract principles of allocation and behavior rather than principles that rely on knowing our own position vis-à-vis others.[11] In the same way, status motivations have distinct observable implications from notions of procedural fairness.[12] Status motivations are focused on distributive outcomes—specifically, maximizing of one's own relative position within a group. They are indifferent to whether allocation rules are consistently applied to everyone, as long as the outcomes generate status for them.

Thus, no matter how they are justified and self-reported, status motivations can frequently be empirically distinguished from fairness concerns, but the distinctions are often subtle. Consider the example of underspending in South Africa. Some politicians spoke to me in fairness terms, saying that it was more fair to wait to build houses or distribute other household-targeted goods until everyone could get one rather than allowing only some to benefit. And it is difficult for me to privilege status motivations over fairness concerns as *the* explanation in the South Africa underspending study without direct evidence that individuals who *did* receive distributed goods worked to preserve their own advantages by trying to keep others down. This is evidence that I do not have. What I can say is that appeals to general and universal fairness principles alone do not easily account for the correlation between changes in black income inequality and spending in that study. The patterns of underspending were not consistent

[10] Rawls. *A theory of justice.*

[11] Giacomo Corneo and Hans Peter Grüner. "Individual preferences for political redistribution." In *Journal of Public Economics* 83.1 (2002), pp. 83–107.

[12] Tom R. Tyler. "Psychological perspectives on legitimacy and legitimation." In *Annual Review of Psychology* 57 (2006), pp. 375–400.

with certain types of fairness concerns, such as attention to fair allocation procedures. For instance, citizens were no more likely in places with rapid changes in black income inequality to think that the political process generating the underspending was corrupt. The 2002 Afrobarometer asked South African citizens, "How many of the following people do you think are involved in corruption: elected leaders, such as . . . local councillors?" to which they could reply "None," "Some of them," "Most of them," or "All of them" (four-point scale).[13] Figure 3.1 shows the average scores on a four-point scale of perceived corruption, broken down by residents who qualified for a government-issued (RDP) house (earning 3,000 Rand per month or less)[14] versus those who did not, both in municipalities where black income inequality increased and where it stayed the same or decreased. The differences in average scores across categories are at most 0.22 on a four-point scale and do not differ in a detectable way between municipalities where black income inequality increased and where it did not. These patterns cast doubt on the possiblity that changes in black income inequality are capturing different degrees of concern about fair *procedures*. So, at the very least, a focus on status motivation helps us narrow down the types of fairness concerns that are analytically relevant.

I am certainly not suggesting that fairness is *never* a useful explanation for domains of political behavior described in this book. Rather, status motivations and fairness principles can each contribute to our understanding of why people behave politically the way they do. For instance, Scheve and Stasavage use compensatory notions of fairness to explain major changes to the American taxation system over time.[15] They show that in certain

[13] I exclude "Don't know" responses.

[14] The law was 3,500 Rand per month or less but the Afrobarometer question on monthly income places respondents in brackets and the relevant cutoff falls in the middle of a bracket (3,000–4,000 Rand per month). The coding in the graph separates people who are definitely RDP qualifiers and those who are not.

[15] Scheve and Stasavage. *Taxing the rich: A history of fiscal fairness in the United States and Europe.*

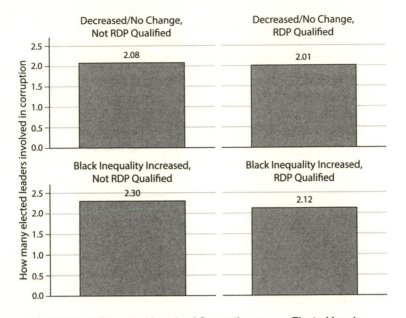

FIGURE 3.1: Perceived Levels of Corruption among Elected Leaders

Note: The 2002 Afrobarometer question asked, "How many of the following people do you think are involved in corruption?" (1 = "None," 2 = "Some of them," 3 = "Most of them," and 4="All of them.")

time periods—particularly in times of war, when the poor and middle class end up making larger sacrifices through conscription—public opinion as a whole becomes more supportive of taxing the rich at higher rates, because a compensatory notion of fairness indicates that the rich should be making equal sacrifices, too. And Fong uses concerns for certain fairness principles—such as the principle that riches earned through hard work should be less subject to redistribution than riches earned through luck—to explain individual-level variation in a cross-section of attitudes toward redistribution.[16] Both arguments help explain some of the puzzling variation in attitudes toward redistribution over time and across individuals.

---

[16] Fong. "Social preferences, self-interest, and the demand for redistribution."

Yet, as I showed in the essay on preferences over redistribution, such fairness principles do not fully account for variation in people's attitudes toward redistributions. Additional variation is accounted for when we allow that people's preferences may also be related to concerns for their relative position within local social groups. Fairness concerns account for the redistributive preferences of *some* people. For instance, although respondents in the South African Social Attitudes Survey who reported engaging in local social comparisons displayed patterns of preferences over redistribution that were consistent with local, within-group status motivations, respondents who reported *not* engaging in local social comparisons displayed patterns of preferences over redistribution that were more consistent with fairness or inequity aversion toward neighbors.

A possible area for future research then would be to examine the interaction of fairness concerns and status motivations. For instance, people may be even more likely to act on their feelings of envy and spite when they find ways to justify these feelings to themselves and others by appealing (even if inappropriately) to fairness principles. Status motivations that are at least partially transformed into an experience of righteous indignation might be the most powerful of all. Such a transformation is not always possible.[17] The circumstances that give rise to envy are personal—that is, they relate to one's *own* disadvantage—so their portrayal as purely about fairness is likely to be contested and often unconvincing.[18] But where it is possible to combine personal motivations for status and a convincing justification of fairness, the behavioral implications might be particularly powerful. The contexts in which this combination is possible deserve future attention.

---

[17] Richard H. Smith. "Envy and the sense of injustice." In *The psychology of jealousy and envy*. Ed. by Peter Salovey. New York, NY: Guilford Press, 1991, pp. 79–99.

[18] Sheskin, Bloom, and Wynn. "Anti-equality: Social comparison in young children."

RELATIVE DEPRIVATION AND STATUS ANXIETY

The arguments presented here may recall earlier political science work on relative deprivation and status anxiety. Those literatures also drew on the insight that being relatively worse off than others is painful. They argued that relative disadvantage produces frustration and discontent. For instance, the mid-twentieth century literature on status anxiety in the United States argued that shifts in prestige across entire communities prompted individuals who had lost status to become Progressives, so that they could push for reforms to gain higher incomes and levels of education.[19] This literature also argued that individuals who are of high status on one dimension (say, education) but of low status on another dimension (say, income) will be particularly troubled and likely to support political parties that favor social change.[20] Meanwhile, relative deprivation theories[21] argued that discontent arises where citizens lose status or where improved absolute standards of living do not meet expectations, given the standard of living of others.[22] This observation was offered as an explanation for violence, among other phenomena. People who find themselves worse off in a relative sense might rebel in order to improve their material circumstances,[23] or they might participate in violence simply to "vent their fury" with their situation.[24]

There are several differences between these earlier arguments and the ones in this book. First, I argue that people sometimes respond to relative disadvantage not by trying to better their

[19] Richard Hofstadter. *The age of reform: From Bryan to FDR*. New York, NY: Vintage, 1955.

[20] David R. Segal and David Knoke. "Social mobility, status inconsistency and partisan realignment in the United States." In *Social Forces* 47.2 (1968), pp. 154–157.

[21] Runciman. *Relative deprivation and social justice: A study of attitudes to social inequality in twentieth-century England*; Gurr. *Why men rebel*; Christopher Reenock, Michael Bernhard, and David Sobek. "Regressive socioeconomic distribution and democratic survival." In *International Studies Quarterly* 51.3 (2007), pp. 677–699.

[22] Gurr. *Why men rebel*. p. 56.

[23] Ibid.

[24] Keen. *The economic functions of violence in civil wars*.

own material circumstances in absolute terms but by trying to "level down" other people's advantages or by trying to preserve their own, even at a cost. This is a distinctive characteristic of status motivations that has not, to my knowledge, received much attention in political science. Relative deprivation arguments still assume that people care most about their absolute welfare but that their attention to absolute welfare is heightened by relative deprivation. Second, according to research in psychology, relative disadvantage is often most salient when it is highly and frequently visible, and among people who are perceived as similar. In previous scholarship, relative deprivation meant more general (and often abstract) comparisons across societies.[25] Third, I argue that there are certain conditions under which status motivations are likely to have consequences for politics. The literature on relative deprivation was criticized for providing little leverage over contextual variation in political outcomes:[26] Relative deprivation—especially when conceptualized on a grand scale—seems to be everywhere.[27] By contrast, I argue that although status motivations may be commonly experienced, they are likely to be most relevant to politics only under certain conditions.

THE TUNNEL EFFECT

In 1973 Albert Hirschman described what he called the "tunnel effect": during the early stages of rapid economic development, people will at first be very tolerant of their place amid new and rising inequality and will become frustrated only later on.[28] He

[25] C.f., Gurr. *Why men rebel.*

[26] Gurney and Tierney. "Relative deprivation and social movements: A critical look at twenty years of theory and research."

[27] Clark McPhail. "Civil disorder participation: A critical examination of recent research." In *American Sociological Review* 36.6 (1971), pp. 1058–1073.

[28] Hirschman and Rothschild. "The changing tolerance for income inequality in the course of economic development."

draws an analogy with waiting in a traffic jam in a two-lane tunnel. When cars in the other lane start moving (other people start becoming richer), at first people are happy at the prospect that they too might soon have the chance to move. If they remain stalled for too long while others continue to move, they become angry. Hirschman compares tolerance for inequality to "a credit that falls due at a certain date."[29] According to this analogy, status motivations should be less salient during times of transition.

The arguments in this book share Hirschman's observation that people's emotional experiences are affected by observing how well others are doing. But the arguments and empirics advanced here suggest that the initial period of tolerating inequality may be short-lived, if it occurs at all. According to the "tunnel effect" argument, in the first years of post-apatheic South African, optimism about the future should have been higher in municipalities with rapidly increasing black income inequality. To borrow the analogy, in those municipalities, cars in the other lane of the tunnel had started moving. On average, citizens there should have been more optimistic and more tolerant of policies that were not equitable. Yet there is little evidence that this was the case. For instance, by merging municipal-level data on changes in black income inequality with responses to an Afrobarometer question on expectations of future living conditions, figure 3.2 examines whether living in a municipality where black income inequality (the decile ratio) had increased between 1996 and 2001 was associated with a greater rate of expressing optimism about one's own future living conditions. Figure 3.2 shows the rate of black respondents indicating "Much better" or "Better," asked in South Africa in 2002,[30] disaggregated by whether black income inequality had increased in a municipality or not. Contrary to the tunnel effect analogy, optimism about future living conditions was not higher where black income inequality had increased.

[29] Ibid., p. 545.
[30] "Looking ahead, do you expect the following to be better or worse: your living conditions in twelve months time?" ("Much better," "Better," "Same," "Worse," or "Much worse.")

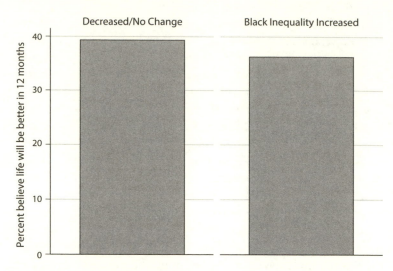

FIGURE 3.2: Optimism about Living Conditions over Next Year, Black Respondents

If anything, it was slightly lower. In municipalities where black income inequality had stayed the same or decreased, 39 percent of black respondents expressed optimism about the future compared to 36 percent in municipalities where black income inequality had increased.

Alternative Interpretations

Even if we accept that status motivations are a distinct and interesting concept, are there other theories of human behavior that might better account for their observable implications? Below I discuss two alternatives: (1) that, instead of status motivations, we are simply observing people's pursuit of their long-term self-interest, and (2) that, instead of status motivations, we are observing geographic sorting on the basis of short-term interests. Both explanations are general objections to status-based explanations for political behavior, but neither is theoretically or empirically sufficient.

LONG-TERM SELF-INTEREST

Is it possible that political behavior that appears to be motivated by status concerns is really about pursuing long-term self-interest? In many ways this was Hobbes's suspicion, as discussed in the introduction. Knocking down those who are more successful might be personally costly in the short term, but it might ensure survival in the long term. There could even be an underlying evolutionary basis for our desire for higher within-group status that links it to concerns for long-term self-interest.[31] Perhaps at some point obtaining a high status, even at a cost, ensured our long-term survival because we would be less likely to be challenged by other group members. Or perhaps high status ensured the survival of subsequent generations by winning us fitter mates.

But the fact that within-group status may have served this purpose at one time in our evolutionary history does not mean that within-group status holds no independent value for individuals today. Fodor writes that the desire for high status has become "to some extent biologically hardwired" such that it influences decisions now even when it is no longer necessary for survival: it "exists as a modular, motivational force that operates independently of information about the effects of its satisfaction."[32] In other words, in this day and age, people may respond to a desire for within-group status even when it is not in their short- or long-term self-interest.

Various lab experiments have shown that envious behavior is distinct from the pursuit of long-term material self-interest. People who participated in the studies of Zizzo and Oswald, Huberman et al., Fehr et al., and Kuziemko et al., among other studies of envy-related behavior, played experimental games anonymously.[33]

---

[31] Beach and Tesser. "Self-evaluation maintenance and evolution."

[32] Jerry A. Fodor. *The modularity of mind: An essay on faculty psychology.* Cambridge, MA: Massachusetts Institute of Technology Press, 1983.

[33] Zizzo and Oswald. "Are people willing to pay to reduce others' incomes?"; Huberman, Loch, and Önçüler. "Status as a valued resource"; Fehr, Hoff, and Kshetramade. "Spite and development"; Kuziemko et al. "'Last-place aversion': Evidence and redistributive implications."

They did not know the identities of the people against whom they were competing for relative position. They were unlikely to interact with them outside of the lab, and, if they did, they would not have known who had the higher relative position in the lab. The costs they paid in the lab to "burn" others' money or to otherwise increase their relative position therefore could not have been related to the pursuit of long-term material gains. By having individuals play one-shot, anonymous games, these studies show that behavior consistent with status motivations is not fundamentally driven by long-term self-interest.

Outside of the lab, distinguishing between status-motivated behavior and long-term self-interested behavior is more difficult. For instance, skeptics might critique the analyses of preferences over redistribution earlier in this book by pointing out that relative local disadvantage could be correlated with support for redistribution not because of envy or spite, but because besting one's neighbors can be important for long-term well-being. Perhaps being in a better position vis-à-vis one's neighbors means a person can more easily afford local goods and services. This is a possibility that is not easily ruled out using observational data, especially since there are no good questions in these surveys about local affordability.

But the available evidence suggests that the role of relative local advantage in shaping preferences over redistribution is not simply one of pursuing long-term material well-being. First, the GSS provides a measure of respondents' socioeconomic status, which could roughly proxy for their quality of life, including their ability to buy goods and services.[34] This measure of socio economic status is correlated with local relative disadvantage but weakly ($r = -0.29$). There is much disjuncture between the the Socioeconomic Index and local relative disadvantage, and the two are certainly not synonymous. Furthermore, the Socioeconomic Index measure is very weakly correlated with supporting more progressive taxation ($r = -0.08$).

[34] The measure here is the respondents' Socioeconomic Index (SEI).

Second, the association between local relative disadvantage and support for redistribution is no stronger within subgroups of respondents for whom relative local disadvantage has clear implications for their long-term self-interest. For instance, if relative local disadvantage were a proxy for redistribution being in an individual's long-term self-interest, then it should be more strongly associated with support for redistribution among people with school-age children than among those without school-age children.[35] For these individuals, living in an area where they are relatively poor means access to better-quality public schools for their children (controlling for family income) if taxes are high.[36] For respondents with school-age children, local relative disadvantage arguably means a stronger relationship between taxes and long-term interests. The GSS measures whether there are children under eighteen in the household of each respondent. But if I consider relative local disparity along with whether the respondent has school-age children in the home, and control for variables discussed in the application to preferences over redistribution, I find that the relationship between relative local disparity and the likelihood of supporting more progressive taxation is no different among people with children than among those without them.

Nor can long-term self-interest fully account for the patterns of underspending we saw in South Africa. Skeptics might have worried, for instance, that potential housing recipients opposed— or were perceived by politicians to oppose—low-income housing construction because they believed opposition would increase the likelihood of receiving additional funds over the long term. Perhaps they opposed low-income housing construction to pre- serve a coalition to lobby for more houses in the future. Yet, although this explanation is appealing, it is ultimately unsatisfy- ing. Municipalities are suppose to return unspent funds to the

[35] Luttmer. "Neighbors as negatives: Relative earnings and well-being."

[36] Schools are usually funded through property taxes, but unfortunately there is no direct question about property tax rates in the survey. One might also think of the variable "children in home" as an indicator of having reasons to think about self-interest (in the sense of the family's self-interest) in the very long term.

TABLE 3.2 (Lack of) Heterogeneous Effects of Relative Local Position on Wanting More Progressive National Tax System, by Children at Home

	Progressive taxation	Progressive taxation
Local relative disadvantage	0.066**	0.083**
	(0.028)	(0.036)
Children in home	−0.061*	−0.048
	(0.036)	(0.057)
Children* local relative disadvantage	−0.015	−0.041
	(0.019)	(0.027)
Household income	0.012	0.083**
	(0.027)	(0.041)
Democrat		0.091*
		(0.048)
Black		0.136
		(0.090)
Hispanic		−0.141
		(0.095)
Hard work		−0.038
		(0.054)
Religious attendance		−0.018
		(0.026)
	N = 1215	N = 574

Notes: GSS (2006). *American community survey*, Washington, DC, 2005. * $p<0.10$, ** $p<0.05$. Standard errors in parentheses, clustered by PUMA. WTSSNR included as probability weights. Change in predicted probability for a one-standard-deviation change in continuous independent variables and for a one-unit change in dummy variables. All other variables are set at their means (if continuous); dummy variables set to values for a white, married, male Democrat. Other controls included in the second column: female, education, age, marital status. The dependent variable is coded 1 if respondent said that taxes on the rich are much too low or too low and said that taxes on the poor are much too high or too high, 0 if responded to the question supporting the status quo or lowering taxes on the rich and/or raising taxes on the poor.

province. When projects did not go forward and the municipality applied for more money to cover all qualifying beneficiaries, the requests were supposed to be denied. It seemed clear that underspending did not help secure more money in the future. Yet municipalities experiencing rapidly increasing black income inequality frequently underspending over a period of several years, unless (as in a few cases) they undertook the risky strategy of vastly overspending their budgets.

The larger point is that although it may be tempting to dismiss behavior consistent with status motivations as really about long-term self-interest, doing so categorically would be a mistake. At one point in our evolutionary history, the pursuit of high status within tribes probably was about long-term well-being, given that securing resources and suitable mates depended on it. But today the relationship between the two is not so tight, even though our desire for within-group status remains entrenched.[37] In the empirical applications in this book, long-term self-interest does not account for the puzzling political behavior in question as well as within-group status motivations do. The same is likely to be true in other domains of politics.

GEOGRAPHIC SORTING AND COMPOSITIONAL CHANGES

Another general, alternative explanation involves geographic sorting. The main arguments in this book often assume relatively fixed reference groups and reference group boundaries. But people can select into and out of many groups. Such selection processes could mean that the relationship between relative position and political actions and attitudes is spurious. Both phenomena could be driven by factors influencing the selection of individuals into particular groups and locations.

For example, I argued earlier that individuals' attitudes toward redistribution policies are influenced in part by their relative positions among coethnic neighbors. In the United States and South Africa, where ethnic and racial groups have historically been divided by social and political institutions, it may be reasonable to assume that membership in these groups is ascriptive and somewhat fixed. Yet, in this day and age, many individuals are not bound to a particular neighborhood or geographic area. Social

---

[37] Eric S. Dickson. "Expected utility violations evolve under status-based selection mechanisms." In *Journal of Theoretical Biology* 254.3 (2008), pp. 650–654; Beach and Tesser. "Self-evaluation maintenance and evolution"; Weiss and Fershtman. "Social status and economic performance: A survey"; Buss. "Evolutionary biology and personality psychology: Toward a conception of human nature and individual differences."

media allows people to compare across wider networks of friends, acquaintances, and other peers. Unless they are destitute, citizens probably live in a particular neighborhood at least in part because they want to. One might therefore wonder whether an underlying selection process is driving both relative economic positions and preferences over redistribution.

Another example is the possible omitted role of migration in my account of underspending in South Africa. Municipalities with decreasing or static inequality might be the places poor people are leaving; those with increasing inequality might be the areas to which they are going. If this were the case and if governments were having difficulty handling the influx of migrants, we might observe lower levels of spending and policy implementation where there is a greater inflow of new residents. Underspending might be explained by geographic sorting rather than by status motivations.

However, these alternatives are unsatisfying both in these specific instances and more generally. In the specific instance of preferences over redistribution, there is little evidence that people who move to a new location exhibit different political reactions to being at a relative local disadvantage than those who stay put. The GSS survey asks people about their mobility since age sixteen. Contrary to the sorting explanation, the association between relative local disadvantage and support for redistribution is no different for people living in the same state or city since age sixteen than it is for people who have moved.

In general, I expect geographic self-selection to generate underestimates of the relationship between an individual's within-group status and her political attitudes and behavior. The processes that drive selection into localities are likely to run counter to a negative relationship between local relative position and support for redistribution. Individuals who choose to "move on up" into a neighborhood—who choose to be a "small fish in a big pond"[38]— are also likely to believe in upward mobility (i.e., that they will become better off in absolute terms over time). Individuals who

---

[38] Frank. *Choosing the right pond: Human behavior and the quest for status.*

TABLE 3.3 (Lack of) Heterogeneous Effects of Relative Local Position on Support for Redistribution, by Lives in Same State

	Supports govt. redistribution	Supports govt. redistribution
Local relative disadvantage	0.039***	0.037**
	(0.013)	(0.016)
Same state	0.012	−0.017
	(0.016)	(0.022)
Same state* local relative disadvantage	−0.018	−0.016
	(0.013)	(0.017)
National position	−0.049***	−0.014
	(0.010)	(0.016)
Pessimism about future		0.064***
		(0.013)
Democrat		0.078***
		(0.022)
Black		0.057
		(0.035)
Hispanic		0.056
		(0.043)
Racial resentment index		−0.034
		(0.042)
Blacks should work way up		−0.055***
		(0.012)
Religious attendance		−0.026**
		(0.011)
	N = 1650	N = 763

Notes: GSS (2006). *American community survey*, Washington, DC, 2005. * p<0.10, ** p<0.05, ***p<0.01. Standard errors in parentheses, clustered by PUMA. WTSSNR included as probability weights. Dependent variable is a seven-point scale of agreement with a statement that the government in Washington should either tax the rich more highly or spend more on the poor. The table reports the estimated change in the predicted probability of choosing 7 on the seven-point scale for a one-standard-deviation change in continuous independent variables, and for a one-unit change in dummy variables. All other variables are set at their means if continuous; dummy variables are set to values for a white, married, male Democrat. The controls in the second column include frequency of female, education, age, marital status.

believe in upward mobility are more likely to *oppose* progressive redistribution in order to protect their future selves from taxation,[39] but I find that these people (in a low local relative position)

---

[39] Benabou and Ok. "Social mobility and the demand for redistribution: The Poum hypothesis."

actually *support* more redistribution. In general, geographic self-sorting has observable implications directly contrary to explanations based on status motivations.

The available data also cast doubt on the sorting story as a sufficient explanation in the specific instance of underspending in South Africa. The 2001 census asked people whether they had lived in the same place five years earlier. Taking the average of those responses at the municipal level yields an estimate of the percentage of the population in each municipality that were recent migrants. Across all municipalities, the average was 11.2 percent recent migrants, ranging from less than 1 percent of the population to 35 percent. Yet the correlation between change in the black income decile dispersion ratio in a municipality and percent migrant is low ($r = 0.01$). If I repeat the analyses from the essay on government underspending but control for percent migrant, the main results are unchanged. Percent change in black income inequality is still negatively correlated with spending and positively associated with being a consistent underspender, while the percentage of the population that had recently migrated is not reliably correlated with spending patterns. These results can be seen in table 3.4.

In other words, in the specific examples discussed in this book, accounting for sorting processes does not diminish the findings based on status motivations. The more general point is that sorting is unlikely to be a satisfactory substitute explanation. While selection into reference groups and geographic areas is an important topic for ongoing study, it is unlikely to be completely fluid. When it does happen, it sometimes has observable implications that are directly contrary to the observable implications of status motivations.

Alternative Approaches to Studying Status Motivations

Even if we are convinced that status motivations are conceptually distinct and that their observable implications cannot be subsumed by alternative theories, why not study dispositional

TABLE 3.4 Relationship between Percent Change in Black Income Inequality and Municipal Budget Spending, Controlling for % Population Moved In during Last Five Years

	Avg % budget spent 2003–2006	Consistent underspending
Percent change in black inequality	−0.02***	0.13**
	(0.01)	(0.06)
% population migrant	0.003	−0.11
	(0.70)	(0.08)
% of pop in informal (2001)	−0.42	0.15**
	(0.524)	(0.07)
Log staff (2003)	−2.08	−0.02
	(4.42)	(0.08)
Years of MM experience (2003)	−0.23	0.00
	(0.39)	(0.05)
% HH black (2001)	−0.36	−0.01
	(0.32)	(0.13)
Log HH (2001)	7.36*	−0.01
	(4.29)	(0.05)
ANC vote % (2000)	0.42	−0.00
	(0.26)	(0.09)
	N = 147	N = 147

Notes: * p<0.10, ** p<0.05, *** p<0.01. Standard errors in parentheses. Province fixed effects included. OLS in first column, logistic regression in the second. The dependent variable in the first column is the percentage of the budget spent, averaged over four years (2003–2006). The dependent variable in the second column is a binary variable indicating whether the municipality underspent in each of those years. That column presents changes in the predicted probabilities of being a consistent underspender associated with a one-standard-deviation change in the independent variables, holding others at their means.

differences in sensitivity to status, or why not study status motivations across groups rather than within them? Why focus on situational factors influencing within-group status motivations?

DISPOSITIONAL PERSPECTIVES

Whereas this book takes a situational approach to understanding the implications of status motivations for politics, an alternative approach would be to treat concerns for status as dispositional. That is, one could treat the desire for status as a function of respondents' attributes rather than their circumstances. Research in psychology certainly supports the notion that some people care more about within-group status than others do. That is, some individuals are more aware of interpersonal differences in status than others and are more inclined to punish others in order to improve their own relative position. There is even a personality trait called Social Comparison Orientation (SCO), which social psychologists measure through a series of questions about how much and how often a person compares her assets and achievements with those of others.[40] Those scoring high on the SCO scale tend to be simultaneously self-referent[41] and highly aware of interpersonal interdependence. They are more likely than those scoring low on the SCO scale to experience obsessions over status.[42]

Another personality trait that correlates with a focus on relative position is "Social Dominance Orientation."[43] It has been argued that people high on the SDO scale exhibit physical signs of discomfort in response to being worse off than others within their reference group—symptoms that can be relieved only by

[40] Frederick Gibbons and Bram Buunk. "Individual differences in social comparison: Development of a scale of social comparison orientation." In *Journal of Personality and Social Psychology* 76.1 (1999), pp. 129–142. Items include: "How often do you compare how your loved ones are doing with how others are doing? Do you pay a lot of attention to how you do things, compared with how others do things? Do you compare your accomplishments with what others have accomplished in life? Do you like to talk with others about mutual opinions and experiences? Agree or disagree with the following statements: Other people are the source of my greatest pleasure and pain; I am greatly influenced by the moods of the people I am with; I am interested in knowing what makes people tick."

[41] That is, the self comes more regularly and immediately to mind in all situations. For instance, one study asked participants to try to guess the translation of foreign pronouns—a technique for measuring how self-oriented someone is. High-SCO scorers tend to guess first-person pronouns, because the self is always at the forefront of their minds.

[42] There is also a recently developed scale to measure interpersonal differences in the tendency toward spite specifically. See Marcus et al. "The psychology of spite and the measurement of spitefulness."

[43] Felicia Pratto et al. "Social dominance orientation: A personality variable predicting social and political attitudes." In *Journal of Personality and Social Psychology* 67.4 (1994), pp. 741–763.

putting others down even when it is costly to do so.[44] People who score high on the SDO scale are more forceful with others, openly admitting that they enjoy imposing their will on others and steering conversations. One study also found that these people tend to view the world literally in more vertical terms than others do. Subjects were shown split-second flashes on vertical and horizontal dimensions of a computer screen. Those with dominant personalities were quicker to notice the flashes on the vertical dimension.[45] High SDO people might be more likely to pursue within-group status at the expense of other goals.[46]

While theories about dispositional factors are fascinating, their analytic usefulness varies depending on the phenomenon one is trying to explain. Unless we expect (and can document) systematic differences in personality traits across societies and across generations, dispositional factors will be less helpful than situational factors for explaining variation in political attitudes and behavior over time and across space. Laboratory experiments also show that a wide variety of individuals randomly assigned to an inferior within-group status can be induced to experience a reduction in happiness and a greater willingness to punish others.[47] In other words, although dispositional factors may lead some individuals to value status more than others, there are also situational factors that, on average, make it more likely that individuals of all personality types place greater weight on the pursuit of within-group status. Indeed, proponents of SCO acknowledge that the measure is not as stable as measures of other personality traits and therefore may

[44] Avi Assor, Joel Aronoff, and Lawrence A. Messé. "Attribute relevance as a moderator of the effects of motivation on impression formation." In *Journal of Personality and Social Psychology* 41.4 (1981), pp. 789–796.

[45] Sara K. Moeller, Michael D. Robinson, and Darya L. Zabelina. "Personality dominance and preferential use of the vertical dimension of space evidence from spatial attention paradigms." In *Psychological Science* 19.4 (2008), pp. 355–361.

[46] However, the empirical relationship could plausibly be the reverse: those high on the SDO scale might be more likely to justify interpersonal inequalities and thus less likely to experience intense envy. More research is needed in order to find out.

[47] Armin Falk, Ernst Fehr, and Urs Fischbacher. "Driving forces behind informal sanctions." In *Econometrica* 73.6 (2005), pp. 2017–2030.

be mostly subject to context.[48] In this way, concerns for status contrast with such motivations as altruism, which appear to be a bit more (though not completely) impervious to situational influences.[49] As discussed in the conclusion, future research might combine the situational approach used here with insights about dispositions, but the situational approach certainly has analytic advantages.

STATUS MOTIVATIONS AND GROUPS

Excellent existing research in the ethnic politics literature focuses on the political consequences of inequality *between* groups,[50] rather than *within* them. For instance, Baldwin and Huber argue that governance is poorer where there is greater between-group inequality,[51] possibly because this type of inequality is accompanied by greater disagreement across groups about policy priorities[52] or because it puts richer groups in a position to dominate and exclude other groups from power.[53] Cramer Walsh argues that divergent preferences over redistribution in the United States are

[48] Gibbons and Bram Buunk. "Individual differences in social comparison: Development of a scale of social comparison orientation."

[49] Robb Willer et al., "The duality of generosity: Altruism and status seeking motivate prosocial behavior." In *Working Paper, Dept. Sociology, Stanford University* (2014).

[50] Tajfel. "Social psychology of intergroup relations"; Donald L. Horowitz. *Ethnic groups in conflict.* Berkeley, CA: University of California Press, 1985; Dawson. *Behind the mule: Race and class in African-American politics*; Kate Baldwin and John D. Huber. "Economic versus cultural differences: Forms of ethnic diversity and public goods provision." In *American Political Science Review* 104.04 (2010), pp. 644–662, John D. Huber and Pavithra Suryanarayan. "Ethnic inequality and the ethnification of political parties." In *World Politics* 68.01 (2016), pp. 149–188.

[51] Baldwin and Huber. "Economic versus cultural differences: Forms of ethnic diversity and public goods provision."

[52] Lieberman and McClendon. "The ethnicity-policy preference link in sub-Saharan Africa."

[53] Andreas Wimmer, Lars-Erik Cederman, and Brian Min. "Ethnic politics and armed conflict: A configurational analysis of a new global data set." In *American Sociological Review* 74.2 (2009), pp. 316–337.

in part influenced by rural residents' resentment of their lower status vis-à-vis elite, urban groups.[54]

Why, then, does this book focus on within-group rather than between-group status concerns? One reason is that scholars of ethnic politics have paid little attention to inequality within groups, and even less attention to individuals' concerns for maximizing within-group status as an end in itself, notwithstanding the observation of other social scientists that status within groups is a significant preoccupation of the human mind. Because within-group status concerns have been more often overlooked in the study of ethnic politics, we first need careful, sustained examinations of those concerns in their own right—their specific manifestations and consequences and the conditions under which they are likely to manifest—before we turn to their interaction (and relative significance) vis-à-vis between-group status concerns. A second reason for focusing on within-group status concerns is that people's reactions to inequality within groups are likely to have important political consequences for the nature of the groups themselves. Within-group status concerns likely affect how well groups hold together. When envy and spite are rife within a group, members watch warily for possible hostile reactions from others and are unlikely to trust each other much.[55] By contrast, as was seen in the field experiment on contentious political participation, when groups can appeal to members' desire for admiration, they may be able to compel individual sacrifices for the benefit of the group. All of this means that within-group status motivations are an important lens through which to explain the cohesion and operation of ethnic groups. Thus, even researchers who think that groups are the only important actors in politics should pay attention to the insights here.

---

[54] Katherine J. Cramer. *The politics of resentment: Rural consciousness in Wisconsin and the rise of Scott Walker*. Chicago, IL: University of Chicago Press, 2016.

[55] Glenn Adams. "The cultural grounding of personal relationship: Enemyship in North American and West African Worlds." In *Journal of Personality and Social Psychology* 88.6 (2005), pp. 948–968.

A next step for future research is to examine more explicitly the interaction between intra- and inter-group status motivations. I have argued that intra-group status motivations shape political behavior even in places where between-group differences are highly salient. That is, within-group status motivations can matter independently of concerns for group status. But when are the two types of status concerns orthogonal to one another, and when do they interact? A body of research in social psychology documents that people can experience admiration, envy, and other status emotions toward members of out-groups as well.[56] This body of research has provided some clues about the conditions under which inter-group social comparison emotions could crowd out intra-group comparisons. For instance, conditions of intense inter-group competition may heighten inter-group envy.[57] Inter-group schadenfreude may be more common when an out-group that has made the in-group feel inferior suffers losses at the hands of a third party.[58] But to my knowledge, no one has teased out the full interplay of intra- and inter-group status motivations in politics. Under what conditions do they influence behavior in the same (or in divergent) directions? When does one override the other? And if there are times when both types of concerns shape citizens' political preferences, how do political elites decide which one to respond to? These are important directions for future research.

Normative Concerns

Many status motivations are ugly. Envy is the only one of the seven deadly sins that brings no pleasure even to the

[56] Cuddy et al. "Stereotype content model across cultures: Towards universal similarities and some differences."

[57] Mina Cikara et al. "Their pain gives us pleasure: How intergroup dynamics shape empathic failures and counter-empathic responses." In *Journal of Experimental Social Psychology* 55 (2014), pp. 110–125.

[58] Colin Wayne Leach and Russell Spears. "Dejection at in-group defeat and schadenfreude toward second-and third-party out-groups." In *Emotion* 9.5 (2009), pp. 659–665.

sinner.[59] Spite is likewise considered socially undesirable, even though it is common.[60] And while the desire for admiration is less offensive than the others, it may still be considered inappropriate for polite conversation.[61]

If these motivations are ugly, should we be indulging them? Should policy makers act on the findings in this book, or would doing so give these motivations too much legitimacy? Rawls was certainly hesitant to design policy and political institutions on the basis of envy or spite. He discusses at some length why his principles for a "just society" are not an expression of envy.[62] Since envy and its kin are undesirable—antisocial, destructive, unseemly—perhaps we should be wary of giving them a political response.

I cannot answer these questions with the skill of a moral philosopher, but I would point readers to what I think might be Grant's response. That is, if we want to design policies and institutions to serve certain principles, we would be wise to recognize human motivations and behavior for what they are in order to get there. That means indulging a full range of human emotions and motivations, even the ugly ones. It involves considering the world as it is, not just as it should be. It means exploring the empirical implications of a full range of human behavior even if that behavior is unsavory.[63] Interestingly, Green argues that even Rawls might allow envy to be taken into consideration under certain circumstances—for example, where there are "excessive inequalities, inequalities not bounded by the difference principle, and inequalities founded on injustice."[64] Green is clear that Rawls' argument would allow envy to enter only into processes of

---

[59] Joseph Epstein. *Envy: The seven deadly sins*. New York, NY: Oxford University Press, 2003.

[60] Fehr, Hoff, and Kshetramade. "Spite and development."

[61] Brennan and Pettit. *The economy of esteem: An essay on civil and political society*.

[62] Rawls. *A theory of justice*, pp. 468–471.

[63] Grant. "Passions and interests revisited: The psychological foundations of economics and politics."

[64] Green. "Rawls and the forgotten figure of the most advantaged: In defense of reasonable envy toward the superrich," p. 136.

legislation and policy implementation and not into the formula-
tion of first principles, but the latter is less relevant here.[65]

Nevertheless, one might worry that appeasing status motivations is a naive strategy. High status is a scarce resource. The desire
for it cannot easily be satisfied in the aggregate. Even as individuals
pursue and achieve higher status within their reference groups,
others necessarily lose status and feel left behind as a result.[66]
The appeasement of the status concerns of some may help achieve
policy ends that would otherwise run into roadblocks if one were
to ignore status motivations altogether, as in the discussion of
underspending in early post-apartheid South Africa. But such an
approach may not end a cycle of inflaming the status concerns of
some, just as the status concerns of others are addressed.

An alternative approach might be to seek ways to transcend
people's baser motivations. When individuals feel more confident
in the integrity of the self, or understand that there are multiple
dimensions along which any person can gain status, or perceive
that their own status rises as others' lives improve they may feel less
inclined to seek psychic benefits from status within any particular
group or along any one dimension.[67] Shklar wrote, "What one
needs is the courage to be loyal to one's own ...way to live,

[65] Green's argument further underscores my suggestion to investigate the
interaction between status motivations and fairness concerns (a point to which I
return in the conclusion). When status concerns can be bolstered with claims about
fairness principles, it might be particularly appropriate to respond with policy
changes.

[66] As has been illustrated elsewhere, there are aggregate arrangements that can
achieve envy-freeness when envy means conflict over possessions and not over
relative position for its own sake. See, e.g., Steven J. Brams, D. Marc Kilgour,
and Christian Klamler. "Maximin envy-free division of indivisible items." In *Group
Decision and Negotiation* 26.1 (2017), pp. 115–131. However, when envy is about
pursuing social standing vis-à-vis other group members for its own sake, rather
than about desiring someone else's possessions, envy cannot be easily appeased in
the aggregate.

[67] Thomas Mussweiler, Shira Gabriel, and Galen V. Bodenhausen. "Shifting
social identities as a strategy for deflecting threatening social comparisons." In
Journal of Personality and Social Psychology 79.3 (2000), pp. 398–409; Amy McQueen
and William Klein. "Experimental manipulations of self-affirmation: A systematic
review." In *Self and Identity* 5.4 (2006), pp. 289–354.

not [as] a way to alter the conduct of other people. In a world of multiple moral hierarchies, this is not only feasible but an act of fidelity to the democratic polity, as well as to oneself."[68] Bolster self-confidence, not vanity, Shklar advises, or at least create multiple dimensions of comparison so that none is crucial. Having reasons to feel good that are independent of social comparisons, or having other dimensions of comparison to turn to when one disappoints, may be the only ways to rise above the pursuit of status. In practice, this might mean encouraging self-affirmation[69] or "self-interest rightly understood," à la Tocqueville,[70] or it might mean fostering pluralism in associational life.

But these notions are probably also naive. As noted in the introduction, deciding unilaterally to turn one's attention away from social comparisons can be lonely and difficult, so these efforts would have to be reinforced by institutions and leaders. In the end, I do not know whether the way forward is to appease, or to transcend, or some other strategy. However, I am confident that we first have to understand how (and under what conditions) status motivations influence political behavior. That has been the task of this book.

[68] Judith N. Shklar. *Ordinary vices.* Cambridge, MA: Harvard University Press, 1984, p. 135.
[69] McQueen and Klein. "Experimental manipulations of self-affirmation: A systematic review."
[70] Tocqueville. *Democracy in America.*

FOUR   Conclusion

W e often think of politics as a contest among individuals and groups to advance their material interests. Many important works in political science reinforce this characterization. Citizens vote based on a desire to maximize their own resources and physical safety.[1] Elites allow regime change when doing so means the least threat to their own income and assets.[2] Conflict arises where material interests are at stake, whether because citizens want to protect their access to resources,[3] or because elites see the instigation of violence as a way to hold on to the spoils of office.[4] Citizens participate in politics when the material and physical costs of doing so decrease.[5] Studies like these shed light on both macro and micro political outcomes.

But this book has provided evidence that the pursuit of within-group status, even at the expense of material interest, is also an analytically useful explanation for political behavior. Status motivations have observable implications that are distinct from those of other psychological drivers of human behavior, including fairness, altruism, in-group bias, and self-interest. These other drivers lead people to prioritize universal principles, others' welfare, group welfare, or their own absolute welfare, while status motivations

---

[1] Posner. *Institutions and ethnic politics in Africa*; Magaloni. *Voting for autocracy: Hegemonic party survival and its demise in Mexico.*

[2] Carles Boix. *Democracy and redistribution.* New York, NY: Cambridge University Press, 2003.

[3] Rafaela M. Dancygier. *Immigration and conflict in Europe.* Cambridge University Press, 2010.

[4] Wilkinson. *Votes and violence: Electoral competition and ethnic riots in India.*

[5] Teitelbaum. *Mobilizing restraint: Democracy and industrial conflict in postreform south Asia*; Chen. *Social protest and contentious authoritarianism in China.*

lead people to sacrifice those other things for a better relative position in income or esteem. Yet while status motivations are a fundamental component of the human psyche, they are likely to be relevant to *political* behavior only under certain conditions— specifically, when social mechanisms for managing them have broken down or are absent, or when elites stoke them for political purposes. These features make status motivations useful for gaining leverage over variation in political behavior.[6] They also mean that status motivations can be an additional tool in our explanatory toolbox; they can enrich, rather than supplant, other characterizations of political behavior.

The arguments in this book have intuitive appeal. We have all experienced a desire for within-group status in its various manifestations (envy, spite, a yearning for esteem) at some point in our lives. Political philosophers and social scientists in economics, psychology, and anthropology have written about it. The desire for within-group status may come from a time when humans lived in small groups of hunter-gathers—when high status within tribes ensured survival and successful procreation. Yet today our desire for within-group status is deeply ingrained, and we often pursue within-group status even when it is contrary to our short- and long-term material self-interest.[7] But beyond its resonance with our everyday experience, this book has shown that our concern for within-group status also has distinct consequences for our politics. In an effort to think broadly about the political role of status motivations, I applied insights about them to three empirical puzzles

[6] The theory offered here is middle range: Daniel Ziblatt. "Of course generalize, but how? Returning to middle range theory in comparative politics." In *American Political Science Association-Comparative Politics Newsletter* 17.2 (2006). Status motivations are common features of human experience. They should have implications across different domains of political outcomes, and should not be limited to particular societies. But the arguments offered here do not constitute an overarching explanation of politics: they apply only under specific conditions.

[7] Dickson. "Expected utility violations evolve under status-based selection mechanisms"; Beach and Tesser. "Self-evaluation maintenance and evolution"; Weiss and Fershtman. "Social status and economic performance: A survey"; Buss. "Evolutionary biology and personality psychology: Toward a conception of human nature and individual differences."

that might not otherwise be considered in tandem—puzzles about preferences over redistribution, government spending, and participation in contentious politics. Although these puzzles are each the subject of a rich existing literature, I explored them in order to underscore the disparate yet core areas of politics on which status motivations might shed light and to explore the different methods that one might use to look for the observable implications of status motivations. The goal was breadth rather than depth, diversity rather than perfect cohesion. However, the puzzles share a basic interest in why people take political positions and actions that are, on balance, materially costly for them. If people care greatly about their own survival and material welfare, why would they support policies and engage in political actions that detract from those goals? Status motivations help us gain more leverage over puzzles like these by drawing attention to something else that people also value: within-group status. People may be willing to support costly policies and undertake costly actions when doing so wins them this other valued good. Status motivations help explain political behavior that is materially costly to the individual but that has within-group distributive implications of income or esteem.

In three empirical essays, I illustrated how status motivations can account for puzzling political outcomes. In the United States and South Africa, respondents who stood to gain status from redistribution policies compared to their neighboring coethnics expressed support for those policies, even though the policies removed money from their pocketbooks. Concerns about status loss (real or perceived) stymied spending on individually and household-targeted goods in South Africa. The promise of higher in-group status pulled participants into a political rally in New Jersey despite countervailing incentives to free-ride. In each case, the political outcomes of interest could not be fully explained by short- or long-term concerns for material self-interest, or by concerns for group welfare, fairness, partisanship, and a host of other alternatives. The patterns were clearest when elites explicitly primed within-group status concerns (as in the contentious politics field experiment) or when social mechanisms for mitigating status concerns had broken down (as in post-apartheid South African municipalities experiencing rapid economic change).

One can easily imagine other domains of politics and political behavior for which status motivations might prove analytically useful. Consider theories of retrospective economic voting. When evaluating an incumbent, citizens may retrospectively consider how the economy has fared during that incumbent's term in office. Each citizen asks himself whether his own economic circumstances have improved or deteriorated (in absolute terms) during that time and perhaps also whether the economy as a whole has improved or deteriorated. The voter then rewards the incumbent for improvement and punishes the incumbent for deterioration.[8] However, if citizens also value how well they have been doing *relative* to other members of their reference groups, then we might have different expectations about how they would vote under a given set of economic conditions. For instance, suppose the incumbent's term had seen general improvement in the overall economy (growth, lower unemployment) as well as improvement in the absolute welfare of a particular voter. Standard theories of retrospective voting would expect this voter to look favorably upon the incumbent. But voters often deviate from these expectations, and in such instances understanding more about status motivations can be analytically useful. We are likely to ask new, and possibly illuminating, questions; for instance, despite enjoying higher welfare in absolute terms, did the voter not do as well as his neighbors during the incumbent's term—that is, did his within-group status decline? Had there previously been a breakdown in social mechanisms for compensating the voter for this loss in status such that he might turn to political solutions? These insights about status concerns provide useful directions for research when confronted with what might seem at first glance like odd behavior.

---

[8] Morris P. Fiorina. "Economic retrospective voting in American national elections: A micro-analysis." In *American Journal of Political Science* (1978), pp. 426–443.

What does all of this mean for the scope and applicability of the arguments offered in this book? What more might be done to understand the conditions under which status motivations influence politics? How can we build on the insights offered here to further clarify and enrich our understanding of the psychological drivers of political behavior, both within and between groups?

Scope Conditions

This book concentrated its empirical analyses in two countries that provided seemingly hard tests for the argument that within-group status motivations shape political behavior. In these two countries, both of which are notorious for salient racial divisions and high levels of between-group inequality, one might have expected that citizens' concerns for group welfare would outweigh concerns for within-group status. In the United States in particular, one might also have expected widespread beliefs in social mobility, individualism, and the American Dream to have muted desires to punish others for their successes. That status motivations promise some additional leverage over political puzzles even in these places suggests that they are useful concepts for political analysis more generally. But it would also be reasonable to wonder whether the findings are likely to generalize to other settings. Future studies should consider the following scope conditions.

One possible scope condition is state capacity. Despite their different levels of economic development, both South Africa and the United States are fairly strong and competent states. Citizens cannot always expect robust state responses to their preferences in either country,[9] but they know that the state is not absent. Citizens might be more likely to see public policy and political participation as an effective means of addressing their

[9] Martin Gilens. *Affluence and influence: Economic inequality and political power in America*. Princeton University Press, 2012; Gwyneth McClendon. "Race and responsiveness: An experiment with South African politicians." In *Journal of Experimental Political Science* 3.1 (2016), pp. 60–74.

status concerns if state capacity is at least moderately high. The arguments presented here might not extend to countries with weaker states.[10]

To that end, India might provide a fruitful place for future research to investigate the generalizability of the theory to different levels of state capacity. India provides wide variation in state capacity across regions and at the local level. Particularly since the 1990s,[11] India has also reportedly experienced a rapid uptick in inequality that has varied in intensity and timing across regions, within regions, among Hindus, and within some castes.[12] India might therefore provide examples of the kinds of transitional moments in which social conventions managing status motivations are weakened while at the same time providing wider variation in state capacity.

One might also wonder whether the arguments in this book are specific to dynamics within social identity and geographic groups from which citizens cannot easily exit. Focusing on countries where racial boundaries are highly salient and at least partially ascriptive and then taking steps to rule out alternative explanations based on self-sorting has methodological advantages. The patterns described in this book are less likely to be spurious as a result. But the flip side of this strategy is that status motivations might be more powerful in these places precisely because people cannot as easily switch their reference group to one in which they are doing relatively better.[13] In places where group boundaries are weak, and where people can easily move from one group to another

[10] Clark, Frijters, and Shields. "Relative income, happiness, and utility: An explanation for the Easterlin paradox and other puzzles."

[11] Michael Bruno, Martin Ravallion, and Lyn Squire. *Equity and growth in developing countries: Old and new perspectives on the policy issues.* Washington, D.C.: World Bank Publications, 1996.

[12] Abhijit Banerjee and Thomas Piketty. "Top Indian Incomes, 1922–2000." In *World Bank Economic Review* 19.1 (2005), pp. 1–20; Shubham Chaudhuri and Martin Ravallion. *Partially awakened giants: Uneven growth in China and India.* Vol. 4069. World Bank Publications, 2006.

[13] Andrew E. Clark and Claudia Senik. "Who compares to whom? The anatomy of income comparisons in Europe." In *Economic Journal* 120.544 (2010), pp. 573–594; Frank. *Choosing the right pond: Human behavior and the quest for status.*

and from one place to another, status motivations might play a less important role. People might never intensely experience envy or spite or the desire for admiration, let alone need to address it through politics, because they can simply choose to belong to a different group in which they are doing relatively well.

Thus a second possible scope condition on the arguments here could be the permeability of group boundaries. This possibility should be investigated empirically. Because status motivations are such a basic feature of the human experience, they may also continue to play a role even when individuals have sorted into "optimal" reference groups. Even where group boundaries are weaker, reference group options are unlikely to be limitless.[14] People may choose their reference group but still be confronted with some disadvantage and become sensitive even to small disparities among group members. One could investigate whether the patterns described here are ever evident in places like Brazil, where racial boundaries are meaningful but weaker than they are in South Africa and the United States.[15] Countries where group boundaries are more porous are promising places to explore the generalizability of the claims made here.

Finally, what about the claim that status motivations shape political behavior either when explicitly primed or when social mechanisms for regulating status emotions break down? Are these conditions generalizable? The claim that status motivations can be explicitly primed by elites seems general enough, but one might worry about the other. For instance, perhaps the early post-apartheid period is sui generis—a dramatic period of legal, economic, and social change from an unusually harsh regime that has no parallel. This is a reasonable concern, but although

---

Salovey and Rodin, "Some antecedents and consequences of social-comparison jealousy."

[14] Frank. *Choosing the right pond: Human behavior and the quest for status*. Posner. *Institutions and ethnic politics in Africa*.

[15] Lieberman. *Boundaries of contagion: How ethnic politics have shaped government responses to AIDS*; Marx. *Making race and nation: A comparison of South Africa, the United States, and Brazil*.

South Africa during this period illustrates the kinds of conditions that throw social conventions around wealth, inequality, and advancement into flux, it is hardly the only example. Conditions of urbanization, recession or dramatic economic growth, social revolution, or large-scale violence, to give some other examples, could trigger the weakening or disappearance of social conventions regulating appropriate displays and practices around wealth, achievement, and esteem. Any shock that leads to serious within-group contestation over the meaning of wealth and achievement would fit the argument. Under such conditions, we might expect people to be more likely to use political measures and mechanisms to assuage status concerns. Like all claims about scope conditions and generalizability, these contentions should be explored through additional empirical work. However, the applications of status motivations to politics are likely to be wide-ranging.

Future Research

While addressing important puzzles, the book also raises questions for future research. As I have suggested several times, one next step is to investigate how status motivations interact with other psychological drivers of political behavior. People deviate from prioritizing their absolute welfare for many reasons, including altruism, a concern for fairness, and outgroup prejudice. The approach in this book has been largely to treat status motivations as additively separable from these other motivations: to show how status motivations have distinct observable implications and can contribute to our understanding of political behavior alongside explanations based on self-interest, fairness, altruism, concerns for group welfare, and so on.

Yet another possibility is that status motivations are a substitute for some motivations of political behavior. For example, in applying status motivations to contentious political participation, I pointed out that status motivations might become most salient when other social rewards are lacking. Status entails distinction from others and is thus best achieved through contentious political behavior when that behavior is valued but also un-usual. By contrast, other social rewards (the feeling of joining together with others, or a sense of belonging) are achieved through contentious political behavior when participation is valued but common. In this example, status motivations may kick in when other social motivations for participants are weak. When there is a reasonable belief that many others will join, the goals of belonging and joining with others can explain participation. But if we acknowledge that people also hold status motivations, then we see that there are also gains to be had when few people are expected to show up, thereby helping to explain why protests occur when the prospects of high turnout are dim. In this example, status rewards function as a substitute for other social rewards.

In fact, appealing to status motivations might also crowd out some other types of motivations. Robb Willer and his coauthors posit that dispositional differences lead some people to be driven by the pursuit of status and other people to be driven by altruism. They divide the world into "egoists," "competitors," and the perpetually "prosocial."[16] The prosocial engage in altruistic acts as a matter of course, independently of situational influences. Meanwhile, egoists and competitors engage in prosocial acts under certain conditions—specifically, when acting prosocially is visible to, and admired by, others.[17] Willer et al.'s argument is consistent with the additively separable approach in this book. The implica-tion of their argument is that assuming a constant distribution of these types, any increase in the salience of status rewards should increase aggregate participation in prosocial acts. Prosocial people should be unaffected by the promise of status, while egoists and competitors should increase their participation in response to the promise of status. This implication is consistent with the

---

[16] Ernst Fehr and Urs Fischbacher. "The nature of human altruism." In *Nature* 425.6960 (2003), pp. 785–791; David De Cremer and Paul A. M. van Lange. "Why prosocials exhibit greater cooperation than proselfs: The roles of social responsibility and reciprocity." In *European Journal of Personality* 15.S1 (2001).

[17] Willer et al. "The duality of generosity: Altruism and status seeking motivate prosocial behavior."

findings in the rally field experiment. The promise of status for participation in collective action increased turnout, on average. But what if, under some conditions, status motivations instead crowd out altruism, or vice versa? Bowles describes this problem with regard to the interaction of monetary incentives and altruism: under some conditions, imposing material incentives for prosocial acts leads those who might otherwise have acted prosocially for altruistic (intrinsic) reasons to *stop* behaving prosocially.[18] For example, members of rural communities in Colombia extracted more from surrounding forests when fines for over-extraction were imposed,[19] and parents of children in daycare in Haifa were more likely to show up late when fines for tardiness were introduced.[20] Offers of monetary incentives can change how altruistic people think about the task. It would be worth examining whether status motivations and altruism interact in similar ways under some conditions or within some groups. For people who are personally inclined to behave altruistically, are there conditions under which the public promise of status rewards for prosocial acts may make those acts less appealing?

Status motivations might also interact synergistically with some psychological drivers of political behavior. For instance, it may be worth exploring whether there are potential synergies between status motivations and fairness concerns. In most of the book, I have argued that status motivations have observable implications that are distinct from those of many types of fairness concerns. That is, we can identify political behavior that is consistent with the pursuit of status and that cannot be fully accounted for by concern for fairness principles alone. The two types of concerns can be treated as additively separable. But, as I suggested in the

---

[18] Samuel Bowles. *The Moral Economy: Why Good Incentives Are No Substitute for Good Citizens.* Yale University Press, 2016.

[19] Juan Camilo Cardenas, John Stranlund, and Cleve Willis. "Local environmental control and institutional crowding-out." In *World Development* 28.10 (2000), pp. 1719–1733.

[20] Uri Gneezy and Aldo Rustichini. "Pay enough or don't pay at all." In *Quarterly Journal of Economics* 115.3 (2000), pp. 791–810.

Elaborations chapter, status motivations may also be *most* powerful when they can be couched in a narrative of fairness. Pursuing fairness is often more socially acceptable than pursuing one's own social standing. The opportunity to justify tearing others down by appealing to principles of fairness might thus bolster inclinations toward that behavior, emboldening a person's pursuit of status in politics. Children certainly understand the value of this combination and often appeal to fairness ("But it's not fair!") when transparently concerned only with their own relative position.[21] But such claims are likely to be credible in politics only when there is large-scale coordination around a fairness narrative, or when individuals do not transparently act spitefully or in other ways that are clearly antithetical to fairness principles. Fairness concerns might amplify status motivations, or status motivations might constrain one's ability to appeal to certain types of fairness concerns. To my knowledge, little work has been done to make sense of these interactions.

As discussed in the Elaborations chapter, more work also needs to be done to understand how within- and between-group status motivations interact. This book has focused on within-group status motivations because we know less about their political consequences than we do about the consequences of between-group status concerns.[22] The book shows that within-group status motivations influence politics even in places where between-group differences are highly salient. But a next step is to ask when the two types of status concerns are orthogonal to one another and when (and how) they interact. I suggested in the essay on contentious

---

[21] Sheskin, Bloom, and Wynn. "Anti-equality: Social comparison in young children."

[22] Tajfel. "Social psychology of intergroup relations"; Horowitz. *Ethnic groups in conflict*; Dawson. *Behind the mule: Race and class in African-American politics*; Baldwin and Huber. "Economic versus cultural differences: Forms of ethnic diversity and public goods provision"; Lieberman. *Boundaries of contagion: How ethnic politics have shaped government responses to AIDS*; Huber and Suryanarayan. "Ethnic Inequality and the Ethnification of Political Parties"; Cramer Walsh. *The politics of resentment: Rural consciousness in Wisconsin and the rise of Scott Walker.*

political participation that, as in other historical examples,[23] the influence of status motivations on political participation might be strongest when the same action can enhance both personal and group status. But in the discussion of preferences over redistribution, poor citizens' opposition to (and rich citizens' support of) redistribution on account of their local relative position seemed to dilute conflict on the basis of class. In general, we do not know enough about whether (and when) within-group status competition amplifies or reduces the salience of between-group status competition.

How do within-group status motivations aggregate? For the most part, this book has taken a micro-level approach to investigating the impact of status motivations on politics. Since status motivations are individually held, this strategy has provided an appropriate first cut at demonstrating how such motivations influence political decision-making and address individual-level puzzles. The approach has also offered macro-political implications. For instance, I argued that individually felt envy could help account for patterns of government spending. But I was not always explicit about how individual status motivations aggregate to influence higher-level outcomes. The background assumption was that in democracies (and possibly also non-democracies), politicians are at least somewhat sensitive to the citizens' preferences and fear losing office, or personal retribution, if citizens are competing with each other for within-group status and cannot manage conflict provoked by intra-group disparities. If citizens' policy preferences are shaped by their willingness to see more-advantaged people in their reference groups punished, even at a cost to themselves, we might expect to see these preferences reflected in policy design and implementation. In the case of local spending in South Africa, politicians certainly seemed to believe that constituents would rather that distributive policies were not implemented at all if they would exacerbate status

[23] Einwohner. "Opportunity, honor, and action in the Warsaw ghetto uprising of 1943."

differences. Politicians' actions thus accorded with sensitivity to those preferences.

Yet if the basic insight that status motivations can shape citizens' political preferences is compelling, more work should be done to probe and theorize the aggregation of these preferences. Important work in American and comparative politics has found that even democratic politicians may be responsive only to certain categories of constituents, such as the wealthy, their coethnics, core or swing voters.[24] Future research could provide additional insight into how elites calculate whether (and when) to respond to citizens' preferences shaped by status motivations. Such insights would help us better tease out the macro-level implications of the theory offered here. They would add more politicking to the accounts of political attitudes and behavior discussed in this book.

Scholars could also explore what happens when reference groups shift. For instance, the introduction of new technologies could change the contours of primary reference groups. An increasing use of social media—wherein people share images and news about their accomplishments and possessions—might mean that people are regularly exposed to salient disparities across larger geographies. The basic arguments in this book are unlikely to change: people are likely to continue to be most sensitive to "similar" others and those to whom they are frequently exposed. But the actors to whom they are most frequently exposed may be shifting, and these new technologies may also offer citizens more choice over which reference groups they use as a benchmark for their own relative standing. As alluded to in the Elaborations chapter, new technologies could produce a general dampening of status motivations' influence on politics, as citizens can more

---

[24] Gilens. *Affluence and influence: Economic inequality and political power in America*; Daniel M. Butler and David E. Broockman. "Do politicians racially discriminate against constituents? A field experiment on state legislators." In *American Journal of Political Science* 55.3 (2011), pp. 463–477; McClendon. "Race and responsiveness: An experiment with South African politicians"; Wilson Prichard. *Taxation, responsiveness and accountability in Sub-Saharan Africa: The dynamics of tax bargaining*. New York, NY: Cambridge University Press, 2015.

easily switch between in-person and social media reference groups depending on which is more troubling. Or new technologies could strengthen status motivations' political influence if social media use means that people are exposed to more upward comparisons among those with whom they share only weak ties.

Finally, as I noted at the start of this book, this study has focused on status emotions as *motivations*—that is, as shaping the goals that people pursue. But there are other ways to think about the potential influence of status emotions on political behavior. For instance, I largely ignored the role that emotions can play in conveying information and in shaping people's beliefs about the world, but research in psychology examines these implications of status emotions for cognition. The experience of emotions such as envy, schadenfreude, spite, pride, and shame gives people information about their status. Likewise, the (often unconscious) display of these emotions can communicate information about status to others.[25] Status emotions can also bias how people process new information about the status hierarchy and other people's position in it.[26] For instance, envy may bias people toward interpreting new information as suggesting they occupy an even lower status than they objectively do.[27] What are the implications of these other functions of status emotions for political behavior? Do status emotions exacerbate status conflict when they bias how people process information? How are status emotions experienced and displayed by politicians and ordinary citizens, and what are the consequences? How do people deal with uncertainty about their social status? These are directions for future research.

≈

I wrote this book amid fervent debates over economic and social inequality. In 2013 President Barack Obama called increasing

---

[25] Steckler and Tracy. "The emotional underpinnings of social status."

[26] Oveis, Horberg, and Keltner. "Compassion, pride, and social intuitions of self-other similarity."

[27] Ibid.

income inequality the "defining challenge of [the] time." Piketty's book on the origins of rising economic inequality became an international best seller.[28] Surveys found that vast majorities of both ordinary citizens and elites in countries all over the world identified economic and social inequality as big problems.[29] Economic inequality featured in the campaign platforms of political candidates across the globe. People strove to make sense of popular frustrations: was material self-interest, prejudice, or a sense of fairness driving people's reactions to rising inequality? It was not the first era in which people have struggled to make sense of the sources and consequences of inequality, nor is it likely to be the last.

The insight of this study is that in order to understand more fully the political implications of inequality in any era, we should focus not only on patterns of national and between-group inequality but also on patterns of local, within-group inequality; we should consider not only that people are self-interested, ingroup biased, and concerned about fairness but also that under some conditions they are willing to pay costs (and even see others harmed) for the sake of within-group status. Even in societies with strong narratives about equal opportunity and equality under the law, we have to pay attention to struggles over status if we want to understand political behavior. And we need to pay attention to concerns for status in all of their manifestations, understanding that people are sensitive to relative disparities in both possessions and respect. By failing to acknowledge the role that within-group status motivations play in politics, we are missing part of the story. In fact, we are missing part of many disparate political stories, from those about redistributive politics to those about political participation. Envy, spite, and the desire for admiration are basic components of the human psyche. They are basic components of political life as well.

---

[28] Thomas Piketty. *Capital in the twenty-first century*. Cambridge, MA: Harvard University Press, 2014.

[29] Andrew Kohut. *Economies of emerging markets better rated during difficult times*. Tech. rep. Pew Research Forum, 2013.

TECHNICAL NOTES

The application to preferences over redistribution uses data from three survey waves: (1) the Afrobarometer [South Africa] [Round 2] [2002], available at http://www. afrobarometer.org, (2) the South African Social Attitudes Survey (SASAS), 2005, available at https://www.datafirst.uct.ac.za/ and (3) the General Social Survey, 2006, provided with IRB approval through NORC at the University of Chicago: Tom W. Smith et al. *General Social Survey*. Chicago, IL, 2006. All three are personal surveys designed to be nationally representative, aided by weighting variables in some cases as noted below and in the main text. The Afrobarometer survey wave contains a clustered, stratified, multistage, area probability sample of 2,400 respondents who were interviewed face-to-face. The SASAS data used in the book consists of 2,850 respondents in the module about inequality and poverty, who were sampled from 500 census enumeration areas, selected while stratifying on province, rural/urban, and majority population group (Black/African, Coloured, White European, Indian). The SASAS dataset includes a weighting variable for analyses at the individual level (benchwgt), which is used as a probability weight in the analyses in that application section of the book where appropriate. The GSS survey wave contains 4,510 respondents in total (including Spanish speakers), with respondents participating in different modules of questions. For instance, only 1,518 respondents were asked the questions about whether taxes on the rich and poor are too high or low. A separate 1,989 respondents were asked the question about whether the government in Washington should reduce the gap between rich and poor (eqwlth). This 2006 wave used a two-stage, sub-sampling design to deal with non-responses. That is, in this year, the GSS engaged in re-sampling from groups and areas from which no response was obtained during the first round of surveying. The WTSSNR weighting variable, provided with the publicly available dataset, weights observations in order to account for sub-sampling of non-respondents, the number of adults in a household, and variation in non-response across geographic areas. Where appropriate and noted, the analyses in the application to preferences over redistribution employ WTSSNR as probability weights. Below I describe the coding of variables used in the analyses in that application.

TABLE E.1 Variables from Afrobarometer 2002

	Question number	Question wording	Coding
Support redistribution (in figure 2.1)	Q63	Which of the following statements is closest to your view? Choose Statement A or Statement B. A: It is alright to have large differences of wealth because those who work hard deserve to be rewarded. B: We should avoid large gaps between the rich and the poor because they create jealousy and conflict.	Coded 1 if Q63 was 3 or 4 ("agree very strongly" or "agree" with Statement B) and coded 0 if Q63 was 1 or 2 ("agree very strongly" or "agree" with Statement A).
Worse rich-poor gap	Q22D	We are now going to compare our present economic system with the economic system a few years ago. Please tell me if the following things are worse or better now than they used to be, or about the same: The gap between the rich and the poor?	Coded 1 if Q22D was 1 or 2 ("much worse" or "worse") and coded zero if Q22D was 3, 4, or 5 ("about the same," "better," or "much better").
Household income	Q90	Before taxes, how much money do you (and your spouse together) earn per month?	Takes a value of the midpoint of the bracket reported in Q90, multiplied by 12. Brackets are: Over R10000, R4001-R10000, R3001-R4000, R2001-R3000, R1401-R2000, R901-R1400, R501-R900, R251-R500, R101-R250, less than R100, None. For the top bracket, coding added 10% to the lower bound and multiplied by 12 and answers of none were coded as R1.

TABLE E.1 (*Continued*)

	Question number	Question wording	Coding
National relative position	Q2B	In general, how do you rate: Your living conditions compared to those of other South Africans?	Same coding as Q2B (from 1 "much worse" to 5 "much better"), with values of 9 in Q2B ("don't know") coded as missing.
Black	Q96new	Respondent's race	Coded as 1 if black/African, and coded as 0 if white, coloured, or Asian and not missing.
National pride	Q56SAFA	Here are some things people say about the way they feel about South Africa. There are no right or wrong answers. We are simply interested in your opinion. Please tell me whether you disagree, neither disagree nor agree, or agree with these statements: It makes you proud to be called a South African.	Same coding as Q56SAFA (from 1 "strongly disagree" to 5 "strongly agree"), with responses of "don't know" and refusals to answer coded as missing.
Unskilled	Q88	What is your main occupation?	Coded 1 if said "Never had a job," "farm worker," "trader/hawker/vendor," "miner," "domestic worker/househelp," "retail worker," "unskilled manual in formal sector," "unskilled manual in the informal sector," or "driver" and zero if other substantive answer and not missing.

TABLE E.1 *(Continued)*

Urban	urbrur	Urban or rural?	Coded 1 if urbrur took a value of 1 (urban), and coded 0 if urbrur took a value of 2 (rural).
Religious attendance	Q86	Excluding weddings and funerals, how often do you attend religious services?	Same values as Q86 (from 1 "never" to 6 "more than once a week"), with responses of "don't know" and refusals to answer coded as missing.
Optimism	Q4B	Looking ahead, do you expect the following to be better or worse: Your living conditions in twelve months time?	Same values as Q4B from 1 ("much worse") to 5 ("much better"), with responses of "don't know" and refusals to answer coded as missing.
Crime top priority	Q44	In your opinion, what are the most important problems facing this country that government should address?	Coded 1 if the respondent mentioned "crime and security" (category 12 in response to Q44PT1, Q44PT2, Q44PT3) as first, second, or third problem/priority.
Economy good	Q1A	In general, how would you describe: The present economic conditions of this country?	Same values as Q1A from 1 ("very bad") to 5 ("very good"), and with responses of "don't know" and refusals to answer coded as missing.
Sex	Q96	Respondent's gender	Coded 1 if Q96 was 2 (female), zero if Q96 was 1 (male).

TABLE E.1 (Continued)

	Question number	Question wording	Coding
Education	Q84	What is the highest level of education you have completed?	Same values as Q84, from 0 ("no formal schooling") to 9 ("post-graduate"), with responses of "don't know" and refusals to answer coded as missing.
Age	Q80	How old were you at your last birthday?	Years (logged).
Attend community meeting	Q25B	Here is a list of actions that people sometimes take as citizens. For each of these, please tell me whether you, personally, have done any of these things during the past year. If not, would you do this if you had the chance: Attended a community meeting?	Coded 1 if Q25B took a value of 2, 3, or 4 ("attended once or twice," "attended several times," "attended often") and coded 0 if Q25B took a value of 1 or 0 ("no, would never do this," "no, but would do if had the chance"), with responses of "don't know" and refusals to answer coded as missing.

TABLE E.2 Variables from SASAS 2005

	Question number	Question wording	Coding
Incomes too unequal	Q117	To what extent do you agree or disagree with the following? In South Africa incomes are too unequal.	Coded 1 if Q117 took a value of 1 ("strongly agree"), coded 0 if Q117 was 2, 3, 4, or 5 ("agree," "neither nor," "disagree," "strongly disagree").
Govt should address	Q118	To what extent do you agree or disagree with the following? The government should take more responsibility to ensure that everyone is provided for.	Coded 1 if strongly agreed, and zero if agreed, disagreed, or strongly disagreed.
Worse off than neighbors	Q120	How does your household income compare with other households in your village/neighbourhood?	Coded 1 if said "much below average" or "below average" and coded 0 if said "average," "above average," or "much above average." When using indicators for those both feeling worse off and feeling better off, "Much worse" is coded 1 if said "much below average" and zero for other substantive answers, while "Much better" is code 1 if said "much above average" and zero for other substantive answers.

TABLE E.2 *(Continued)*

	Question number	Question wording	Coding
Household income	Q311	Please give me the letter that best describes the total monthly household income of all the people in your household before tax and other deductions. Please include all sources of income, i.e., salaries, pensions, income from investment.	Same coding as Q311 (from 1 to 14), treating codes of 97 ("refuse to answer") and 98 ("uncertain/don't know") as missing. Brackets included: None, R1–R500, R501–R750, R751–R1000, R1001–R1500, R1501–R2000, R2001–R3000, R3001–R5000, R5001–R7500, R7501–R10000, R10001–R1500, R15001–R20000, R20001–R30000, and R30000+.
Black	Q264	Race of respondent.	Coded 1 if Q264 was 1 (black/African), coded zero if Q264 was 2, 3, or 4 (coloured, Indian/Asian, white).
Economy improved	Q2	In the last 5 years, has life improved, stayed the same, or gotten worse for most people in South Africa?	Reverse coded such that 1 is "gotten worse," 2 is "stayed the same," and 3 is "improved."
Prioritize crime	Q1	Please tell me what you think are the 3 most important challenges facing South Africa today?	Coded 1 if Q1(1), Q1(2), or Q1(3) took a value of 5 ("crime and safety"), coded 0 otherwise.
No Interracial marriage	Q84	Please tell me to what extent you agree or disagree with these statements. People should marry someone of the same race group.	Reverse coded so that values of 1 and 2 correspond to "strongly agree" or "agree," 3 corresponds to "neither agree nor disagree," and 4 and 5

TABLE E.2 (Continued)

National pride	Q46	It makes me feel proud to be called a South African.	Coded 1 if strongly agree or agree, coded 0 if disagree or strongly disagree.
Unemployed	Q273	Current employment status?	Coded 1 if said "unemployed, not looking," "unemployed, looking," "housewife looking for work," "permanently disabled," "temporarily sick," or "aged/retired" and zero otherwise.
Optimistic	Q5	Do you think that life will improve, stay the same, or get worse in the next 5 years for people like you?	Coded 1 if Q5 was 1 ("improve"), coded 0 if Q5 was 2 or 3 ("stay the same" or "get worse").
Religious attendance freq	Q278	Apart from special occasions such as weddings, funerals, and baptisms, how often do you attend services or meetings connected with your religion?	Reverse coded from Q278, such that, on a scale from 1 to 8, 1 is "never" and 8 is "several times a week." "Do not know" and "refused to answer" responses treated as missing.
Sex	Q247	Gender of respondent.	Coded 1 if female and 0 if male.
Education	Q268	What is the highest education level you have ever completed?	Takes values from 0 ("no schooling") to 20 ("post-graduate degree or diploma").
Age	Q249	Age of respondent in completed years.	Years (logged).
Urban	geotype	Environmental milieu.	Coded 1 if geotype was 1 or 2 (urban formal or urban informal); coded 0 if geotype was 3 or 4 (tribal or rural formal).

TABLE E.2 *(Continued)*

	Question number	Question wording	Coding
Local comparison	Q119	Who do you compare your income mostly with?	Coded 1 if said "neighbors," "others in the village," "people in the township" (if urban resident), "people in the rural area" (if rural resident), or "people in the city" (if urban resident). Coded 0 if said "People in South Africa as a whole," "work colleagues," "people in the township" (if rural resident), "people in rural areas" (if urban resident), or "people in the cities" (if rural resident).
Attached to neighbors	Q45	To what extent do you feel attached to the following types of people: those who live in your neighbourhood?	Coded 1 if Q45 took a value of 1 ("very attached") and coded 0 if took a value of 4, 3, or 2 ("not at all attached," "not very attached," or "slightly attached").

TABLE E.3 Variables from GSS 2006

	Question number	Question wording	Coding
Progressive	taxrich/ taxpoor	Generally, how would you describe taxes in America today. We mean all taxes together, including Social Security, income tax, sales tax, and all the rest. For those with high incomes, are taxes … For those with low incomes, are taxes … much too low, too low, about right, too high, or much too high?	Coded 1 if a respondent thinks taxes on those with high incomes are much too low/too low and thinks taxes on those with low incomes are much too high/too high; coded 0 otherwise unless said "can't choose" or gave no answer in which case treated as missing.
Tax rich	taxrich	Generally, how would you describe taxes in America today. We mean all taxes together, including Social Security, income tax, sales tax, and all the rest. For those with high incomes, are taxes … much too low, too low, about right, too high, or much too high?	Coded 1 if taxrich took a value of 5 or 4 ("much too low" or "too low"), and coded 0 if taxrich took a value of 3, 2, or 1 ("about right," "too high," or "much too high"). "Can't choose" and no answer responses treated as missing.
Support redistribution	eqwith	Some people think that the government in Washington ought to reduce the income differences between the rich and the poor, perhaps by raising the taxes of wealthy families or by giving income assistance to the poor. Others think that the government should not concern itself with reducing this income difference between the rich and the poor. What score between 1 and 7 comes closest to the way you feel?	Reverse coding (1–7) of eqwith. Original question said: "Here is a card with a scale from 1 to 7. Think of a score of 1 as meaning that the government ought to reduce the income differences between rich and poor, and a score of 7 meaning that the government should not concern itself with reducing income differences." New coding is such that 7 means the government out to reduce the income differences between rich and poor.

TABLE E.3 (*Continued*)

	Question number	Question wording	Coding
Household income	income06	In which of these groups did your total family income, from all sources, fall last year—2005—before taxes?	Takes the same coding as income06. The 25 brackets included: Under $1000, 1000–2999, 3000–3999, 4000–4999, 5000–5999, 6000–6999, 7000–7999, 8000–9999, 10000–12499, 12500–14999, 15000–17499, 17500–19999, 20000–22499, 22500–29999, 30000–34999, 35000–39999, 40000–49999, 50000–59999, 60000–74999, 75000–89999, 90000–109999, 110000–129999, 130000–149999, and 150000+.
Perceived national position	finrela	Compared with American families in general, would you say your family income is far below average, below average, average, above average, or far above average?	Same coding as finrela (1—"far below average," 2—"below average," 3—"average," 4—"above average," 5—"far above average").
Pessimistic about future	goodlife	The way things are in America, people like me and my family have a good chance of improving our standard of living—do you agree or disagree?	Same coding (scale 1 to 5) as goodlife, with "don't know" and refusals treated as missing. When using binary version, coded 1 if "neither agree nor disagree," "disagree," or "strongly disagree," and 0 if said "strongly agree" or "agree."

TABLE E.3 (Continued)

Democrat	partyid	Generally speaking, do you usually think of yourself as a Republican, Democrat, Independent, or what?	Coded 1 if partyid took a value of 0, 1, or 2 ("strongly Democrat," "not very strong Democrat," "Independent, close to Democrat"); coded 0 otherwise.
Black	race	What race do you consider yourself?	Black is coded 1 if race took a value of 2 ("Black") and coded 0 if race took a value of 1 or 3 ("White" or "Other").
Hispanic (not black/white)	hispanic/ race	Are you Spanish, Hispanic, or Latino/Latina? What race do you consider yourself?	Coded 0 if Hispanic took a value of 1 ("not Hispanic") or race took a value of 1 or 2 ("Black or White"). Hispanicnotblackwhite was coded 1 if Hispanic did not equal 1 and if race did not equal 1 or 2.
Individual should help self	helppoor	Some people think that the government in Washington should do everything possible to improve the standard of living of all poor Americans; they are at Point 1 on this card. Other people think it is not the government's responsibility, and that each person should take care of himself; they are at Point 5. Where would you place yourself on this scale, or haven't you made up your mind on this?	Same coding as helppoor, with don't know responses and refusals to answer treated as missing.

TABLE E.3 *(Continued)*

	Question number	Question wording	Coding
Hard work	getahead	Some people say that people get ahead by their own hard work; others say that lucky breaks or help from other people are more important. Which do you think is most important?	Coded 1 if getahead took a value of 1 ("Hard work most important") and coded 0 if getahead took a value of 2 or 3 ("Hard work, luck equally important" or "Luck most important").
Black should work way up	wrkwayup	Do you agree strongly, agree somewhat, neither agree nor disagree, disagree somewhat, or disagree strongly with the following statement: Irish, Italians, Jewish, and many other minorities overcame prejudice and worked their way up. Blacks should do the same without special favors.	Reverse coded such that a value of 5 corresponds to "agree strongly" and a value of 1 corresponds to "disagree strongly."
Racial resentment index	racdif1-4	On the average (Blacks/African-Americans) have worse jobs, income, and housing than white people. Do you think these differences are . . . mainly due to discrimination?/because most (Blacks/African-Americans) have less in-born ability to learn? (reversed)/don't have the chance for education that it takes to rise out of poverty?/don't have the motivation or will power to pull themselves up out of poverty?	Adds the values of racdif4 (reversed), racdif3, racdif2 (reversed), and racdif1 and divides by four.

TABLE E.3 (Continued)

Religious attendance	attend	How often do you attend religious services?	Same coding as attend, from 0 "never" to 8 "more than once a week."
Female	sex	Sex of respondent.	Coded 1 if sex took a value of 2 (female) and coded 0 if sex took a value of 1 (male).
Education	educ	Respondent's highest level of education.	Same coding as educ from 0 (no schooling) to 20 (eight years of higher education or more).
Age	age	Year of birth.	Years (logged).
Marital status	marital	Are you currently – married, widowed, divorced, separated, or have you never been married?	Coded 1 if marital took a value of 1 ("married") and coded 0 if marital took a value of 2, 3, 4, or 5 ("widowed," "divorced," "separated," or "never married").
Spend social in neighborhood	socommun/ socfrend	Which answer comes closest to how often you do the following things: Spend a social evening with someone who lives in your neighborhood? Or, Spend a social evening with friends who live outside the neighborhood?	Coded 1 if the score given for in neighborhood is greater or equal to the score for outside the neighborhood, and zero otherwise.
Rural	srcbelt	belt code	Coded 1 if srcbelt takes a value of 6 ("counties having no towns of 10,000 or more") and coded zero if srcbelt takes a value less than six.

TABLE E.3 *(Continued)*

	Question number	Question wording	Coding
Children in house	adults/hompop	Number of members 18 yrs or older; Householdsize and composition	Subtracts the number of adults in the interviewed household (adults) from the total number of people in the home and then recodes any value greater than zero as 1.
Samestate	mobile16	When you were 16 years old, were you living in this same (city/town/county)?	Coded 1 if mobile16 takes a value of 1 or 2 ("same state, same city" or "same state, different city") and coded 0 if mobile 16 takes a value of 3 ("different state").

BIBLIOGRAPHY

Adams, Charles Francis. *The works of John Adams*. Boston, MA: Little Brown, 1850.

Adams, Glenn. "The cultural grounding of personal relationship: Enemyship in North American and West African worlds." In *Journal of Personality and Social Psychology* 88.6 (2005), pp. 948–968.

Addison, Douglas M. "The quality of budget execution and its correlates." In *World Bank Policy Research Working Paper* 1.6657 (2013).

Afrobarometer Data [South Africa][Round 2]. Cape Town, 2002.

Albertson, Bethany, and Shana Kushner Gadarian. *Anxious politics: Democratic citizenship in a threatening world*. New York, NY: Cambridge University Press, 2015.

Alesina, Alberto, and Paola Giuliano. "Culture and institutions." In *Journal of Economic Literature* 53.4 (2015), pp. 898–944.

Alesina, Alberto, and Edward L. Glaeser. *Fighting poverty in the US and Europe: A world of difference*. Vol. 26. Oxford, UK: Oxford University Press, 2004.

Alexander, Peter. "Rebellion of the poor: South Africa's service delivery protests—a preliminary analysis." In *Review of African Political Economy* 37.123 (2010), pp. 25–40.

American Community Survey. Washington, DC, 2005.

Anderson, Cameron, Oliver P. John, Dacher Keltner, and Ann M. Kring. "Who attains social status? Effects of personality and physical attractiveness in social groups." In *Journal of Personality and Social Psychology* 81.1 (2001).

Anderson, Cameron, Michael W. Kraus, Adam D. Galinsky, and Dacher Keltner. "The local-ladder effect: Social status and subjective well-being." In *Psychological Science* 23.7 (2012), pp. 764–771.

Anderson, Lisa. "Demystifying the Arab spring." In *Foreign Affairs* 90.3 (2011), pp. 2–7.

Ansolabehere, Stephen, Marc Meredith, and Erik Snowberg. "Mecro-economic voting: Local information and micro-perceptions of the macro-economy." In *Economics & Politics* 26.3 (2014), pp. 380–410.

Aristotle. *Complete works of Aristotle: The revised Oxford translation*. Trans. by Jonathan Barnes. Vol. 1. Princeton, NJ: Princeton University Press, 2014.

Ashforth, Adam. *Witchcraft, violence, and democracy in South Africa*. Chicago, IL: University of Chicago Press, 2005.

Assor, Avi, Joel Aronoff, and Lawrence A. Messé. "Attribute relevance as a moderator of the effects of motivation on impression formation." In *Journal of Personality and Social Psychology* 41.4 (1981), pp. 789–796.

Baldwin, Kate, and John D. Huber. "Economic versus cultural differences: Forms of ethnic diversity and public goods provision." In *American Political Science Review* 104.04 (2010), pp. 644–662.

Bales, Robert F., Fred L. Strodtbeck, Theodore M. Mills, and Mary E. Roseborough. "Channels of communication in small groups." In *American Sociological Review* 16.4 (1951), pp. 461–468.

Banerjee, Abhijit, and Thomas Piketty. "Top Indian incomes, 1922–2000." In *World Bank Economic Review* 19.1 (2005), pp. 1–20.

Banks, Antoine J. *Anger and racial politics: The emotional foundation of racial attitudes in America*. Cambridge University Press, 2014.

Barr, A., and M. Stein. "Status and egalitarianism in traditional communities: An analysis of funeral attendance in six Zimbabwean villages." In *Mimeograph* (2008).

Bartels, Larry M. *Unequal democracy*. New York, NY: Russell Sage Foundation, 2008.

Beach, Steven R. H., and Abraham Tesser. 2000. "Self-evaluation maintenance and evolution." In *Handbook of social comparison: Theory and research*. Ed. by Jerry Suls, and Ladd Wheeler, New York, NY: Springer, 123–140.

Beissinger, Mark R. *Nationalist mobilization and the collapse of the Soviet State.* New York, NY: Cambridge University Press, 2002.

———. "The semblance of democratic revolution: coalitions in Ukraine's orange revolution." In *American Political Science Review* 107.03 (2013), pp. 574–592.

Benabou, Roland, and Efe A. Ok. "Social mobility and the demand for redistribution: The Poum hypothesis." In *The Quarterly Journal of Economics* 116.2 (2001), pp. 447–487.

Bihar. *White paper on state finances and development.* Tech. rep. Finance Department, Government of Bihar, 2006.

Bobo, Lawrence. "Social responsibility, individualism, and redistributive policies." In *Sociological Forum* 6.1 (1991), pp. 71–92.

Boix, Carles. *Democracy and redistribution.* New York, NY: Cambridge University Press, 2003.

———. "Origins and persistence of economic inequality." In *Annual Review of Political Science* 13 (2010), pp. 489–516.

Boltz, Marie, Karine Marazyan, and Paola Villar. "Preference for hidden income and redistribution to kin and neighbors: A lab-in-the-field experiment in Senegal." Unpublished Paper, Paris School of Economics (2015).

Bowles, Samuel. *The moral economy: Why good incentives are no substitute for good citizens.* Yale University Press, 2016.

Boyce, Christopher J., Gordon D. A. Brown, and Simon C. Moore. "Money and happiness: Rank of income, not income, affects life satisfaction." In *Psychological Science* 21.4 (2010), pp. 471–475.

Brader, Ted. *Campaigning for hearts and minds: How emotional appeals in political ads work.* Chicago, IL: University of Chicago Press, 2006.

Brams, Steven J., D. Marc Kilgour, and Christian Klamler. "Maximin envy-free division of indivisible items." In *Group Decision and Negotiation* 26.1 (2017), pp. 115–131.

Brañas-Garza, Pablo, Antonio M. Espin, Filippos Exadaktylos, and Benedikt Herrmann. "Fair and unfair punishers coexist in the Ultimatum Game." In *Scientific Reports* 4 (2014).

Bratton, Michael, and Nicolas van de Walle. "Popular protest and political reform in Africa." In *Comparative Politics* 24.4 (1992), pp. 419–442.

Brennan, Geoffrey, and Philip Pettit. *The economy of esteem: An essay on civil and political society*. Oxford, UK: Oxford University Press, 2004.

Brosnan, Sarah F., Hillary C. Schiff, and Frans B. M. de Waal. "Tolerance for inequity may increase with social closeness in chimpanzees." In *Proceedings of the Royal Society of London B: Biological Sciences* 272.1560 (2005), pp. 253–258.

Bruno, Michael, Martin Ravallion, and Lyn Squire. *Equity and growth in developing countries: Old and new perspectives on the policy issues*. Washington, D.C.: World Bank Publications, 1996.

Buck, Ross. "Social and emotional functions in facial expression and communication: The readout hypothesis." In *Biological Psychology* 38.2 (1994), pp. 95–115.

Buss, David M. "Evolutionary biology and personality psychology: Toward a conception of human nature and individual differences." In *American Psychologist* 39.10 (1984), pp. 1135–1147.

Butler, Daniel M., and David E. Broockman. "Do politicians racially discriminate against constituents? A field experiment on state legislators." In *American Journal of Political Science* 55.3 (2011), pp. 463–477.

Butler, Emily A., Tiane L. Lee, and James J. Gross. "Emotion regulation and culture: Are the social consequences of emotion suppression culture-specific?." In *Emotion* 7.1 (2007), pp. 30–48.

Camerer, Colin. *Behavioral game theory: Experiments in strategic interaction*. Princeton, NJ: Princeton University Press, 2003.

Campos, Joseph J., Eric A. Walle, Audun Dahl, and Alexandra Main. "Reconceptualizing emotion regulation." In *Emotion Review* 3.1 (2011), pp. 26–35.

Cardenas, Juan Camilo, John Stranlund, and Cleve Willis. "Local environmental control and institutional crowding-out." In *World Development* 28.10 (2000), pp. 1719–1733.

Carpenter, Daniel. "Recruitment by petition: American antislavery, French Protestantism, English suppression." In *Perspectives on Politics* 14.03 (2016), pp. 700–723.

Carpenter, Daniel, and Colin D. Moore. "When canvassers became activists: Antislavery petitioning and the political mobilization of American women." In *American Political Science Review* 108.03 (2014), pp. 479–498.

Carson, Clayborne. *In struggle: SNCC and the black awakening of the 1960s*. Cambridge, MA: Harvard University Press, 1981.

Cavaillé, Charlotte. "Demand for redistribution in the age of inequality." PhD thesis. Harvard University, 2014.

Cederman, Lars-Erik, Nils, B. Weidmann, and Kristian Skrede Gleditsch. "Horizontal inequalities and ethnonationalist civil war: A global comparison." In *American Political Science Review* 105.03 (2011), pp. 478–495.

Chaudhuri, Shubham, and Martin Ravallion. *Partially awakened giants: Uneven growth in China and India*. Vol. 4069. World Bank Publications, 2006.

Chen, Xi. *Social protest and contentious authoritarianism in China*. New York, NY: Cambridge University Press, 2012.

Chong, Dennis. *Collective action and the civil rights movement*. Chicago, IL: University of Chicago Press, 1991.

Cialdini, Robert B., Raymond R. Reno, and Carl A. Kallgren. "A focus theory of normative conduct: Recycling the concept of norms to reduce littering in public places." In *Journal of Personality and Social Psychology* 58.6 (1990), pp. 1015–1026.

Cikara, Mina. "Intergroup schadenfreude: Motivating participation in collective violence." In *Current Opinion in Behavioral Sciences* 3 (2015), pp. 12–17.

Cikara, Mina, E. Bruneau, J. J. Van Bavel, and R. Saxe. "Their pain gives us pleasure: How intergroup dynamics shape empathic failures and counter-empathic responses." In *Journal of Experimental Social Psychology* 55 (2014), pp. 110–125.

Clark, Andrew E., Paul Frijters, and Michael A. Shields. "Relative income, happiness, and utility: An explanation for the Easterlin paradox and other puzzles." In *Journal of Economic Literature* 46.1 (2008), pp. 95–144.

Clark, Andrew E., and Claudia Senik. "Who compares to whom? The anatomy of income comparisons in Europe." In *Economic Journal* 120.544 (2010), pp. 573–594.

Corneo, Giacomo, and Hans Peter Grüner. "Individual preferences for political redistribution." In *Journal of Public Economics* 83.1 (2002), pp. 83–107.

Cramer Walsh, Katherine J. *The politics of resentment: Rural consciousness in Wisconsin and the rise of Scott Walker*. Chicago, IL: University of Chicago Press, 2016.

Crocker, Jennifer, and Brenda Major. "Social stigma and self-esteem: The self-protective properties of stigma." In *Psychological Review* 96.4 (1989), pp. 608–630.

Cuddy, Amy, Susan T. Fiske, Virginia Kwan, et al. "Stereotype content model across cultures: Towards universal similarities and some differences." In *British Journal of Social Psychology* 48.1 (2009), pp. 1–33.

Cusack, Thomas, Torben Iversen, and Philipp Rehm. "Risks at work: The demand and supply sides of government redistribution." In *Oxford Review of Economic Policy* 22.3 (2006), pp. 365–389.

Dancygier, Rafaela M. *Immigration and conflict in Europe*. Cambridge University Press, 2010.

Dawson, Hannah. "Youth politics: Waiting and envy in a South African informal settlement." In *Journal of Southern African Studies* 40.4 (2014), pp. 861–882.

Dawson, Michael C. *Behind the mule: Race and class in African-American politics*. Princeton University Press, 1994.

De Cremer, David, and Paul A. M. van Lange. "Why prosocials exhibit greater cooperation than proselfs: The roles of social responsibility and reciprocity." In *European Journal of Personality* 15.S1 (2001).

Della Porta, Donatella, and Mario Diani. *The Oxford handbook of social movements*. Oxford, UK: Oxford University Press, 2015.

DellaVigna, Stefano, John List, and Ulrike Malmendier. "Testing for altruism and social pressure in charitable giving." In *Quarterly Journal of Economics* 127.1 (2012), pp. 1–56.

Dickson, Eric S. "Expected utility violations evolve under status-based selection mechanisms." In *Journal of Theoretical Biology* 254.3 (2008), pp. 650–654.

Dreber, Anna, and David G. Rand. "Retaliation and antisocial punishment are overlooked in many theoretical models as well as behavioral experiments." In *Behavioral and Brain Sciences* 35.01 (2012), pp. 24.

Druckman, James N., Erik Peterson, and Rune Slothuus. "How elite partisan polarization affects public opinion formation." In *American Political Science Review* 107.01 (2013), pp. 57–79.

Dundes, Alan. *The evil eye: A casebook*. Vol. 2. Madison, WI: University of Wisconsin Press, 1981.

Easterly, William, and Ross Levine. "Africa's growth tragedy: policies and ethnic divisions." In *Quarterly Journal of Economics* (1997), pp. 1203–1250.

Einwohner, Rachel L. "Opportunity, honor, and action in the Warsaw ghetto uprising of 1943." In *American Journal of Sociology* 109.3 (2003), pp. 650–675.

Ellis, Frank. "We are all poor here: Economic difference, social divisiveness and targeting cash transfers in sub-saharan Africa." In *Journal of Development Studies* 48.2 (2012), pp. 201–214.

Englund, Harri. "Witchcraft, modernity and the person: the morality of accumulation in central Malawi." In *Critique of Anthropology* 16.3 (1996), pp. 257–279.

Ensor, Linda. "Municipal leaders 'should account for underspending of grants.' " In *Business Day* 10 (Oct. 2010).

Epstein, Joseph. *Envy: The seven deadly sins*. New York, NY: Oxford University Press, 2003.

Exline, Julie J., and Anne L. Zell, "Antidotes to envy: A conceptual framework." In *Envy: Theory and research. Series in affective science*. Ed. by Richard H. Smith. Oxford, UK: Oxford University Press, 2008, pp. 315–331

Fairbanks, Eve. "Why South African students have turned on their parents' generation." In *Guardian* (2015).

Falk, Armin, Ernst Fehr, and Urs Fischbacher. "Driving forces behind informal sanctions." In *Econometrica* 73.6 (2005), pp. 2017–2030.

Feather, Norman T. "Attitudes towards the high achiever: The fall of the tall poppy." In *Australian Journal of Psychology* 41.3 (1989), pp. 239–267.

Fehr, Ernst, and Urs Fischbacher. "The nature of human altruism." In *Nature* 425.6960 (2003), pp. 785–791.

Fehr, Ernst, Karla Hoff, and Mayuresh Kshetramade. "Spite and development." In *American Economic Review* 98.2 (2008), pp. 494–499.

Fehr, Ernst, and Klaus M. Schmidt. "A theory of fairness, competition, and cooperation." In *Quarterly Journal of Economics* (1999), pp. 817–868.

Feldman, Stanley. "Structure and consistency in public opinion: The role of core beliefs and values." In *American Journal of Political Science* (1988), pp. 416–440.

Feldman, Stanley, and Leonie Huddy. "Racial resentment and white opposition to race-conscious programs: Principles or prejudice?." In *American Journal of Political Science* 49.1 (2005), pp. 168–183.

Festinger, Leon. "A theory of social comparison processes." In *Human Relations* 7.2 (1954), pp. 117–140.

Fiorina, Morris P. "Economic retrospective voting in American national elections: A micro-analysis." In *American Journal of Political Science* (1978), pp. 426–443.

Fischer, Claude S. *To dwell among friends: Personal networks in town and city*. Chicago, IL: University of Chicago Press, 1982.

Fischer, David Hackett. *Fairness and freedom: A history of two open societies, New Zealand and the United States*. New York, NY: Oxford University Press, 2012.

Fiske, Susan T. *Envy up, scorn down: How status divides us*. New York, NY: Russell Sage Foundation, 2011.

Fodor, Jerry A. *The modularity of mind: An essay on faculty psychology*. Cambridge, MA: Massachusetts Institute of Technology Press, 1983.

Fong, Christina. "Social preferences, self-interest, and the demand for redistribution." In *Journal of Public Economics* 82.2 (2001), pp. 225–246.

Foster, George M., R. J. Apthorpe, H. Russell Bernard, et al. "The anatomy of envy: A study in symbolic behavior [and comments and reply]." In *Current Anthropology* (1972), pp. 165–202.

Frank, Robert H. *Choosing the right pond: Human behavior and the quest for status.* New York, NY: Oxford University Press, 1985.

Franzsen, Riël. *Property taxation in South Africa.* United Kingdom: Ashgate, 1999.

Funk, Patricia. "Social incentives and voter turnout: Evidence from the Swiss mail ballot system." In *Journal of the European Economic Association* 8.5 (2010), pp. 1077–1103.

Gächter, Simon, and Ernst Fehr. "Collective action as a social exchange." In *Journal of Economic Behavior & Organization* 39.4 (1999), pp. 341–369.

Gardner, Wendi L., Shira Gabriel, and Laura Hochschild. "When you and I are 'we,' you are not threatening: The role of self-expansion in social comparison." In *Journal of Personality and Social Psychology* 82.2 (2002), pp. 239–251.

Gerber, Alan S., Donald P. Green, and Christopher W. Larimer. "Social pressure and voter turnout: Evidence from a large-scale field experiment." In *American Political Science Review* 102.01 (2008), pp. 33–48.

Gershman, Boris. "The economic origins of the evil eye belief." In *Journal of Economic Behavior & Organization* 110 (2015), pp. 119–144.

Ghosh, Amitav. "The relations of envy in an Egyptian village." In *Ethnology* 22.3 (1983), pp. 211–223.

Gibb, Matthew. "The 'global' and the 'local': A comparative study of development practices in three South African municipalities." PhD thesis. Rhodes University, 2006.

Gibbons, Frederick, and Bram Buunk. "Individual differences in social comparison: Development of a scale of social comparison orientation." In *Journal of Personality and Social Psychology* 76.1 (1999), pp. 129–142.

Gilbert, Daniel T., R. Brian Giesler, and Kathryn A. Morris. "When comparisons arise." In *Journal of Personality and Social Psychology* 69.2 (1995), pp. 227–236.

Gilens, Martin. *Affluence and influence: Economic inequality and political power in America*. Princeton, NJ: Princeton University Press, 2012.

———. *Why Americans hate welfare: Race, media, and the politics of antipoverty policy*. Chicago, IL: University of Chicago Press, 2009.

Gneezy, Uri, and Aldo Rustichini. "Pay enough or don't pay at all." In *Quarterly Journal of Economics* 115.3 (2000), pp. 791–810.

Godwin, Peter. *When a crocodile eats the sun*. New York, NY: Little Brown, 2007.

Goudie, S. C., F. Khan, and D. Kilian. "Transforming tourism: Black empowerment, heritage and identity beyond apartheid." In *South African Geographical Journal* 81.1 (1999), pp. 22–31.

Grant, Ruth W. "Passions and interests revisited: The psychological foundations of economics and politics." In *Public Choice* 137.3–4 (2008).

Green, Jeffrey Edward. "Rawls and the forgotten figure of the most advantaged: In defense of reasonable envy toward the superrich." In *American Political Science Review* 107.01 (2013), pp. 123–138.

Gross, James J. "The emerging field of emotion regulation: An integrative review." In *Review of General Psychology* 2.3 (1998), pp. 271–299.

Guest, Avery M., and Susan K. Wierzbicki. "Social ties at the neighborhood level: Two decades of GSS evidence." In *Urban Affairs Review* 35.1 (1999).

Guha, Ranajit. *Elementary aspects of peasant insurgency in colonial India*. Durham, NC: Duke University Press, 1999.

Gurney, Joan Neff, and Kathleen J. Tierney. "Relative deprivation and social movements: A critical look at twenty years of theory and research." In *Sociological Quarterly* 23.1 (1982), pp. 33–47.

Gurr, Ted Robert. *Why men rebel*. Princeton, NJ: Princeton University Press, 1970.

Guthrie, George M. "A social-psychological analysis of modernization in the Philippines." In *Journal of Cross-Cultural Psychology* 8.2 (1977), pp. 177–206.

Habyarimana, James, Macartan Humphreys, Daniel N. Posner, and Jeremy M. Weinstein. *Coethnicity: Diversity and the dilemmas of collective action*. New York, NY: Russell Sage Foundation, 2009.

Henrich, Joseph Patrick. *Foundations of human sociality: Economic experiments and ethnographic evidence from fifteen small-scale societies*. Oxford, UK: Oxford University Press, 2004.

Herrmann, Benedikt, Christian Thöni, and Simon Gächter. "Antisocial punishment across societies." In *Science* 319.5868 (2008), pp. 1362–1367.

Hirsch, Fred. *Social limits to growth*. New York, NY: Routledge, 1976.

Hirschman, Albert O., and Michael Rothschild. "The changing tolerance for income inequality in the course of economic development." In *Quarterly Journal of Economics* 87.4 (1973), pp. 544–566.

Hobbes, Thomas. *Leviathan*. New York, NY: Oxford University Press, 1998.

Hochschild, Arlie R. *The Managed heart*. Berkeley, CA: University of California Press, 1983.

Hochschild, Jennifer L. *What's fair? American beliefs about distributive justice*. Cambridge, MA: Harvard University Press, 1986.

Hofferth, Sandra L., and John Iceland. "Social capital in rural and urban communities." In *Rural Sociology* 63.4 (1998), pp. 574–598.

Hofstadter, Richard. *The age of reform: From Bryan to FDR*. New York, NY: Vintage, 1955.

Hoggett, Paul, Hen Wilkinson, and Phoebe Beedell. "Fairness and the Politics of Resentment." In *Journal of Social Policy* 42 (July 3, 2013), pp. 567–585.

Hopkins, Daniel J. "The diversity discount: When increasing ethnic and racial diversity prevents tax increases." In *Journal of Politics* 71.01 (2009), pp. 160–177.

Horowitz, Donald L. *A democratic South Africa?: Constitutional engineering in a divided society*. Vol. 46. University of California Press, 1991.

————. *Ethnic groups in conflict.* Berkeley, CA: University of California Press, 1985.

Huber, John D., and Pavithra Suryanarayan. "Ethnic inequality and the ethnification of political parties." In *World Politics* 68.01 (2016), pp. 149–188.

Huberman, Bernardo A., Christoph H. Loch, and Ayse Önçüler. "Status as a valued resource." In *Social Psychology Quarterly* 67.1 (2004), pp. 103–114.

Immordino-Yang, Mary Helen, Andrea McColl, Hanna Damasio, and Antonio Damasio. "Neural correlates of admiration and compassion." In *Proceedings of the National Academy of Sciences* 106.19 (2009), pp. 8021–8026.

ISER. *Living in Rhini: Research report series.* Tech. rept. Institute of Social and Economic Research, 2007.

Iversen, Torben, and David Soskice. "An asset theory of social policy preferences." In *American Political Science Review* 95.4 (2001), pp. 875–894.

James, William. *Principles of psychology.* New York, NY: Dover, 1890.

Jensen, Keith. "Punishment and spite, the dark side of cooperation." In *Philosophical Transactions of the Royal Society of London B: Biological Sciences* 365.1553 (2010), pp. 2635–2650.

Kahneman, Daniel, and Amos Tversky. "Prospect theory: An analysis of decision under risk." In *Econometrica: Journal of the Econometric Society* (1979), pp. 263–291.

Kebede, Bereket, and Daniel John Zizzo. "Social preferences and agricultural innovation: An experimental case study from Ethiopia." In *World Development* 67 (2015), pp. 267–280.

Keen, David. *The economic functions of violence in civil wars.* New York, NY: Routledge, 2005.

Killian, Mitchell, Ryan Schoen, and Aaron Dusso. "Keeping up with the Joneses: The interplay of personal and collective evaluations in voter turnout." In *Political Behavior* 30.3 (2008), pp. 323–340.

King, Gary, Jennifer Pan, and Margaret E. Roberts. "How censorship in China allows government criticism but silences collective expression." In *American Political Science Review* 107.02 (2013), pp. 326–343.

Kingdon, Geeta Gandhi, and John Knight. "Community, comparisons and subjective well-being in a divided society." In *Journal of Economic Behavior & Organization* 64.1 (2007), pp. 69–90.

Kirchsteiger, Georg. "The role of envy in ultimatum games." In *Journal of Economic Behavior & Organization* 25.3 (1994), pp. 373 – 389.

Kitts, James A. "Collective action, rival incentives, and the emergence of antisocial norms." In *American Sociological Review* 71.2 (2006), pp. 235–259.

———. "Mobilizing in black boxes: Social networks and participation in social movement organizations." In *Mobilization: An International Quarterly* 5.2 (2000).

Klandermans, Bert. "How group identification helps to overcome the dilemma of collective action." In *American Behavioral Scientist* 45.5 (2002), pp. 887–900.

Knight, John, Song Lina, and Ramani Gunatilaka. "Subjective well-being and its determinants in rural China." In *China Economic Review* 20.4 (2009), pp. 635–649.

Kohut, Andrew. *Economies of emerging markets better rated during difficult times.* Tech. rep. Pew Research Forum, 2013.

Kolodny, Niko. "The explanation of amour-propre." In *Philosophical Review* 119.2 (2010), pp. 165–200.

Kracker Selzer, Amy, and Patrick Heller. "The spatial dynamics of middle class formation in postapartheid South Africa: Enclavization and fragmentation in Johannesburg." In *Political Power and Social Theory* 21 (2010), pp. 171–208.

Krugell, Waldo, Hannelie Otto, and Jacky van der Merwe. "Local municipalities and progress with the delivery of basic services in South Africa." In *North-West University Working Paper No. 116* (2009).

Kuziemko, Ilyana, Ryan W. Buell, Taly Reich, and Michael I. Norton. "'Last-place aversion': Evidence and redistributive implications." In *Quarterly Journal of Economics* 129.1 (2014), pp. 105–149.

LaFraniere, Sharon. "China curbs fancy tombs that irk the poor." In *New York Times* (Apr. 2011), A1.

Larson, Jennifer M., and Janet I. Lewis. "Ethnic networks." In *American Journal of Political Science* 61.2 (2017), pp. 350–364.

Lasswell, Harold. *Politics: Who gets what, when, how*. New York, NY: Peter Smith, 1936.

Leach, Colin Wayne, and Russell Spears. "Dejection at in-group defeat and schadenfreude toward second- and third-party out-groups." In *Emotion* 9.5 (2009), pp. 659–665.

Lemanski, Charlotte. "Augmented informality: South Africa's backyard dwellings as a by-product of formal housing policies." In *Habitat International* 33.4 (2009), pp. 472–484.

Levine, David K. "Modeling altruism and spitefulness in experiments." In *Review of Economic Dynamics* 1.3 (1998), pp. 593–622.

Lieberman, Evan S. *Boundaries of contagion: How ethnic politics have shaped government responses to AIDS*. Princeton, NJ: Princeton University Press, 2009.

———. "How South African citizens evaluate their economic obligations to the state." In *Journal of Development Studies* 38.3 (2002), pp. 37–62.

———. "The perils of polycentric governance of infectious disease in South Africa." In *Social Science & Medicine* 73.5 (2011), pp. 676–684.

Lieberman, Evan S., and Gwyneth H. McClendon. "The ethnicity-policy preference link in sub-Saharan Africa." In *Comparative Political Studies* 46.5 (2013), pp. 574–602.

Lohmann, Susanne. "A signaling model of informative and manipulative political action." In *American Political Science Review* 87.02 (1993), pp. 319–333.

López-Cálix, José R, and Alberto Melo. *Creating fiscal space for poverty reduction in Ecuador: A fiscal management and public expenditure review*. Inter-American Development Bank, 2005.

Lü, Xiaobo, and Kenneth Scheve. "Self-centered inequity aversion and the mass politics of taxation." In *Comparative Political Studies* 49.14 (2016), pp. 1965–1997.

Luttmer, Erzo F. P. "Group loyalty and the taste for redistribution." In *Journal of Political Economy* 109.3 (2001), pp. 500–528.

——. "Neighbors as negatives: Relative earnings and well-being." In *The Quarterly Journal of Economics* 120.3 (2005), pp. 963–1002.

Magaloni, Beatriz. *Voting for autocracy: Hegemonic party survival and its demise in Mexico*. New York, NY: Cambridge University Press Cambridge, 2006.

Mail and *Guardian* Staff. "State to Spend R800bn on Infrastructure." In *Mail and Guardian* (Feb. 2011).

Major, Brenda. "From social inequality to personal entitlement: The role of social comparisons, legitimacy appraisals, and group membership." In *Advances in Experimental Social Psychology* 26 (1994), pp. 293–293.

Marcus, David K., Virgil Zeigler-Hill, Sterett H. Mercer, and Alyssa L. Norris. "The psychology of spite and the measurement of spitefulness." In *Psychological Assessment* 26.2 (2014), pp. 563–574.

Marcus, George E. "Emotions in politics." In *Annual Review of Political Science* 3.1 (2000), pp. 221–250.

Marx, Anthony W. *Making race and nation: A comparison of South Africa, the United States, and Brazil*. Cambridge University Press, 1998.

McAdam, Doug, Sidney Tarrow, and Charles Tilly. *Dynamics of contention*. New York, NY: Cambridge University Press, 2001.

McCall, Leslie. *The undeserving rich: American beliefs about inequality, opportunity, and redistribution*. New York, NY: Cambridge University Press, 2013.

McClendon, Gwyneth. "Race and responsiveness: An experiment with South African politicians." In *Journal of Experimental Political Science* 3.1 (2016), pp. 60–74.

McPhail, Clark. "Civil disorder participation: A critical examination of recent research." In *American Sociological Review* 36.6 (1971), pp. 1058–1073.

McQueen, Amy, and William Klein. "Experimental manipulations of self-affirmation: A systematic review." In *Self and Identity* 5.4 (2006), pp. 289–354.

Meltzer, Allan H, and Scott F. Richard. "A rational theory of the size of government." In *Journal of Political Economy* 89.5 (1981), pp. 914–927.

Mill, John Stuart. *On liberty and other essays*. New York, NY: Oxford University Press, 1998.

Moeller, Sara K., Michael D. Robinson, and Darya L. Zabelina. "Personality dominance and preferential use of the vertical dimension of space evidence from spatial attention paradigms." In *Psychological Science* 19.4 (2008), pp. 355–361.

Moene, Karl Ove, and Michael Wallerstein. "Earnings inequality and welfare spending: A disaggregated analysis." In *World Politics* 55.04 (2003), pp. 485–516.

Mussweiler, Thomas, Shira Gabriel, and Galen V. Bodenhausen. "Shifting social identities as a strategy for deflecting threatening social comparisons." In *Journal of Personality and Social Psychology* 79.3 (2000), pp. 398–409.

Nisbett, Richard E., and Dov Cohen. *Culture of honor: The psychology of violence in the South*. Boulder, CO: Westview Press, 1996.

Olson, Mancur. *The logic of collective action*. Cambridge, MA: Harvard University Press, 1965.

Opp, Karl-Dieter, and Bernhard Kittel. "The dynamics of political protest: Feedback effects and interdependence in the explanation of protest participation." In *European Sociological Review* (2009), pp. 97–109.

Oveis, Christopher, Elizabeth J. Horberg, and Dacher Keltner. "Compassion, pride, and social intuitions of self-other similarity." In *Journal of Personality and Social Psychology* 98.4 (2010), pp. 618–630.

Panagopoulos, Costas. "Affect, social pressure and prosocial motivation: Field experimental evidence of the mobilizing effects of pride, shame and publicizing voting behavior." In *Political Behavior* 32.3 (2010), pp. 369–386.

Park, Namsu, Kerk F. Kee, and Sebastián Valenzuela. "Being immersed in social networking environment: Facebook groups, uses and gratifications, and social outcomes." In *Cyber Psychology & Behavior* 12.6 (2009), pp. 729–733.

Pearlman, Wendy. "Emotions and the microfoundations of the Arab uprisings." In *Perspectives on Politics* 11.02 (2013), pp. 387–409.

Petersen, Roger D. *Understanding ethnic violence: Fear, hatred, and resentment in twentieth-century Eastern Europe*. Cambridge University Press, 2002.

Piketty, Thomas. *Capital in the twenty-first century*. Cambridge, MA: Harvard University Press, 2014.

Platteau, Jean-Philippe. "Redistributive pressures in Sub-Saharan Africa: Causes, consequences, and coping strategies." In *Africa's Development in Historical Perspective*. Ed. by Emmanuel Akyeampong et al. New York, NY: Cambridge University Press, 2014, pp. 153–207.

Ponte, Stefano, and Lance van Sittert. "The chimera of redistribution in post-apartheid South Africa: Black Economic Empowerment (BEE) in industrial fisheries." In *African Affairs* 106.424 (2007), pp. 437–462.

Posner, Daniel N. *Institutions and ethnic politics in Africa*. Cambridge University Press, 2005.

Pratto, Felicia, James Sidanius, Lisa M. Stallworth, and Bertram F. Malle. "Social dominance orientation: A personality variable predicting social and political attitudes." In *Journal of Personality and Social Psychology* 67.4 (1994), pp. 741–763.

Prichard, Wilson. *Taxation, responsiveness and accountability in Sub-Saharan Africa: The dynamics of tax bargaining*. New York, NY: Cambridge University Press, 2015.

Putnam, Robert D., Robert Leonardi, and Raffaella Y. Nanetti. *Making democracy work: Civic traditions in modern Italy*. Princeton, NJ: Princeton University Press, 1994.

Ramphele, Mamphela. *Steering by the stars: Being young in South Africa*. Cape Town, SA: Tafelberg, 2002.

Range, Friederike, Lisa Horn, Zsófia Viranyi, and Ludwig Huber. "The absence of reward induces inequity aversion in dogs." In *Proceedings of the National Academy of Sciences* 106.1 (2009), pp. 340–345.

Rawls, John. *A theory of justice*. New York, NY: Oxford University Press, 1971.

Reenock, Christopher, Michael Bernhard, and David Sobek. "Regressive socioeconomic distribution and democratic survival." In *International Studies Quarterly* 51.3 (2007), pp. 677–699.

Renshon, Jonathan. *Fighting for status: Hierarchy and conflict in world politics*. Princeton, NJ: Princeton University Press, 2017.

Rogerson, Christian M. "Tourism, small firm development and empowerment in post-apartheid South Africa." In *Small firms in tourism*. Ed. by Rhodri Thomas. New York, NY: Routledge, 2013, pp. 13–35.

Rose-Ackerman, Susan. *Corruption and government: Causes, consequences, and reform*. Cambridge, UK: Cambridge University Press, 1999.

Rotheram-Borus, Mary J. "Adolescents' reference-group choices, self-esteem, and adjustment." In *Journal of Personality and Social Psychology* 59.5 (1990), pp. 1075–1081.

Rousseau, Jean-Jacques. *The basic political writings*. Trans by Donald A. Cress. Indianapolis, IN: Hackett, 1987.

Rueda, David, and Daniel Stegmueller. "The externalities of inequality: Fear of crime and preferences for redistribution in Western Europe." In *American Journal of Political Science* 60.2 (2015), pp. 472–489.

Runciman, Walter Garrison. *Relative deprivation and social justice: A study of attitudes to social inequality in twentieth-century England*. Berkeley, CA: University of California Press, 1966.

Salovey, Peter, and Judith Rodin. "Some antecedents and consequences of social-comparison jealousy." In *Journal of Personality and Social Psychology* 47.4 (1984), pp. 780–792.

Sauermann, Jan, and André Kaiser. "Taking others into account: Self-interest and fairness in majority decision making." In *American Journal of Political Science* 54.3 (2010), pp. 667–685.

Scacco, Alexandra. "Anatomy of a riot: Participation in ethnic violence in Nigeria." In Book Manuscript, New York University (2012).

Schensul, Daniel. "Remaking an apartheid city: State-led spatial transformation in post-apartheid Durban, South Africa." PhD thesis. Brown University, 2009.

Scheve, Kenneth, and David Stasavage. "Religion and preferences for social insurance." In *Quarterly Journal of Political Science* 1.3 (2006), pp. 255–286.

———. *Taxing the rich: A history of fiscal fairness in the United States and Europe*. Princeton, NJ: Princeton University Press, 2016.

Schoeck, Helmut. *Envy*. Boston, MA: Liberty Press, 1969.

Seekings, Jeremy, and Nicoli Nattrass. "Class, distribution and redistribution in post-apartheid South Africa." In *Transformation: Critical Perspectives on Southern Africa* 50.1 (2002), pp. 1–30.

Seekings, Jeremy, Tracy Jooste, Singumbe Muyeba, Marius Coqui, and Margo Russell. *The social consequences of establishing mixed neighbourhoods*. Cape Town, SA: Centre for Social Science Research, 2010.

Segal, David R., and David Knoke. "Social mobility, status inconsistency and partisan realignment in the United States." In *Social Forces* 47.2 (1968), pp. 154–157.

Senik, Claudia. "Direct evidence on income comparisons and their welfare effects." In *Journal of Economic Behavior & Organization* 72.1 (2009), pp. 408–424.

Shayo, Moses. "A model of social identity with an application to political economy: Nation, class, and redistribution." In *American Political Science Review* 103.02 (2009), pp. 147–174.

Sheskin, Mark, Paul Bloom, and Karen Wynn. "Anti-equality: Social comparison in young children." In *Cognition* 130.2 (2014), pp. 152–156.

Shklar, Judith N. *Ordinary vices*. Cambridge, MA: Harvard University Press, 1984.

Sinclair, Betsy. *The social citizen: Peer networks and political behavior*. Chicago, IL: University of Chicago Press, 2012.

Smith, Adam. *An Inquiry into the Nature and Causes of the Wealth of Nations*. Ed. by Edwin Cannan. London, 1904

———. *The Theory of Moral Sentiments*. Cambridge: Cambridge University Press, 2002.

Smith, Richard H. "Envy and the sense of injustice." In *The psychology of jealousy and envy*. Ed. by Peter Salovey. New York, NY: Guilford Press, 1991, pp. 79–99.

———. *Envy: Theory and research*. Oxford, UK: Oxford University Press, 2008.

Smith, Tom W., Peter Marsden, Michael Hout, and Jibum Kim. *General social survey*. Chicago, Illinois, 2006.

Soetevent, Adriaan R. "Anonymity in giving in a natural context: A field experiment in 30 churches." In *Journal of Public Economics* 89.11 (2005), pp. 2301–2323.

South African Census, Version 1.1. Pretoria, 2001.

Steckler, Conor M., and Jessica L. Tracy. "The emotional underpinnings of social status." In *The psychology of social status*. Ed. by Joey T. Cheng, and Jessica L. Tracy. New York, NY: Springer, 2014, pp. 201–224.

Steinberg, Jonny. *Sizwe's test: A young man's journey through Africa's AIDS epidemic*. New York, NY: Simon and Schuster, 2008.

Sundberg, Mark, and Mandakini Kaul. "Bihar: towards a development strategy." In *World Bank, India* (2005).

Swidler, Ann. "Culture in action: Symbols and strategies." In *American Sociological Review* (1986), pp. 273–286.

Tajfel, Henri. "Social psychology of intergroup relations." In *Annual Review of Psychology* 33.1 (1982), pp. 1–39.

Tarrow, Sidney G. *Power in movement: Social movements, collective action and politics*. New York, NY: Cambridge University Press, 1994.

Teitelbaum, Emmanuel. *Mobilizing restraint: Democracy and industrial conflict in postreform south Asia*. Ithaca, NY: Cornell University Press, 2011.

Tissington, Kate. *A resource guide to housing in South Africa 1994–2010*. Tech. rep. Socio-Economic Rights Institute of South Africa, 2011.

Tocqueville, Alexis de. *Democracy in America*. Trans by Henry Reeve. New York, NY: Adlard and Saunders, 1838.

Tomba, Luigi. "Creating an urban middle class: Social engineering in Beijing." In *China Journal* 51 (2004), pp. 1–26.

Tyler, Tom R. "Psychological perspectives on legitimacy and legitimation." In *Annual Review of Psychology* 57 (2006), pp. 375–400.

Valentino, Nicholas A., Vincent L. Hutchings, Antoine J. Banks, and Anne K. Davis. "Is a worried citizen a good citizen? Emotions, political information seeking, and learning via the internet." In *Political Psychology* 29.2 (2008), pp. 247–273.

Van der Berg, Servaas. "Consolidating South African democracy: The political arithmetic of budgetary redistribution." In *African Affairs* 97.387 (1998), pp. 251–264.

Viterna, Jocelyn. *Women in war: The micro-processes of mobilization in El Salvador.* Oxford, UK: Oxford University Press, 2013.

Watt, Nicholas, and Shiv Malik. "Nick Clegg wealth tax 'the politics of envy,' says senior Tory." In *Guardian* (Aug. 2012).

Wegner, Daniel M., Ralph Erber, and Sophia Zanakos. "Ironic processes in the mental control of mood and mood-related thought." In *Journal of Personality and Social Psychology* 65.6 (1993), pp. 1093–1104.

Wegner, Eva, and Miquel Pellicer. "Demand for redistribution in South Africa." In *Special IARIW-SSA Conference on Measuring National Income, Wealth, Poverty, and Inequality in African Countries, Cape Town, South Africa.* 2011.

Weiss, Yoram, and Chaim Fershtman. "Social status and economic performance: A survey." In *European Economic Review* 42.3 (1998), pp. 801–820.

Wilkinson, Steven I. *Votes and violence: Electoral competition and ethnic riots in India.* New York, NY: Cambridge University Press, 2006.

Willer, Robb. "Groups reward individual sacrifice: The status solution to the collective action problem." In *American Sociological Review* 74.1 (2009), pp. 23–43.

Willer, Robb, Matthew Feinberg, Francis J. Flynn, and Brent Simpson. "The duality of generosity: Altruism and status-seeking motivate prosocial behavior." In working paper, Dept. of Sociology, Stanford University (2014).

Wills, Thomas A. "Downward comparison principles in social psychology." In *Psychological Bulletin* 90.2 (1981), pp. 245–271.

Wimmer, Andreas, Lars-Erik Cederman, and Brian Min. "Ethnic politics and armed conflict: A configurational analysis of a new global data set." In *American Sociological Review* 74.2 (2009), pp. 316–337.

Wong, Cara J. *Boundaries of obligation in American politics: Geographic, national, and racial communities.* New York, NY: Cambridge University Press, 2010.

Wood, Elisabeth. "The emotional benefits of insurgency in El Salvador." In *The Social Movements Reader: Cases and Concept.* Ed. by Jeff Goodwin, and James M. Jasper. John Wiley and Sons, 2001, pp. 143–152.

Young, Lauren E. "Mobilization Under Threat." In *Working Paper, Columbia University* (2016).

Ziblatt, Daniel. "Of course generalize, but how? Returning to middle range theory in comparative politics." In *American Political Science Association-Comparative Politics Newsletter* 17.2 (2006).

———. "Why some cities provide more public goods than others: A subnational comparison of the provision of public goods in German cities in 1912." In *Studies in Comparative International Development* 43.3–4 (2008), pp. 273–289.

Zizzo, Daniel John. "Inequality and procedural fairness in a money burning and stealing experiment." In *Research on Economic Inequality* 11 (2004), pp. 215–247.

Zizzo, Daniel John, and Andrew J. Oswald. "Are people willing to pay to reduce others' incomes?" In *Annales d'Economie et de Statistique* (2001), pp. 39–65.

INDEX